Pascal
and the
Paradox® Engine
Full-powered
Windows applications

Pascal
and the
Paradox® Engine

Full-powered
Windows applications

Robert Signore
Michael Vernick
Michael O. Stegman

Windcrest®/McGraw-Hill

New York San Francisco Washington, D.C. Auckland Bogotá
Caracas Lisbon London Madrid Mexico City Milan
Montreal New Delhi San Juan Singapore
Sydney Tokyo Toronto

NOTICES

Borland®	Borland International, Inc.
Paradox®	
ObjectWindows™	
Database Framework™	
Windows™	Microsoft Corp.

FIRST EDITION
FIRST PRINTING

Library of Congress Cataloging-in-Publication Data

Signore, Robert.
   Pascal and the paradox engine : full-powered Windows applications
 / by Robert Signore, Michael Vernick, and Michael O.
 Stegman.
      p.   cm.
   Includes index.
   ISBN 0-8306-4325-7 (paper)
   1. Windows (Computer programs) 2. Turbo Pascal (Computer file)
 3. Paradox (Computer file) I. Vernick, Michael. II. Stegman,
 Michael O. III. Title.
 QA76.76.W56S499   1993
 005.75'65—dc20   93-23113
                                                                      CIP

Acquisitions Editor: Brad Schepp
Editorial team: Robert Ostrander, Executive Editor
               John C. Baker, Book Editor
               Jodi L. Tyler,Indexer
Production team: Katherine G. Brown, Director
                Wanda S. Ditch, Layout
                Brenda S. Wilhide, Layout
                Susan E. Hansford, Coding
                Nancy K. Mickley, Proofreading
Design team: Jaclyn J. Boone, Designer
             Brian Allison, Associate Designer   4345
Cover design and marble paper: Margaret Karczewski, Vienna, Va.   WP1

Dedication

For Nancy, Audrey, and Jeanne

Contents

Acknowledgments　　　　　　　　　　　　　　　　　*xi*

Introduction　　　　　　　　　　　　　　　　　　*xiii*

Who needs this book?　xiv
Overview by chapter　xiv
What's new in this book　xvi
Conventions　xvi
Naming conventions　xvii
Requirements　xvii

1　*Relational databases and Paradox*　　　　　　　　　　*1*

Starting out　1
Object-oriented programming and database design planning　2
An overview of relational databases　2
Planning a relational database application　3
Databases and relational databases: terms for Paradox users　4
Paradox objects and their uses　10
The Paradox Engine and the Paradox family　13
Introducing the Paradox Engine　13
Planning tip one: setting up a table　13
Planning tip two: fielding a useful form　14
Conclusion　14

2　*An application planning process*　　　　　　　　　　*17*

The planning sessions　17
Preparing the code for the tables　28

3 The Resource Workshop and the user interface   37

Session 5: planning the user interface menus   37
The main menu bar   38
Screen design   39
The three foundation screens   46
Conclusion   59

4 The objects of our application   61

The Pascal database framework hierarchy   62
Own own objects   65
The new objects and their ancestors   67
Messages and the new objects   69
The three messages   69
The new objects and their code   75
Conclusion   142

5 Integrating the user interface and the Engine   143

Cranking up the Engine for the first time   143
Conclusion   162

6 Performing data validity checking with the Engine   163

The TValidator and other validators   164
The ObjectWindows validators   169
Integrating the validators into a user interface   171
Initiating a validity check   173

7 Maintaining database integrity with the Engine   181

Basic integrity constraints   181
Introducing the DCursor object type   184
Using the DCursor with the Engine   188
Integrating DCursor into the user interface   189
Source code for the DCursor object type   191

8 Query processing and the Engine   241

Optimizing a query   242
The query object types described   244
The fields and object types for a query   244
Integrating the query objects and the user interface   250

Appendix Source code listings   317

Starting out   317
The heart of the matter   317
The windows and dialogs   318
Querying the database   318

Index   319

About the Authors   323

Acknowledgments

In writing this book, we've been fortunate to have the strong and enthusiastic support of many individuals. Thanks to Brad Schepp, Acquisitions Editor at TAB/McGraw-Hill, whose enthusiasm for this band of merry men has kept us out of the darkest parts of the forest; to Lisa Black, also of TAB/McGraw-Hill, who fielded our questions; to Nan Borreson, Borland, whose support for this project was unfailing and generous to a fault; to Klaus Krull and Rich Jones, Borland, for their valuable insights; and to Karen Giles, Borland, whose deft humor managed the tangle of working with not one, but three authors; and to Len Dorfman who kept us going.

Thanks also to Thomas Finn for his technical assistance with this book.

Nancy Signore, Audrey Vernick, and Jeanne Stegman know, as only they can, how vital their support has been during our writing, and beyond.

Introduction

The simplest description of a *database management system* would reveal it to be a place to store information and a means to get at it. The more data, the greater the need for an efficient way to store and retrieve that information. A computer's database, in its simplest form, can store information more efficiently than other storage mediums such as paper or microfilm.

The Paradox relational database management program and its related programming tools, the Paradox Application Language (PAL and ObjectPAL), offers an application's developer one of the most sophisticated and extensive programming environments currently available.

This book will provide a programmer with the necessary tools to write a Windows application that creates and manipulates Paradox database tables.

This book's first goal is to demonstrate to programmers who have worked with Pascal or want to begin working with Pascal with Objects that they can and should create Windows applications for Paradox with Pascal. The main stumbling block at the threshold between Pascal and the Paradox Engine is that the Engine does not explicitly offer important features found in the interactive Paradox environment such as validity checking, relational integrity, and queries. This book removes that stumbling block.

If you have ever wanted to improve your PAL or Pascal applications so that their possibilities opened out into other languages—ones which you have worked hard to master and could not reach from either place before—then find a comfortable place to read and sit back as we go full throttle with the Paradox Engine. We are going to take it through its paces with an application that will wring out all of the speed and functionality already built into the Engine and show you how to add in some features that will allow you to write applications that really will crank some speed out of your machine.

To convince you that this process will dramatically increase your ability to deliver applications in less time, we will be developing our application using Borland's ObjectWindows as our application framework. Borland's Resource Workshop and ObjectWindows' extensive set of objects for creating a user interface will overcome the first programming bottleneck. The advantage that Pascal programming offers comes from developing an application using object-oriented programming techniques. It doesn't hurt that Borland also has adopted an object-oriented approach for all of its products, including the latest versions of Paradox. Even a cursory glance at the programming style suggested and reinforced throughout its manuals for Paradox 4.5 will convince you that Borland doesn't make a move without some object in mind.

Who needs this book?

PAL, ObjectPAL, and all Pascal programmers who want to create efficient Windows applications using Paradox tables are the first audience for this book. The second audience includes any programmer who has wished for a thorough introduction to object-oriented programming techniques and how to apply them to a business application. Readers already familiar with Pascal with Objects will appreciate this book's detailed use of object-oriented programming techniques, starting with the planning sessions for an application.

Overview by chapter

Chapter 1, "Relational databases and Paradox," explores the general concept of database tables and how they store information. The chapter discusses the advantages that a relational database model offers and how Paradox uses this model. We will be exploring the hows and whys of database concepts—such as rows, columns, key fields, and primary and secondary indexes—and the appropriate Paradox implementations of these ideas. With this background, a reader will know what is needed to complete an intelligent application planning process.

Chapter 2, "An application planning process," recreates the key moments in a step-by-step planning process that arrives at all of the dimensions and requirements for a full-featured business application. Two guidelines determined our choices for planning this application:

- A reader should be able to compile this application, as is, and end up with a completely usable, full-featured, general business application, including order entry, inventory, and customer information elements.

- A programmer should be able to see a concise demonstration of as many of the Paradox Engine's functions as possible within the context of a normal application.

Realizing that these guidelines might conflict with each other, we designed an application with a wide range of functions but skipped over many of the redundancies that a commercially salable application would have to include. All concepts in this application that we have not explicitly coded merely repeat other modules within the application. For example, while you will not find every validity check enforced in every place one would be expected, every rule for validity checking is included and an example for each is provided. Still, a reader will find just about everything in place and ready to run.

Chapter 3, "Creating a user interface," covers how to create the input screens for a Paradox database application using Borland's Resource Workshop to create a Windows resource file for the user interface. After showing how to write the main menu window, the chapter explores the basic building blocks for every window in the application's user interface and begins to suggest how the Paradox Engine powers these windows. This chapter will include how to create an application compliant with the Windows' Multiple Document Interface (MDI).

We'll feature step-by-step directions for working with Borland's Resource Workshop to create the resources needed by the application.

Chapter 4, "The objects of our creation," introduces the objects that we have written that manage the connections between the Windows resources and a Paradox database. These particular objects are designed as fully re-usable plug-and-play modules to shorten your coding time. They create objects that associate the Windows control elements and the Engine's objects for manipulating and navigating a database. Inherit this set of objects for field, button, and static controls, and that hard work of tying a resource to a database is well on its way. The Windows messages needed to trigger these events also are here and fully integrated.

Chapter 5, "Integrating the user interface and the Engine," discusses the framework of the Paradox Engine object layer and demonstrates how to integrate it into the user interface. The chapter covers all aspects of how to initiate the Engine and access information.

Chapter 6, "Performing data validity checking with the Engine," covers how to ensure the accuracy of data within the application's table through validity checking. We'll be tracing the advantages of the validity checking objects defined in the *Validate* unit available through the ObjectWindows application framework.

Chapter 7, "Maintaining database integrity with the Engine," introduces the first of the two chapters in the book devoted to objects that we have explicitly written to provide operations that the Engine does not itself account for. In this chapter, we present an object type that links tables together to maintain referential integrity throughout our application's tables. Of special note here will be how we use a secondary index to accomplish this.

Chapter 8, "Query processing and the Engine," demonstrates how to write a query object type that performs simple, single table queries of Paradox tables. A programmer also can use this object to perform table queries within any Pascal application using Borland's Pascal, version 7.0, and the Paradox Engine, version 3.01.

The appendix includes the complete listings of all code excerpted in a chapter. Any files that are completely listed within a chapter are not duplicated here.

What's new in this book

The programming books currently available for Borland's Pascal platform cover the major areas of Windows programming, but none provides all of the necessary code to hook the power of Borland's Paradox Engine and Database Framework into such an environment. Additionally, the object types that we demonstrate for linking and querying tables are not available from the Engine directly. With access to Crystal Reports, bundled with the Engine and its Database Framework, and this book's features, you now have all of the Paradox programming tools that you'll need to save time and money as you write Windows database applications. With this book, a harried programmer can write Paradox applications quickly and with a minimum of fuss.

Now that you have all of this time, we encourage you to send us improvements or intriguing code that you come up with from using this book.

Conventions

The text of this book generally will follow Borland's own typography conventions and include the following:

Alternate font type   Program code

ALL CAPS The names of database tables within this application, the names of any file included in this application.

Boldface In the text, Pascal functions (like **procedure**), Pascal and Engine object types (like **TApplication** or **TCursor**), reserved words or keywords (like **virtual**), and Paradox field types (like **$**).

Italics In the text, ObjectWindows and Engine Database Framework procedure, functions, variable names, or identifiers; similarly for all functions, variable names, and identifiers for this application. We also might use italics simply for emphasis.

Naming conventions

Throughout the code, we have followed the standard naming practice for our functions: no spaces between words or abbreviated versions of words, lower case first letter and upper case for the start of each word within the function name, as in *firstName*. All classes will follow the Borland mnemonics for ObjectWindows classes, including starting with a capital letter. Classes derived from ObjectWindows classes will begin with a capital *T*. With the exception of **DCursor**, our own Engine-related objects also begin with a capital *T*. Also, all functions using table names follow the DOS-format name of the table.

As a general rule, the complete code listings for all elements of the application directly related to the user interface are described in the appendix and can be found on the enclosed diskette. The complete code listing for the **DCursor** and **TQuery** objects, as well as the code for the reusable objects we are including in chapter 4, are listed in their respective chapters.

Requirements

If you want to compile this application and use it, you will need to meet the following requirements:

- The Borland Paradox Engine and Database Framework, 3.0, including the maintenance release for the Engine, version 3.01
- Borland Pascal with Objects, 7.0, and ObjectWindows
- All hardware and software requirements for the Borland Paradox Engine and Database Framework, version 3.0; similarly, for Borland Pascal with Objects, version 7.0, and Borland ObjectWindows Application Framework
- A mouse

1
Relational databases and Paradox

You won't have to read too far into this chapter to realize that we will be covering some familiar ground. The ground here might seem so familiar that it has paved paths from one end to the other. Okay, we admit that we're going to discuss rows and columns, but this quick romp through the database field also will work in some tips on planning an application from an object-oriented perspective and establishing the elements that we will begin to accumulate as we write a Paradox application using Pascal and the Borland Paradox Engine.

Starting out

Planning any application begins with assessing the amount and types of data that users need to perform their tasks successfully. The planning sessions for an application often begin by determining the general information needed, the elements of that general information, then the natural sets or groupings of those elements. The terminology of databases gives names like table to a grouping of information, records to a complete set of general information in a table, and fields to the specific elements of each record. The advantage that a relational database provides includes the means for easily fitting the information requirements of an application into its management environment.

To assist your plans for an application, this chapter will quickly cover the database basics needed to complete the initial design stages of any application. We will be especially conscious of the power that you can incorporate into your application when you join a relational database to the productivity of the object-oriented programming environments of Borland's Pascal and Paradox Engine.

Object-oriented programming and database design planning

Conceptually, a relational database suggests a close relation to object-oriented programming. The support of abstract data types that define a set of similar objects and a collection of ways to manipulate them is one of the most important qualities of object orientation. We also can include a relational database in this category if it features separate, independent objects, or tables, and the means for communicating between them. Furthermore, information hiding, a primary characteristic of an object-oriented language, is defined as when an object is accessed and modified only through an external interface and operations defined by that interface so that a user never sees the details, data structure, storage strategy, nor restrictions and operations that allow the user to access and modify an object. In the database world, this strategy would be called a data-entry screen. That screen, in addition to being the means for accessing information and manipulating it, might gather or inherit (another OOP term) its information from several tables (or OOP objects) without the user knowing how any of this came about.

This extremely brief analogy of relational database design and object-oriented programming ought to suggest a symbiotic relationship between good design procedures for planning a Paradox application and the execution of those ideas through Pascal's object-orientation.

Chapter 2 will lay out the set of tables and their relations for the Paradox application that we then will write using Pascal and the Borland Paradox Engine. To accomplish this goal, our planning uses techniques for designing a relational database that also could resemble the planning for the object types that we have written in Pascal. In fact, they have to.

An overview of relational databases

The difference between a database and a relational database is the difference between a glove compartment crammed full of tape cassettes and a Wurlitzer jukebox. With organization, you can be more efficient at storing and finding what you need most. However, because even the beautiful old Wurlitzers have long been replaced by Carousel CD players, organizing information with computers has become the premier method for information storage and retrieval. The relational database management program allows for independent groups of information to appear neatly arranged into tables for immediate use.

A relational database allows you to build discrete data groups to maintain specialized pieces of data and also link these together by explicit relationships with other groups of information. These relations allow you to develop more efficient and space-saving databases because you do not have to duplicate information throughout all of the files. Instead, these relations allow link information using what often is called the *relational model.* A relational database program such as Paradox relates this information between groupings or sets of information, then presents compilations of these sets as its management job. This means that Paradox's effectiveness depends on a carefully thought-out application design. Paradox merely facilitates the access, while the design must envision the best way to incorporate and interrelate all of the information needed for a successful and useful application.

With the recent introduction of Paradox's ability to store any binary object—often referred to as a *Binary Large Object* (BLOB)—its tables will no longer simply store character data but now will be able to store as a field almost anything that you can copy to a disk, including whole programs, scanned photographs, graphics, digitized sounds, text, and more. A binary object cannot be viewed as if it were a table of information. Its mnemonic indicates the lack of a defined tabular shape that distinguishes this type of data from the usual alphabetical or numeric information databases usually store. Being able to include a BLOB in a database allows you to have more than just a mere index of information.

A natural use for our application might be to create an online catalog from scanned images of the product or to include a customer's signature for verifying checks or credit cards.

Planning a relational database application

To plan our application, we first will consider the ways in which a relational database operates, determine how the functions of the Paradox Engine perform these operations, then demonstrate how to accomplish all of this using object-oriented programming techniques facilitated by Pascal.

Distinct from traditional structured programming, the object orientation of Pascal's ObjectWindows environment does not require that you go in and change the actual source code of a tool such as a Windows object for a menu. Instead, a programmer groups functions and constructs modules. The end result of this modular programming style reduces the complexity of the overall system and speeds programming because tasks can be allocated across a team of programmers. While the team must communicate with each other more at the start of a project, they do not need to do so as much later on nor during the maintenance cycle of a project. Further, existing modules can be reused in other programs, reducing the cost and speeding the completion of a new application.

To write this book, the team has adopted planning and programming techniques suited to an object-oriented project. Each of the objects that we have created first was planned by the group, then executed by a member of the team as we moved towards completing the application. From the start, Borland's Pascal and ObjectWindows library shaped the process. With the release of the latest version of the Paradox Engine organized with its own OOP layer, the Database Framework, we were able to blend its objects in with those for our user interface, then incorporate the objects that we created to overcome areas that the Engine does not deal with explicitly.

Databases and relational databases: terms for Paradox users

While a *database* is most simply defined as a collection of data, a *relational database* allows a user to interrelate independent bases of data, or tables, to each other in ways that produce information that no one collection contains wholly within itself. A relational database should be able to accomplish the following tasks:

- Create and modify data structures, that is, tables.
- Create, edit, manipulate, and delete data within these structures.
- Manage the security and integrity of data during any of the above operations.
- Custom fit the previous operations to suit a particular use such as an application.
- Automate or improve on the use of other features in the relational database management program.

We will be using Borland Pascal and the Paradox Engine to accomplish these five basic operations within an application that will adhere to the data structures of any Paradox database. So, before we jump into planning the application itself, let's review an outline of the Paradox database management system.

Tables

Paradox defines the basic organizing structure of a collection of data as a table and invites a user to interrelate these tables. While each Paradox table, or data structure, can contain its own grouping of information, each table also allows for a way to relate the information to other Paradox tables. Keeping track of these relationships and maintaining the integrity of the data stored throughout the database, the job of the database management program, is achieved through the process of referential integrity.

In this way, no matter how the information is stored, a user can access and display that information in ways that make sense easily. They do not need to get into the guts of programming a management system that maintains an inventory of programmed routines that organize, reorganize, add, delete, sort, check, and present data in a database's tables. Paradox handles these housekeeping chores for itself. In our application, however, we will be managing them directly using our own object type, **DCursor**, to maintain the integrity of the application's data when the application requires access to a table or tables. The discussion of referential integrity in chapter 7 will show how to create and implement this object type.

Rows, columns, records, and fields

A *table* presents information in tabular form using *rows* and *columns* of data, the standard terms for explaining how a relational database stores and displays its information. Paradox defines each row as a record. The different types of data within each record are each stored in a field that appears in columns when the interactive Paradox displays the records in a table. Each of these fields differs from any other field in the table, both in the name used to identify it and the information stored there.

From the fields in a record, the design team and the programmer of an application often will designate one field as a key field. Paradox then uses such a key field to uniquely identify each record so that another scheme, such as an index, can organize access to a table more efficiently when an application process searches for and needs to display the information from a record; hence, its function as the key to that record.

The information stored in these fields often is entered by application users from forms created for this purpose. In this way, data security, and often data integrity, becomes an easier job because the form displays only those fields or that information that the design of the application has allowed for a particular task. By creating a menu-driven or screen-driven application, a programmer can develop an application in which the user never sees the complete information for any record in a table unnecessarily and might not even be aware that the information asked for by the form or displayed on the screen might be drawn from several data tables.

This type of control then simplifies the use of a database and promotes its acceptance because users work only with the information needed for a limited range of tasks. Of course, the many types of actions related to a complete application will present users with different arrays of information. For example, the information needed to accomplish a customer sale by a salesperson differs completely from that of the warehouse manager who needs to make ordering decisions based on the current stock for any item.

So, the design of a relational database application often focuses its first efforts on the relations between the tables storing the information and the screen used to gather and display that information. With this information, a programmer designs an appropriate user interface and plans for the proper use of programmed routines for managing data.

Keys and linking tables with them

A design team or programmer might designate two or more fields as the keys for each record. In those cases, it is possible to have identical information in the first keyed field of a record. Paradox then uses the second or later keyed fields to break ties with the first keyed field when it searches for or organizes the data in a table. The design for our application uses such a composite key to define the records in the table for all sale items.

There, we use the sale number plus the item number to define a unique record and later organize all the items of one sale.

Our application uses a record's fields to interrelate tables using a field common to each table to constitute the relation or link between them. Establishing a relation between tables begins with conceiving of one of the tables as the master table—the table to which other tables will be linked. These tables are called *detail tables*, mostly because they contain details that the master table describes only in a general way through some key that links them to avoid any unnecessary duplication of information.

The table or tables which are linked to that master table need some hook, or link, to the master table for a relation to exist. Paradox uses a specialized field or set of fields, a key, to accomplish the link. Because a relation between tables depends upon a key unique to each record, the planning process designates a field or group of fields as the unique identifier, or key, for each record in the table. Paradox requires that you match some or all of the key fields in the detail table with fields in the master table. These matching key fields then determine the link between the tables and are used by Paradox to display multiple tables in a form. Further, Paradox demands that, for any link between tables, you must use the first key field in a composite key and as many others as you want as long as they are all grouped together as the first fields in a table's structure. Certainly, the abstract notion of a valid relation can exist between two nonkeyed fields also. Queries and PAL scripts then could display the related data without using the keys.

Paradox might require this, but our application doesn't. Because, by necessity, we had to write our own linking routines (the Engine doesn't do this explicitly), we established our own rules for linking tables together and created a design to allow us to establish links between the master and detail tables using both the usual keyed fields, as does Paradox, and any field for which we have created a secondary index, which Paradox does not allow for.

Those of you familiar with database design can lower your eyebrows from their amazed position and struggle to resist the temptation to check this feature out right now by skipping to chapter 7, "Referential integrity and the Engine." Anyone whose eyebrows are raised to the quizzical position should lower them a notch and read on, trusting that we will explain secondary indexes and why this linking feature qualifies as cool stuff.

Data types in fields and their lengths

The efficiency of any application increases as it takes advantage of natural moments within its design to create and store the information compactly not only to conserve the resources needed to display and manipulate it, but also to speed the manipulation of the data itself. If a field is limited to only one type of data, then the resources of the management program are not unnecessarily taxed when it seeks to manipulate the information in such a field. The second advantage that we gain from limiting the type of data within a field shows up as the rudimentary beginnings of validating the data's integrity within such a field.

To assist its management duties, Paradox 3.5 stores data in its table in one of five ways: alphanumeric, numeric, currency, date, and short. Paradox 4.0 adds four new data types: memo, formatted memo, binary, and graphic. These data types each increase the efficiency with which an application can manipulate them. Using the term BLOB (Binary Large Object) to describe them, the engine considers memo, formatted memo, graphics, and binary data types as a BLOB field type but does provide a way to specify these field types as subtypes. Although Paradox for Windows and the Paradox Engine, 3.0, support OLE type objects, we will not use an OLE type object in this application.

Alphanumeric Alphanumeric fields can include letters, numbers, special symbols—such as %, &, #, -, (,), and =—or any other ASCII characters, including those with diacritical marks, except the ASCII null character (ASCII 0). The length of any alphanumeric field ranges between 1 to 255 characters only.

Numeric Numeric fields contain only positive or negative real numbers ranging from -10^{307} to 10^{308} with 15 significant digits, including the decimal place. Values exceeding 15 significant digits are rounded and stored in scientific notation.

This data type is best used when you need to perform calculations on the values in such a field. In an inventory, the number of products on hand might be best expressed by defining the field as a number data type. The phone number of the supplier of that product, because it might contain parentheses for the area code and a hyphen for the telephone number, would be better defined as an alphanumeric field. Hyphens and parentheses are allowed with an alphanumeric data type but are not valid in a numeric field.

Currency A currency data type is a number field that defaults to two decimal places. During internal calculations, however, Paradox accounts for up to four decimal places on currency fields.

Date A date field recognizes any valid date between January 1, 100 and December 31, 9999. Paradox and the Engine handle leap years and leap centuries correctly for this data type and automatically check all dates for validity.

Short This data type is another special numeric data type, as is currency. A short data type allows a range of signed integers between –32,767 and 32,767.

Memo This data type is specifically designed to contain text that exceeds the 255 character limit of an alphanumeric data type and allows you to include line breaks and tabs for simple formatting of the text. A memo field is identical to an alphanumeric field except that, unlike the maximum fixed length of an alphanumeric field, memo fields have no explicit total length to restrict them. A single memo field can be up to 512Mb in size, so disk space will determine how much you can store.

When you create a memo field, you assign a length value of between 1 to 240 characters. Paradox stores all characters up to 240 or the field length that you specify in the table itself and stores the remainder of the contents of this memo field outside the table in a separate file from which it retrieves the data as needed. Because the entire contents of the field are not always stored in the table itself, Paradox does not allow you to use this type for searches or as a record's key.

As with an alphanumeric field, a memo field can contain letters, numbers, special symbols, or any other ASCII characters except the ASCII NULL character.

The Engine considers this type of field as a binary field.

Binary A binary data type, often called a Binary Large Object or BLOB, contains information stored in a binary format only. While Paradox cannot display or interpret binary fields, the Engine can access them. In such a field, you can store data that cannot be interpreted by Paradox such as sound or other data that is in machine-readable form. You cannot use a binary field as a key or part of any composite key. This eliminates this field type from use during links and searches because these two functions rely on exact matches for their success.

Data atomicity

This process arrives at what often is called the *atomicity* of an element. Practically, determining an element's atomic value might include considerations that include the mission, operating practices, etiquette, and selling strategy for the business itself.

Suppose you were creating an application for a nonprofit organization that prided itself on its close relations with its donors. If you were to build in a mass mailing process that sent properly addressed letters with a "Dear Donor" salutation, then the goodwill that such an organization constantly seeks to build might suffer from this impersonal approach. So, not only would you need a field or fields for the names of each donor, but it also might be an advantage to include a field for a letter's salutation.

This is fine, but now how do you determine the punctuation of that salutation? Should you use a comma, or a colon, and when is each appropriate?

A thoroughly planned application that suits the particular needs of an organization might have to reach into such arcana, but the attention paid to such details will assist the mission of that organization, sometimes obviously, often subtly. Neglecting such details might have its price in the complete success of the application. So, getting them worked into the planning process early is, finally, a better planning strategy and less costly than jimmying them in later.

Naming the fields

Once the planning process has determined the level of precision or atomicity needed for each field, you must name the fields clearly. The best names are unique, brief, descriptive, and singular (State, not States). The more obvious the name, the more someone who might need to revise your application later will thank you. Because we're planning a Pascal application that allows us to use longer names, the fields can have even more descriptive names to facilitate an understanding of their purpose. Our naming convention for a field's logical name includes the name of the table in which the field occurs (SALE_SALE_NUMBER) with each word separated by an underscore. When we create the actual Paradox table, we will map these names to field names within each table that a user will recognize more easily, such as Sale Number.

There remain only two aspects of a field that we still need to plan for: each field's data type and length. The Paradox data types provide some real assistance here, but the length of alphanumeric (and now memo fields) can present some difficult planning moments that require, once again, an attention to detail, with mailing labels widths only the beginnings of considerations that might include bills of lading, printed invoices, and an entire paper trail leading off from our current path. Now, the memo field practically invites verbosity.

Along with any consideration of the data type for a field is the definition of the actual length of that field. The design for any application should consider the most efficient amount of space needed to store data and the practical uses of that data such as those described above.

Valid data within a field: validity checks

To increase the reliability and accuracy of a database's information, the fields in its records might require more restrictions than merely data type and field length. As long as you are settling the requirements of the application, listing the additional restrictions for a field beyond length and data type during these early planning meetings will take advantage of the synergy and freshness of the topic and supply you with the basis for your later coding work.

You should consider the following qualities that might restrict a field by checking for the validity of any data entered. While the Paradox Engine does not automatically handle all validity checks, chapter 6 will assist you when you need to create them. The validity checks for an application verify that the information matches one or more of the following types of conditions:

- The data type for that field
- An accepted range of values (the quantity ordered cannot exceed the inventory on hand)
- Is unique (a record's key)

- Matches an expected format (a telephone number) or value (at least 1 for each item ordered)
- Automatically defaults to some value (the identifier for the person completing the form)
- Is required before the record is complete (a method of payment)
- Is found in some field of some table

A range of values Restricting a field to a range of values usually involves working with the standard mathematical comparison operators: equals, greater than, less than, greater than or equal to, and lesser than or equal to. The data types that you can restrict include dates, numbers, currency values, alphanumeric, and even alphabetical (a-z, A-Z) data. For example, we will use a function to make sure that the quantity ordered for any item is 1 or greater than 1.

The uniqueness of a value This restriction would test to make sure that no other value in that database matched the data about to be entered. This test would ensure, for example, that no other record contains the same information absolutely needed to identify the record, such as a primary key.

Expected values Recognizing that detail and consistency will increase the accuracy, efficiency, and value of information, you might want to incorporate particular restrictions on the order, spacing, and contents of a field. A phone number with a parenthesis where there ought to be a number is useless; a social security number with only eight and not nine digits is similarly useless.

Default values If a field must contain data of some sort and that field is left empty by a user, creating a way to place a default value in such a field automatically also will make the information in that field consistent. For example, you might want to ensure that a screen for recording sales always makes sure that the data in a field identifying the sales clerk always defaults to that clerk's identifier so that it does not have to be keyed in for each transaction.

Required values Another way to handle empty fields or fields that have been mistakenly left empty by a user would be to force a value to the field, like a default value except that the information can be hidden from the user. Another scenario would force the user to enter some particular value before the record is created or updated.

Paradox objects and their uses

So far, we have been walking through the structure of a generic relational database model. Paradox fully implements all of the concepts that we've presented so far and meets or exceeds the external standards that a scholarly approach to database theory might want to mention. Beyond these professorial concerns, Paradox does more than just set up tables stored as files on a disk. Paradox also creates files, or objects, that handle specific tasks such as indexes. Paradox defines as a family all objects associated with one table to manage the efficiency of its operations. The complete list of the objects Paradox can create as one family includes the following:

- Table*
- Memos from a table*
- Form
- Report
- Script
- Compiled Script
- Image Settings
- Graph Settings
- Validity Checks
- Primary Index*
- Secondary Index*

Consult the various user manuals for Paradox if you want to learn more about each one. We will be concerned only with those that the Engine supports, indicated in the previous list by an asterisk.

Our Pascal application uses the Paradox Engine to generate Paradox tables and includes the code necessary to create these tables properly. Beyond a table object, many of the other objects in a Paradox family are covered by the code within an application itself. For example, the Engine does not contain functions for creating or managing a form, or user interface, so the programmer is responsible for accomplishing this with the added advantage that a user interface written in, say, Pascal will outperform one that requires the complete overhead of Paradox to work successfully. Also, because an application is a type of extended script anyway, the Paradox Engine does not support or create a script object, here an unproductive redundancy.

The types of objects with their file extensions and an explanation of those that the Engine supports follows.

Table object (.DB)

The Table object contains the complete set of records for a table, including the names of the fields and their lengths and data types. While a relational database can consist of a set of tables related to each other, a Paradox family consists only of the files related to one table. This table's name gives its name to the rest of the files in that family. If there is a designated primary key, the table is kept sorted over the key.

Primary index object (.PX)

Whenever you create a table and designate a primary key with single or multiple fields for a table using Paradox interactively, the program generates a primary index object using the name of the table with the extension .PX. A primary index includes only the first key from each page and lists the table in key-field order, preventing records with duplicate keys. Additionally, this primary index accesses records more rapidly. While keyed tables and maintained indexes speed processing, there is a trade-off because Paradox must spend some time maintaining the indexes.

The order of the records in both the table and the index depends upon the type of sort order you define. There are four available: ASCII (the default), International (Intl), Norwegian/Danish (NorDan), and Swedish/Finnish (SwedFin). Each sort order treats the alphabet according to specific rules based on the languages that they are associated with. Generally, the ASCII sort order, the standard computer sorting order, follows the sequence of the ASCII alphabet based on each character's ASCII value, grouping the capital letters first, followed by the small letters. The ASCII order does not handle letters with diacritical marks such as accents in a strictly alphabetical sequence because these characters follow all of the unaccented characters in the ASCII alphabet. Consequently, the International order, and its two subgroups Norwegian/Danish and Swedish/Finnish, combines all of the special characters into a unified sequence so that the case of letters and any diacritical marks do not affect the alphabetical position of a letter. In this ordering, a small letter precedes its capital.

Secondary indexes objects (.Xnn and .Ynn)

A secondary index further speeds the access to information in a table because it stores records sorted by the designated fields. Often, Paradox will create such a secondary index temporarily, but you also can create a permanent one should your application benefit from this feature. A secondary index functions best if a particular field does not contain numerous duplicate values. The more distinct the values are within a field the more beneficial it is to develop a secondary index for that field.

Whenever you think about secondary indexes, remember that Paradox works with two different types: maintained and nonmaintained. A nonmaintained index contains the key and a physical pointer to the data record associated with it. These nonmaintained indexes are not updated if a record's field changes for which the index was defined or if a record is deleted or added. This type of index is for fast access because a key can be looked up and its associated record found with two or three disk accesses. A maintained index contains the key and the primary key of an associated record. Lookup is slower because a search finds the needed key, then the primary index is searched for the primary key, then the record is found. This process might take one or two extra disk accesses.

We will create a secondary index on the second field of a composite primary index. Sound complex? Not to worry, because the Engine maintains the references to the first field of the composite index so that the ordering of records in the secondary index has an intimate and, therefore, efficient relation to any record in the actual table itself.

The Paradox Engine and the Paradox family

Within the family of objects that Paradox itself can generate to maintain its own efficiency, the Engine currently cannot provide explicit access to forms, reports, graph specifications, image settings, or validity checks. While the interactive quality of Paradox allows a user to edit a database to suit spontaneous needs, this spontaneity carries with it a certain amount of ability and responsibility towards the material in a database and its importance in a larger context, such as a business operation. For the casual user—or in the case of an application for a particular business or purpose, the employee who needs to enter or look up data—the function of a database application largely replaces the serendipitous possibilities of a programming language in favor of simplicity, ease of use, and confidence in the integrity of the information entered and retrieved.

This does not mean that these interactive features are completely lost to a developer using the Engine, but it does mean that a developer must deal with these interactive and fluid aspects of Paradox explicitly, either using PAL or one of the Engine's supported languages. This book will later demonstrate how a Pascal Paradox application can create forms, validity checks, referential integrity, and querying information within a specific application.

Introducing the Paradox Engine

The next link in this programming chain between Paradox database tables and a Pascal application framework is the Paradox Engine itself. The Engine, which gives you seamless access to Paradox tables from within the frame of a Pascal application, also implements seamless connections to third-party libraries, including the entire Borland Pascal arsenal of programming tools. A Paradox Engine application can operate side by side with interactive Paradox or PAL applications. Rather than complicate the intent of this book by demonstrating how to coordinate Paradox and PAL scripts with an Engine oriented application, we will focus on writing an application independent of PAL and the interactive Paradox environments. To accomplish this, we will demonstrate features not available from the Engine itself, such as referential integrity, validity checking, queries, basic screen views, and entry forms. For these added capabilities, we will rely on Pascal as our programming tool.

The latest release of the Engine has, for the first time, included an application programming interface that eases the use of Pascal and its object-oriented programming approach.

Planning tip one: setting up a table

The following sections contain a few tips that you might want to keep in mind when you are setting up a table.

List the application's input and output

The early planning sessions for an application begin by determining what input and output the application will have to support. You can gather these end results in a number of ways, including polling a focus group of end users, working with a planning team that includes expert insights, or simply surveying similar applications in the field.

List the elements or data needed for each input and output

This list, randomly organized at first and later focused and organized through planning sessions, forms the basis for determining the elements needed to accomplish each of the requirements on the list.

From these elements, the next planning step determines the pieces of information needed to satisfy each of the requirements.

Group the elements

Grouping these pieces of information leads you to the tables you might create. While a group of the elements might suggest that we are done with planning a table, an element might not be sufficiently defined to be truly useful. Do not assume that each element is necessarily the only description that we need to consider.

For example, if one of your elements is listed as an address, then it's clear that there are some benefits to defining City, State, and ZIP as components of the address. So, while address is an element of such a table's design, it is not all there is to that element. That next level of definition will determine the actual components or fields within a table.

Planning tip two: fielding a useful form

The previous planning step encourages you to determine the information elements for the tables in an application. However, if you go no further than to say that one of the elements in a table needs to be a person's name and leave it at that, you might not have defined your elements carefully enough to be useful later on. After all, we generally alphabetize names using the person's last name. If there were no way to determine the last name from your element, a list of customers might prove useless or at least difficult to read. Hence, the benefit of focusing each field carefully and thoughtfully.

Conclusion

This chapter has introduced some of the elementary concepts needed to plan any application. An application design will need to consider the categories of data that it will store and manipulate. While your design for a user interface might present screens according to your own best sense of practical aesthetics, these screens might not necessarily present that information in the classic row and columns or tabular record and fields formats. However, defining the data, data types, and field lengths still are integral to any application. While users might not need to know that the information in front of them was culled from several tables, a programmer must know how to plan for such an arrangement.

2
An application planning process

This chapter will present a series of planning sessions that outline the steps leading up to the successful coding of the application. Although chapter 4 will illustrate how to incorporate the Engine into the user interface, the final steps of this planning process will present the user interface screens and how to create some of them using the Resource Workshop provided with Pascal with Objects. The planning for this application also will keep in mind the advantages of an object-oriented program so that later revisions or emendations of the application will be easier to implement.

This simulation will merely summarize the conclusions of typical planning sessions. Similarly, we have eliminated most of the redundancies in any commercially available application and have deliberately presented a user interface that incorporates a wide range of features. In this way, you can choose the format and complexity of the user interface that suits your own application, then merely excerpt and duplicate what you need. Each entry screen that we discuss will add some new element to the mix so that this entire application will cumulatively present a rich assortment and combination of functions.

The planning sessions

The following sections contain "planning sessions," which break down the tasks that you should perform when conducting the initial planning for your application.

Session one: establishing the application's requirements

The following list presents a group of users and the tasks they might need to perform. This is a bare bones list, and we have deliberately skewed it to allow us to demonstrate objects from Borland's ObjectWindows and the complete range of the Engine's functions that the Database Framework incorporates when we demonstrate how to write the application itself. You will notice that this planning session lists information common to most any data-entry application situation.

We will make extensive use of ObjectWindows, Borland's application framework for Microsoft Windows, and create our own set of objects that explicitly manage the application's connections to the Paradox Engine through its Database Framework.

Similar to ObjectWindows, the Paradox Engine Database Framework provides an object-oriented application program interface to the Paradox Engine. This sample application will exploit the advantages of both ObjectWindows and the Paradox Engine to create the basis for a full-featured Paradox application that joins the world of relational database design with a user's world as seen through Microsoft's Windows.

Figure 2-1 outlines the tasks and results of this first planning session where we outline the duties associated with a typical order-entry operation. As we atomize this listing of tasks, we will look toward grouping them into subsets that will allow us to begin to think ahead to the entry screens that we can associate with the various jobs of each user. Because the tasks from one user to another do intersect each other a lot, we'll create an application consisting of interface screens that, with your changes and emendations, can be fleshed out into a complete application.

2-1 Planning session one: general information.

Defining who will use the application
Employees
1. Sales
   Managers
   Order-entry Personnel
2. Warehouse
   Managers
   Shipping Personnel

Defining what they will do with the application.
General
• Enter/scan/edit information
• React to information from the application
• Managers will have access to information unavailable to such as personnel files and customer purchasing history.

Specific Tasks, by job description

1. Sales

Sales managers

- Enter new employee information
- View or edit employee information
- Assign password protection level
- View purchasing history for customers
- Create and view statistical information regarding employees and customers such as total sales by employee or most recent purchase by a customer.
- Order-entry Personnel
- Enter new customer information
- Verify and or edit old customer information
- Enter new sales order and verify that items are in stock
- Select a shipping method
- Verify credit if a credit card sale
- Edit previous sales order
- View previous sales order
- Delete sales order

2. Warehouse

Warehouse Manager

- Enter new employee information
- View or edit employee information
- Assign password protection level
- Manage inventory and reordering
- Add new vendors/items
- Update items/vendors
- Delete items/vendors

Warehouse Shipping Personnel

- Obtain latest list of unfilled orders
- Fill orders
- Record changes in inventory

Session two: normalizing the database—step 1

The second session further defines each employee's task by detailing the data required. This session begins the atomizing and normalizing process for creating a relational database. Our process follows the usual steps for accomplishing normalization. If you wish, you might consult almost any readily available book on database design for additional suggestions. In the end, a normalized set of database tables will reflect the unique elements of information, the various tasks required, and the interrelation between the tables and those tasks. As our start, FIG. 2-2 lists the specific responsibilities for each employee group and the types of information needed.

2-2 Planning session two: specifying responsibilities.

Sales

Sales managers

Enter new employee information.
- Employee ID Number
- Employee Name
- Employee Address
- Employee Phone
- Employee Position: Sales, Warehouse, Management
- Employee Security level with password
- Social Security Number
- Salary

View or Edit employee information. Prevent unauthorized access.
- Employee Name
- etc.
- Assign security level.
- Employee ID Number
- Employee Name
- Employee Password
- Employee Security Level

View purchasing history for customers
- Customer Number
- Customer Name
- Sales Order Number
- Date(s) of order(s)

Create and view statistical information regarding employees and customers such as total sales by employee or most recent purchase by customer.
- Employee Name
- Employee Number
- Customer Number
- Customer Name
- Customer Order Number(s)

Order-entry Personnel

Enter new customer information.
- Customer ID Number
- Customer Name
- Customer Address
- Customer Phone
- Customer Credit Card Information
- Customer Memo

Verify and/or edit old customer information.
- Customer ID Number
- Customer Name
- Customer Address
- Customer Phone

- Customer Credit Information
- Customer Memo

Enter new sales order and verify that items are in stock.
- Sales Order Number
- Customer ID Number
- Customer Address
- Inventory Item Number
- Inventory Item Description
- Sales Quantity Ordered
- Inventory Item Unit Price
- Inventory Quantity on hand
- Shipping Method

Verify credit if a credit card sale.
- Customer ID Number
- Credit Card Information
- Sales Order Number
- Credit Verification Number

Edit previous sales order.
- Customer ID Number
- Sales Order Number
- Inventory Item number(s)
- Inventory Item Description
- Sales Quantity Ordered
- Inventory Unit Price
- Inventory Quantity on hand

View previous sales order.
- Customer ID Number
- Sales Order Number
- Inventory Item number(s)
- Inventory Item Description
- Sales Quantity Ordered
- Inventory Unit Price

Delete sales order.
- Customer ID Number
- Sales Order Number
- Inventory Item number(s)
- Inventory Item Description
- Sales Quantity Ordered
- Inventory Unit Price

Warehouse

Warehouse Manager

Enter new employee information.
- See Sales Manager.

View or Edit employee information.
- See Sales Manager.

```
Assign security level.
     • See Sales Manager.
Manage inventory and reordering.
     • New Vendors/Items, Updating Items/Vendors, Deleting
       Items/Vendors
     • Inventory Item ID number
     • Inventory Description
     • Inventory Unit Price
     • Inventory Quantity on Hand
     • Vendor ID Number
     • Vendor Name
     • Vendor Address

Warehouse Shipping Personnel
Obtain latest list of unfilled orders, fill orders, and record
changes in inventory.
     • Sales Order Number(s)
     • Inventory Item Number(s)
     • Inventory Description(s)
     • Sales Quantity Ordered
     • Inventory Item Quantity on Hand
     • Customer ID Number
     • Customer Name
     • Customer Address
```

As you will later see, we will not create a user interface that reflects every single aspect of an employee's job description. Adding in the details that are in this fairly complete list will not be a problem for you, because you will need to extend only the types of fields and their appropriate locations and table associations already presented in the code itself. It will require some additional cutting and pasting and typing on your part, but no new coding principles for completing the work will be needed.

Session three: normalizing the tables—step 2

In this session, we need to group the elements into entities and name the tables. To accomplish this, we eliminated similar elements from each task as we grouped them. Additionally, we determined a unique element within each of the groupings, now beginning to resemble the design of a database's tables, and defined it as the table's primary key. Because Paradox allows more than one element, or field, to be defined as a key field, we determined that the SALES ITEM table would use two fields as keys.

In the SALES ITEMS table, the first element of the key uses the order number; however, because there might be several items ordered at one time, we designated the item number as the second key field. In this way, the combination of both the field order number and the item number would, as a composite key, reference a single record.

The database's entities, as described in FIG. 2-3, begin to atomize the information, group them by sets of information, and identify the unique attribute that will function as the key for a record. Because the tables for vendors (VENDOR) and personnel (PERSONNEL) resemble the same types of information stored in the customer table (CUSTOMER), we will not include it in the sample application. This will give you the chance to write them as you need to and apply the principles that we present in the code for this sample application. In most cases, you will need to be concerned only with the various definitions for each table's variables and the special needs of any data validation that you might require. Also, even though we have not included every field mentioned here for the same reasons, you will still find that our sample application is pretty well defined anyway.

2-3 Planning session three: defining database entities.

Entity	Key	Element
SALE	*	Sale Number
		Customer ID Number
		Shipping Method
		Payment Method
		Credit Card Number
		Credit Card Expiration Date
SALES ITEMS	*	Sale Number
	*	Item Number
		Quantity
INVENTORY	*	Item ID
		Description
		Quantity in stock
		Current Unit Price
		Vendor ID
CUSTOMER	*	Customer ID
		Name
		Address
		Phone

Note: The asterisk indicates that this unique element composes the table's primary key. The SALE ITEMS requires a composite key.

Session four: defining the fields and the relations between tables

With each table and its key selected, we now can move on to isolating each element of a table into discrete units, or establish an entity's atomicity. For example, we have noted only that each customer has an address. Now, we want to define more carefully the actual fields of that address, such as the street address, the city, state, and ZIP code. Further, we will need to specify the data types and restrictions for each field. We want to ensure that the field indicating the state follows the standard postal service names including capitalization so that, when we create the record for a customer's address, the application can check for correctness by matching the contents of the field with a list of state names and also check that both letters in the field are capitalized before allowing the record to be created. In this way, we begin to define the conditions needed to define using the validity checking operations included with Borland's latest ObjectWindows. We'll cover validity checking in greater detail in chapter 6.

The qualities of each field that we now will define include a unique field name that identifies the field and the table it is a part of. We have done this for two reasons: one, Paradox requires that a programmer handle name conflicts; and two, it simplifies writing and reading the code as we go along if we resolve name conflicts early in our planning process. With these names, members of a team of programmers can work separately and confidently on sections of the application.

The design of this application has declared that a sale is its primary task. Accordingly, the SALE table is the application's base, or master, table. Hence, FIG. 2-4 lists how the information the SALE table collects becomes the attributes for each of its records and forms a real world picture of a single sale. In the sample application, we have not included any of the code related to the vendors or personnel information described in this planning session.

2-4 The attributes of a record for the SALE figure.

SALE_NUMBER
  A sale identifier. SALE_NUMBER also is the primary key for this table. The SALE_NUMBER field along with an item identifier(SALES_ITEMS_ITEM_NUMBER) constitutes the link to the actual items ordered, information stored in the SALES ITEMS table using the SALES_ITEMS_SALE_NUMBER and SALES_ITEMS_ITEM_NUMBER fields as a composite key for the SALES ITEMS table.

SALE_CUSTOMER_ID
  A customer identifier. SALE_CUSTOMER_ID joins this sale to more de-tailed customer information such as name and address. This field links the SALE table to the CUSTOMER table through CUSTOMER_CUSTOMER_ID.

SALE_SHIP_METHOD, SALE_PAYMENT_METHOD, SALE_CARD_NUMBER, SALE_CARD_DATE
  These fields record information concerning the shipping method and payment method for each sale.

With the SALE table established, we can define its relation to the SALES ITEMS table. The SALES ITEMS table records the items ordered, the quantity ordered and its shipping status. The field SALES_ITEMS_SALE_NUMBER links the SALES ITEMS table to the SALE table as the field SALES_ITEMS_ITEM_DESCRIPTION links the table to the full inventory description of the item found in the INVENTORY table's INVENTORY _ITEM_NUMBER field. The two fields, SALES_ITEMS_SALE_NUMBER and SALES_ITEMS_ITEM_NUMBER, constitute the primary key for this table and identify each record as unique because a single sale will not have repeated records of the same item if each item has a discrete identifier.

The SALES_ITEMS_ITEM_NUMBER also can reference the INVENTORY table so that we can include a fuller description of the product in any table view or report.

Note that, in the sample application itself, we have not created a table with all of these fields. This planning idea incorporates some of the thinking that would go into a full-feature application.

The remainder of the tables in this application use a simple primary key.

One way of expressing the relations between these tables uses the relational schema demonstrated in FIG. 2-5 where field names preceded by an asterisk indicate a table's complete primary key. We have taken advantage of the Paradox feature that allows that this primary key consist of more than one field. In this application, only the SALES ITEMS table requires this composite primary key; INVENTORY uses INVENTORY_VENDOR merely to reference the VENDOR table's information.

2-5 A relational schema for the application's database. The tables are SALE, SALES ITEMS, CUSTOMER, and INVENTORY. Italics indicate each table's key.

```
SALE (SALE_NUMBER, SALE_CUSTOMER_ID, SALE_SHIP_METHOD,
SALE_PAYMENT_METHOD, SALE_CARD_NUMBER, SALE_CARD_DATE)

Foreign Key: SALE_CUSTOMER_ID references CUSTOMER_ID in
CUSTOMER table.

SALES ITEMS (SALES_ITEMS_SALE_NUMBER, SALES_ITEMS_ITEM_NUMBER,
SALES_ITEMS_QUANTITY)

ForeignKey:SALES_ITEMS_SALE_NUMBER references
SALE_SALE_NUMBER in SALE table.

CUSTOMER (CUSTOMER_ID,CUSTOMER_LAST_NAME, CUSTOMER_FIRST_NAME,
CUSTOMER_ADDRESS, CUSTOMER_CITY, CUSTOMER_STATE, CUSTOMER_ZIP,
CUSTOMER_TELEPHONE)

INVENTORY(INVENTORY_ITEM_NUMBER,INVENTORY_DESCRIPTION,
INVENTORY_QUANTITY, INVENTORY_UNIT_PRICE)
```

Figure 2-6 lists the general information elements in the table and how each of them is further separated into the actual fields of the table, the data type associated with that field, the domain of the field, and any rules for that field. We also selected unique fields from tables to define the relations between the tables once we had normalized the contents of the tables. Our naming convention includes the full table name as a part of the field name to make the relations clear throughout the tables for this application.

Figure 2-6 presents a completely normalized set of database tables for this application. In addition to the field name, data type and length, we have planned for the domain and restrictions that can govern a field. The validity checking facility for the application manages this aspect of a database system so that each field is filled in properly.

Another way of completing this process, which can later aid the programming team responsible for writing the code that will create these ta-

2-6 The application's database fields, data types, lengths, and restrictions.

Field	Type	Length	Domain	Rules
SALE				
SALE_SALE_NUMBER	A	12	>0	Unique
SALE_CUSTOMER_ID	A	12	>0	Unique
SALE_SHIP_METHOD	S		0,1,2	Required
SALE_PAYMENT_METHOD	S		0,1,2	Required
SALE_CARD_NUMBER	A	30		Required
SALE_CARD_DATE	D			mm/dd/yyyy
SALES ITEMS				
SALES_ITEMS_SALE_NUMBER	A	12	>0	Unique
SALES_ITEMS_ITEM_NUMBER	A	12	>0	Unique
SALES_ITEMS_QUANTITY	S		>0	Required
CUSTOMER				
CUSTOMER_CUSTOMER_ID	A	12	>0	Unique
CUSTOMER_LAST_NAME	A	15		Required
CUSTOMER_FIRST_NAME	A	15		Required
CUSTOMER_ADDRESS	A	30		Required
CUSTOMER_CITY	A	30		Required
CUSTOMER_STATE	A	2	Postal Rules	Required, uppercase.
CUSTOMER_ZIP	A	5	Postal Rules	Required - #####
CUSTOMER_TELEPHONE	A	14		Required (###)###-####
INVENTORY				
INVENTORY_ITEM_NUMBER	A	12	>0	Unique
INVENTORY_DESCRIPTION	A	20		Required
INVENTORY_QUANTITY	S		>=0	Required
INVENTORY_UNIT_PRICE	$		>=.01	Required

bles correctly, imitates the parameters the Engine requires for its field descriptors. For an advance look at this aspect of the Engine consult the description of the **TFieldDesc** object type in the Pascal Database Framework for the Engine. You will see there that a collection of these field descriptors becomes the means for defining the table's structure. Figure 2-7 simply abstracts that descriptor so that coding will be easier later on and strings them together into a fill-out form for your planners.

You can establish a complete record structure for any table by providing the planners with a fill-in sheet similar to the one we show in FIG. 2-7.

2-7 A planning instrument to assist with defining a table.

Planning Instrument for defining a table

Application Working title:

Project Team:

Number of tables in the application:

TABLE NAME:

Number of fields in this table:

Field Name Constants (Constants for the field handles)
                                    KEY (Y,N)

1

     (Ex. TABLENAME_FIELD_NAME)

2

3

4

5

6

7

8

Field # 1			Field # 5		
Field Name Constant (fldNum)			Field Name Constant (fldNum)		
Field Name	(fldName)		Field Name	(fldName)	
Field Type	(fldTpye)		Field Type	(fldTpye)	
Field SubType	(fldSubType)		Field SubType	(fldSubType)	
FieldLength	(fldLen)		FieldLength	(fldLen)	

Field # 2			Field # 6		
Field Name Constant (fldNum)			Field Name Constant (fldNum)		
Field Name	(fldName)		Field Name	(fldName)	
Field Type	(fldTpye)		Field Type	(fldTpye)	

Field SubType	(fldSubType)
FieldLength	(fldLen)

Field SubType	(fldSubType)
FieldLength	(fldLen)

Field # 3
Field Name Constant (fldNum)	
Field Name	(fldName)
Field Type	(fldTpye)
Field SubType	(fldSubType)
FieldLength	(fldLen)

Field # 7
Field Name Constant (fldNum)	
Field Name	(fldName)
Field Type	(fldTpye)
Field SubType	(fldSubType)
FieldLength	(fldLen)

Field # 4
Field Name Constant (fldNum)	
Field Name	(fldName)
Field Type	(fldTpye)
Field SubType	(fldSubType)
FieldLength	(fldLen)

Field # 8
Field Name Constant (fldNum)	
Field Name	(fldName)
Field Type	(fldTpye)
Field SubType	(fldSubType)
FieldLength	(fldLen)

Preparing the code for the tables

As long as we have all of the details for the tables in hand, let's create the code that we will use throughout the program whenever we need to work with a table. In this code, we will be establishing not only the definitions of each table's field, but also the constants that we will use, for example, to establish the size of a data entry window for the field.

This file, TABLEDIC.PAS, contains a dictionary of all table information and opens with the unit header that defines the name of this unit, which here is *tabledic*. The reserved word interface begins the public part section of this *tabledic* unit and defines those elements that other programs or units might use: the various constants and the arrays of information needed to define each table and its fields. This "public" part of the unit ends with the "implementation" code that includes the procedures for creating the field descriptions (FieldDesc). As you can see, the interface section of this unit begins by informing the compiler which other units it will need. Because this is an ObjectWindows application, we will use the Objects unit so that we can declare constants, procedures and functions, and variables in this unit. The Database Framework unit for the Engine, OopXEng, also is included here because we will need it to create the tables. The OopXEng unit conditionally pulls in the units needed for Windows Engines.

With "Objects," we now have **TObject** defined as the base object that allows us to use **TCollection** for storing dynamic collections of various records and objects. We will need **TCollection** for this unit because we need to create a collection of objects as field descriptors using the Engine's **TFieldDesc** object to define the field structure for our tables.

The code for this is simply:
```
Unit tabledic; {Unit name}
interface
uses Objects,
      OopXEng;
```

The next section of the code contains the constants that we will be declaring for use throughout the application. As you can see, we declare field handles for all of the fields that we will use to assist us in understanding the code as we go along. The constants that we declare for the various field lengths are used here to define the length of each field. Later, we will use these same field length constants to define the length of text controls for our data input. The code, as shown in FIG. 2-8, also includes the means for creating the various arrays that we need for establishing the number of fields in each table, the key counts for each table, and the table names.

2-8 This excerpt from TABLEDIC.PAS presents the constants and the names assigned to them as part of the process for preparing the code to create the application's tables.

```
{ Field lengths }

    CUST_NAME_LEN          = 15;
    SALE_NUMBER_LEN        = 12;
    CUST_ID_LEN            = 12;
    DATE_LEN               = 10;
    TIME_LEN               =  5;
    CARD_NUMBER_LEN        = 30;
    STREET_LEN             = 30;
    CITY_LEN               = 30;
    STATE_LEN              =  2;
    ZIP_LEN                =  5;
    TELEPHONE_LEN          = 14;
    ITEM_NUMBER_LEN        = 12;
    QUANTITY_LEN           =  5;
    ITEM_DESC_LEN          = 50;
    SOCIAL_SECURITY_LEN    = 11;
    UNIT_PRICE_LEN         = 10;


{ Number of tables }
```

```
  TOTAL_TABLES  = 4;

{ Table names: NOTE ——> They are PChar }

  CUSTOMER_DB_NAME      = 'CUSTOMER';
  SALE_DB_NAME          = 'SALE';
  SALES_ITEMS_DB_NAME = 'SALEITEM';
  INVENTORY_DB_NAME     = 'INVENTOR';

{ Answer table name for queries }

  ANSWER_DB_NAME        = 'ANSWER';

{ Define the number of fields in each table. }

  CUSTOMER_FIELD_COUNT    = 8;
  SALE_FIELD_COUNT        = 6;
  SALES_ITEMS_FIELD_COUNT = 3;
  INVENTORY_FIELD_COUNT   = 4;

{ Constants for the CUSTOMER field handles }

  CUSTOMER_CUSTOMER_ID = 1;
  CUSTOMER_LAST_NAME   = 2;
  CUSTOMER_FIRST_NAME  = 3;
  CUSTOMER_ADDRESS     = 4;
  CUSTOMER_CITY        = 5;
  CUSTOMER_STATE       = 6;
  CUSTOMER_ZIP         = 7;
  CUSTOMER_TELEPHONE   = 8;

{ Constants for the SALE field handles }

  SALE_SALE_NUMBER     = 1;
  SALE_CUSTOMER_ID     = 2;
  SALE_SHIP_METHOD     = 3;
  SALE_PAYMENT_METHOD  = 4;
  SALE_CARD_NUMBER     = 5;
  SALE_CARD_DATE       = 6;

{ Constants for the SALEITEMS field handles }

  SALES_ITEMS_SALE_NUMBER = 1;
  SALES_ITEMS_ITEM_NUMBER = 2;
  SALES_ITEMS_QUANTITY    = 3;
```

```
{ Constants for the INVENTORY field handles }

   INVENTORY_ITEM_NUMBER        = 1;
   INVENTORY_DESCRIPTION        = 2;
   INVENTORY_QUANTITY           = 3;
   INVENTORY_UNIT_PRICE         = 4;

{ Individual table primary key counts }

   CUSTOMER_KEY_COUNT    = 1;
   SALE_KEY_COUNT        = 1;
   SALES_ITEMS_KEY_COUNT = 2;
   INVENTORY_KEY_COUNT   = 1;

{ Put the field counts in an array. }

   tableFieldCounts: array [1..TOTAL_TABLES] of Integer =
   (
     CUSTOMER_FIELD_COUNT,
     SALE_FIELD_COUNT,
     SALES_ITEMS_FIELD_COUNT,
     INVENTORY_FIELD_COUNT
   );

 { Array of these key counts }

   tableKeyCounts: array [1..TOTAL_TABLES] of integer =
   (
     CUSTOMER_KEY_COUNT,
     SALE_KEY_COUNT,
     SALES_ITEMS_KEY_COUNT,
     INVENTORY_KEY_COUNT
   );

 { Put the table names into an array. }

   tableNames: array [1..TOTAL_TABLES] of string =
   (
     CUSTOMER_DB_NAME,
     SALE_DB_NAME,
     SALES_ITEMS_DB_NAME,
     INVENTORY_DB_NAME
   );

{ CUSTOMER table fields }
```

```
CUSTOMER_FIELD_DESC: array [1..CUSTOMER_FIELD_COUNT] of
TFieldDesc =
(
  { Field #1 (Customer ID) }
(
     fldNum:     CUSTOMER_CUSTOMER_ID;
     fldName:    'Customer ID';
     fldType:    fldChar;
     fldSubtype: fldstNone;
     fldLen:     CUST_ID_LEN
),

  { Field #2 (Last name) }

  (
     fldNum:     CUSTOMER_LAST_NAME;
     fldName:    'Last Name';
     fldType:    fldChar;
     fldSubtype: fldstNone;
     fldLen:     CUST_NAME_LEN
  ),

  { Field #3 (First name) }

  (
     fldNum:     CUSTOMER_FIRST_NAME;
     fldName:    'First Name';
     fldType:    fldChar;
     fldSubtype: fldstNone;
     fldLen:     CUST_NAME_LEN
  ),

  { Field #4 (Address) }

  (
     fldNum:     CUSTOMER_ADDRESS;
     fldName:    'Address';
     fldType:    fldChar;
     fldSubtype: fldstNone;
     fldLen:     STREET_LEN
  ),

  { Field #5 (City) }

  (
```

```
    fldNum:       CUSTOMER_CITY;
    fldName:      'City';
    fldType:      fldChar;
    fldSubtype:   fldstNone;
    fldLen:       CITY_LEN
),

{ Field #6 (State) }

(
    fldNum:       CUSTOMER_STATE;
    fldName:      'State';
    fldType:      fldChar;
    fldSubtype:   fldstNone;
    fldLen:       STATE_LEN
),

{ Field #7 (ZIP) }

(
    fldNum:       CUSTOMER_ZIP;
    fldName:      'Zip';
    fldType:      fldChar;
    fldSubtype:   fldstNone;
    fldLen:       ZIP_LEN
),

{ Field #8 (Telephone) }

(
    fldNum:       CUSTOMER_TELEPHONE;
    fldName:      'Telephone';
    fldType:      fldChar;
    fldSubtype:   fldstNone;
    fldLen:       TELEPHONE_LEN
)
);
```

We finally come to the definitions of the field descriptors for each table. You will notice here that the code follows the fill-in worksheet that we presented earlier in FIG. 2-7. In this example, we have included only the information for the CUSTOMER table; the remaining tables follow the same principles.

The code for TABLEDIC.PAS concludes with the implementation segment of this unit. Here, we have written the procedures needed to create the arrays of table descriptors we will need for each table. See FIG. 2-9 for this code.

2-9 This excerpt from TABLEDIC.PAS presents the code for creating the arrays of table descriptors that we will need when we create a table and its indexes.

```
implementation
var
  fieldLoop: integer;
  tmpIndexRec: PIndexRecord;

begin

{ Create a table descriptor for each table, also fill in the }
{ secondary index array.                                      }

{ CUSTOMER table }

  tableFieldDesc[1] := new(PTableDesc, Init(10, 5));
  secondaryIndexArray[1] := NIL;

  for fieldLoop := 1 to CUSTOMER_FIELD_COUNT do
  begin
    tableFieldDesc[1]^.insert(@CUSTOMER_FIELD_DESC[fieldLoop]);
  end;

{ SALE table }

  tableFieldDesc[2] := new(PTableDesc, Init(10, 5));

  for fieldLoop := 1 to SALE_FIELD_COUNT do
  begin
    tableFieldDesc[2]^.insert(@SALE_FIELD_DESC[fieldLoop]);
  end;

{ The second field of the SALE table has a secondary index on it. }

  tmpIndexRec := new(PIndexRecord);
  tmpIndexRec^.FieldsToIndex[1] := 2;
  tmpIndexRec^.Count := 1;

  secondaryIndexArray[2] := tmpIndexRec;

{ SALES ITEMS table }

  tableFieldDesc[3] := new(PTableDesc, Init(10, 5));
  secondaryIndexArray[3] := NIL;
```

```
for fieldLoop := 1 to SALES_ITEMS_FIELD_COUNT do
begin
  tableFieldDesc[3]^.insert(@SALES_ITEMS_FIELD_DESC[fieldLoop]);
end;
{ INVENTORY table }

  tableFieldDesc[4] := new(PTableDesc, Init(10, 5));
  secondaryIndexArray[4] := NIL;

  for fieldLoop := 1 to INVENTORY_FIELD_COUNT do
  begin
    tableFieldDesc[4]^.insert(@INVENTORY_FIELD_DESC[fieldLoop]);
  end;
```

With the TABLEDIC.PAS file, we have established all the constants, variables, and arrays of field descriptors that we will use throughout the program. The arrays of field descriptors are used in the program by the procedure that the "Tools ¦ Create Database" menu option calls when selected. This procedure, **TMDIPosWindow.CreateDatabase**, relies on the arrays that TABLEDIC.PAS has established to perform its tasks. We will explain this procedure fully in chapter 5 when we cover the code needed for integrating the user interface and the procedures that access the Paradox Engine. Still, the code for creating the tables and their primary indexes follows in FIG. 2-10 so that you can see how our work here in TABLEDIC.PAS is used when it is needed. Figure 2-10 is an excerpt from TMDIPOS.PAS.

2-10 This excerpt from TMDIPOS.PAS shows how the application creates a table and indexes from the code provided by TABLEDIC.PAS.

```
{ Create the table. }

  errCode := ERROR(getDatabase^.createTable(tableNames[tableLoop],
    tableFieldDesc[tableLoop]), tableNames[tableLoop]);

{ If there was an error, then skip the other operations. }

  if(errCode <> PXSUCCESS) then continue;

{ Create the primary index, if any. }

  if(tableKeyCounts[tableLoop] > 0) then
  begin
    ERROR(getDatabase^.createPIndex(tableNames[tableLoop],
    tableKeyCounts[tableLoop]), tableNames[tableLoop]);
  end;
```

3

The Resource Workshop and the user interface

With the tables set, our planning turns to creating the user interface screens for the application. Working with the Resource Workshop makes prototyping input screens a fast and easy task because the Workshop handles much of the overhead for you and leaves you to drag and drop or point and click your way to success. We'll be showing you how to put together a clever set of graphical and text elements that stretch out some of the usual features of a user interface. The first associates a field in a database table with an area that is protected from access by the user. This display element will combine a window element normally used for displaying static text into which we will pump data from a table so that the text is anything but static. The second cleverness shows how to combine several child windows into a unified data entry form that will permit us to display, navigate, and update the contents of several tables simultaneously.

Before we max out with this last window, we'll jump in with how to use the Resource Workshop to create the menu bar and the simplest of screens.

Session 5: planning the user interface menus

The planning for this user interface will adhere to the specifications already defined as defaults in Borland's ObjectWindows or defined by the Borland Windows Custom Controls DLL (BWCC). We will not be changing the screen colors for the menu bars, dialogue boxes, highlight colors, active buttons, etc.

This session, designing the user interface, uses the following set of design specifications:

- All menu selections will have keyboard shortcuts. These shortcuts will be accessed using a combination of the Alt key and a unique letter within the static text of the menu bar or drop down menu.
- All menu selections will be accessible using a mouse.
- To enforce entity validity, basic information regarding a sale—such as the sales number, customer identification, and other information such as the total number of records and the current record—will appear on screens as values the user cannot alter.
- When a user creates information for a sale, inventory, or customer, the system automatically will assign an identification number for that operation. This number will constitute the record's key and the application will generate it using elements from the system's calendar and clock. The identification number will consist of a 12 digit number composed of the year (2 digits), month (2), day (2), and time (6 digits) from the system clock. We chose this method for generating keys because it uses easily available information.
- A user will be able to search for information already on the system, such as customer information and product information, including current inventory.
- A user will be able to view information that cannot be changed.
- Any delete operation will always prompt the user to confirm the deletion.
- A user will have the following basic options: Ok, to complete an operation; and Cancel, to cancel that operation without changing anything. In addition a screen might offer other options such as Add, Edit, Delete, First, Previous, Next, Last, and so on.

The main menu bar

The main menu bar displayed in FIG. 3-1 presents the choices for the application: Sales, History, Merchandise, Tools, and Window. The choices are located at the top of the screen.

Sales

The Sales choice allows a user to create a new sale. It first will prompt the user to supply a customer. If the customer does not exist, then the user will have the option of adding the customer to the database.

History

The History choice allows a user to view the contents of a sale or sales made to a particular user.

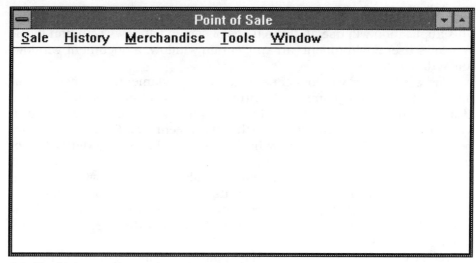

3-1 The Main menu bar and application window.

Merchandise

The Merchandise menu covers all aspects of inventory: adding new items, editing this information, and so on.

Tools

The Tools menu bar choice has two offerings: Create Database and Query. This first choice, Create Database, automatically will create all of the tables and indexes required for the application. The second choice, Query, will allow a user to assemble a simple, single table query using QBE techniques.

Window

The Window option allows a user to arrange document windows within the application window. When more than one "Sale" window is open, this menu option will allow a user to arrange the various windows or their icons.

Screen design

Once we get beyond the design for the main application window and its menu bar, the entire application is based on variations of three user entry screens that we'll refer to as our foundation screens. They form the true center of the coding for the application. When you work with the application or peruse its code, you'll begin to recognize them as the leitmotifs for the entire user interface.

The Windows windows

This application will use all three types of screen windows common to the Windows user environment: an application window, a document window, and a dialog box.

The application window constitutes the fundamental framework, or desktop, for data and commands within the application. It is movable and sizable, and virtually all activity for an application takes place within it. The exceptions really are stylistic rather than technical. For example, suppose that an application window has been resized so that a dialog box or menu drop-down no longer fits inside it. Should this happen, the dialog box or menu box then might appear partially outside the window. Similarly, movable dialogs can be moved outside the primary application window. Do any of these possibilities actually affect the operation of the application or the code needed to account for such things? No, Windows manages these resources.

As part of the design process, the application window ought to include some other elements that are a part of the parameters for the object used to create it: a sizable frame and a title bar that contains at least the title of the application. The other elements of an application window are described in the following sections.

Window frame All windows have frames even when they fill the entire screen. In such a case, the frame simply coincides with the screen edge. While the frames of dialog boxes are not sizable, those for the application and documents and most other windows are.

Title bar A title bar can contain a title, a Control-menu box (also known as a System-menu box), a Maximize button (if the window does not then fill the screen), or a Restore button (if the window is currently maximized). We will disable the Control-menu box for our Inventory dialog, which prevents a user from closing the dialog without one of the command buttons and forces the user either to create the record fully or delete it explicitly.

Menu bar The menu bar is used in our application to provide access to commands and entry screens in the application. Document windows and dialogs generally do not have a menu bar. Our menu bar contains the titles of the operations of the application. The menu can contain items with drop-down menus for commands or be commands themselves.

In this application, only the Tools menu title offers further command choices via a drop-down menu. The other menu titles are commands that initiate a process such as order entry or adding merchandise to the inventory.

Scroll bar Scroll bars along the right side and bottom of a window allow a user to move the contents of a window so that whatever is clipped by the edge of the window may be viewed. Only our main application window includes scroll bars for conditions when a document window is displayed and clipped. The dialog boxes, because they can extend in front of and beyond the edges of the main application window of desktop if it is not maximized, do not require scroll bars to be viewed. Because they themselves are not resizeable, they do not require scroll bars for themselves. These remaining elements of a window are not included in this application, though you might want to use them yourself.

Message bar and status bar   These two types of informational bars generally found at the bottom of a window are optional and let the application request information from the user or display help information. A status bar is a more elaborate form of a message bar that displays information about the current state of an application. Word processors, like Word for Windows, use a status bar to indicate the current page, section, line and column location of the cursor, and so on. This application will not use this type of messaging service for the user; however, we will incorporate information such as the record totals in a table and the current record location of the cursor within a table as part of a dialog box.

Control bars   Control bars can include ribbons, rulers, toolboxes, and palettes. While we will not use control bars containing rulers, toolboxes, or palettes for this application, we certainly will need ways to issue common commands—the general domain of ribbon control bars. We'll place them in a convenient location on the screen, generally close to the locations of the data entry boxes. The style of ribbon control bars—commonly found beneath the menu bar of word processing applications and so on—really is not appropriate for the needs of this application.

However, we will demonstrate a control area within the frame of our own dialog boxes to issue the commands we need to manipulate the display of data from our tables. The principles for creating a ribbon control bar are similar and really a matter of style and locating these functions in a place where a user can get to them with a minimum amount of mousing around.

The menu bar

To begin prototyping the application's main window and its menu, we will need to create a menu bar. The Application's menu bar and main window follow standard Windows conventions. We will incorporate three types of menu bar choices: immediate selection, drop-down menu choices, and a cascading menu choice box. The first three choices on our menu bar immediately issue a command that moves a user to an entry screen; the fourth, Tools, uses a drop-down menu to offer two choices: Create Database and Queries. The second choice also includes a pop-up, or fly-out menu box, with further choices. Figure 3-2 illustrates the menu bar with the choices for Tools visible.

Using the Resource Workshop to create the menu bar

First off, there is a difference between what we'll be doing in the Resource Workshop and the Pascal code for the program itself. A resource created with the Workshop doesn't "do" anything; the program itself does the work. Consequently, for each resource, there must be a corresponding element in the code itself performing some function or procedure. The Resource Workshop, however, provides an excellent arena for prototyping the application's menu and interfaces and testing them in a rudimentary way to make sure they anticipate a user's needs.

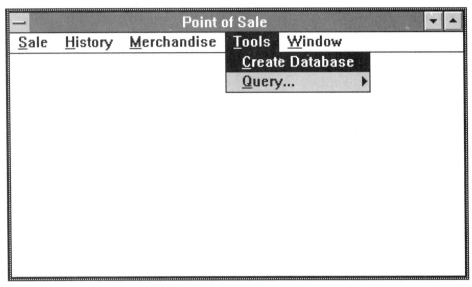

3-2 The Main menu bar showing the choices for the Tools option.

To begin to create a menu, launch the Resource Workshop, select the New option from the File menu and choose the .RES (for resource) file type in the New project dialog box that appears. Click Ok and the full Resource menu will appear with an "untitled.res" window on the desktop. From the Resource menu select New, then select Menu as the type of resource to create.

Using the Menu option, you can quickly assemble a menu for this application. All our menu choices, with the exception of Tools and Window, are MENUITEM resources. Tools and Window are POPUP resources. Keep track of the ID number for each of the menu items because you will need to assign these as the constant values for the menu's various options.

After you have completed the menu, save the resource. We will include this resource containing this menu and all of the dialog boxes for this application in the file containing our main program (POS.PAS) as one of the compiler directives. To do this, we simply include this line as part of the file's header:

{$R POS.RES}

Now, all you need to do to reference a resource and use it is to remember the constant that the recourse workshop, or you, assigned each element. To hook this resource to the objects that actually do the work so that the menu does more than look good on a color monitor, here's how to write the first elements of the necessary code.

Once we have added a resource file to an executable file, we have to load it explicitly before we can make use of it. Because a window's menu is one of its creation attributes, we have to specify its characteristics before the window's corresponding element is created. Therefore, we can specify a menu in the window type's constructor by using the *LoadMenu* Windows function with the menu identifier when a new window object is constructed. For the moment, all you need to worry about here is the section of the code that loads the menu. The other intriguing code in FIG. 3-3 (an excerpt from POS.PAS) illustrates how we are creating our own instance of a **TApplication** object with **TPosApplication** and constructing the Main Window of the application. Because we want this main window to handle some specialized Engine tasks like cranking up the Engine and establishing a pointer to the database, we have written our own descendant object **TMDIDBFWindow**, a **TMDIWindow** object type to manage initializing the Engine, and its descendant **TMDIPosWindow**, which is the object that actually contains the code for the procedures especially written for a particular application, and so on. When we discuss the reusable objects that we have created for you to work with in your applications, we will discuss the role that **TMDIDBFWindow** plays in this scheme.

As you can see in FIG. 3-3, the menu handle *'Pos_Main_Menu'* establishes this resource as the main menu of our application's **TMDIWindow** object. With that in place, we now can point to the resource identifiers for the menus pop-up and dialog resources.

As you prepare to write the code for your resources, you'll want to establish the constants and assign them to mnemonic variables for your convenience in the interface section of the unit. Because we also will be including the standard child window menu in this MDI window, we'll need to locate that also. Our menu bar displays four choices, and we want the final option

3-3 This excerpt from POS.PAS shows how to construct a main window and load the main menu for our application.

```
procedure TPosApplication.InitMainWindow;
begin

{ Create a TMDIDBFWindow object as the main window for the
application. The }
{ constructor to TMDIWindow takes a handle to a menu.  This
is the { application's main menu.
}

  MainWindow := New (PMDIPOSWindow, Init('Point of Sale',
            LoadMenu(HInstance, 'Pos_Main_Menu')));
end;
```

to be the child window Windows option, making its position the fifth and its offset the integer 4 because the first position at the uppermost left hand corner is zero. The field *ChildMenuPos* handles this for us, as you will see in FIG. 3-4. Remembering the constants for our menu resources and our "Windows" offset, we can write the code shown in FIG. 3-4. The Windows constant

3-4 This excerpt from TMDIPOS.PAS shows how to define the constants for the main menu bar and the child window menu in this unit's interface section.

```
const

{ The offset of the Window menu in the application }
  MENU_WINDOW_OFFSET    = 4;
{ Sale menu }
  id_New_Sale           = 100;
{  Inventory menu }
  id_Inventory          = 104;
{ History Menu }
  id_History            = 108;
{ Tools menu }
  id_Create             = 109;
  id_Query_Customers    = 101;
  id_Query_Inventory    = 102;
  id_Query_Sales        = 103;
  id_Query_Items        = 105;

{ Define the new types we are going to use in the program }

type

(*********************************************************************
 * OBJECT:       TMDIPOSWindow
 *
 * INHERITS:   TMDIWindow
 *
 * DESCRIPTION:  This object overrides TMDIDBFWindow and makes a specific
 *               object used in the POS application.
 *
 *********************************************************************)
  PMDIPOSWindow = ^TMDIPOSWindow;
  TMDIPOSWindow = object(TMDIDBFWindow)

{ Override the constructor to set up the Window Menu }
  constructor Init(Atitle: PChar; AMenu: HMenu);

{ A procedure to respond to the Sale menu selection }
  procedure CMNewSale(var Msg: TMessage); virtual cm_First + id_New_Sale;
```

```
{ A procedure to respond to the History menu selection }
  procedure CMHistory(var Msg: TMessage); virtual cm_First + id_History;

{ A procdeure to respond to the Inventory menu selection }
  procedure Inventory(var Msg: TMessage);
        virtual cm_First + id_Inventory;

{ Define a procedure that will create all the tables in the database. }
{ This procedure should be called when the user selects the           }
{ Tools¦Create database (id_Create) menu choice.                      }
  procedure CreateDatabase(var Msg: TMessage);
        virtual cm_First + id_Create;

{ Procedures to query tables when a user selects the Tools¦Query option.}
  procedure QueryCustomers(var Msg: TMessage);
        virtual cm_First + id_Query_Customers;
  procedure QueryInventory(var Msg: TMessage);
        virtual cm_First + id_Query_Inventory;
  procedure QuerySales(var Msg: TMessage);
        virtual cm_First + id_Query_Sales;
  procedure QueryItems(var Msg: TMessage);
        virtual cm_First + id_Query_Items;
  .
  .
  .
end;
```

cm_First offsets our menu and dialog constants to ensure that we will not be interfering with any of the default constants Windows itself has claimed.

Each of the previous procedures will need control objects that define the tasks for each menu choice. To begin that process, let's take a look at how to create the necessary dialog boxes this application uses.

Dialog boxes and child windows

With a menu resource done, we move on to creating the resources for the dialog boxes that these menu choices will call. The entire application is based upon variations of the following three screens. The first two of them—dialog boxes—are best done with the Resource Workshop, and the third—a document child window—presents some interesting coding situations. In its case, we'll simply show the design of it here and how to do the code for it when we begin to dig more deeply into the application's code.

The three foundation screens

The following sections describe the three foundation screens used by the application: new customer, select customer, and new sale.

Foundation screen one: new customer

Figure 3-5 lays out the entry screen for the information the CUSTOMER table requires. Following the design guidelines for a Windows interface, the screen will require the following elements:

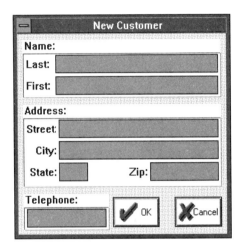

3-5 The Windows resources needed for the New Customer dialog box: a simple data entry dialog box.

- A frame. This screen is a dialog box that we will be able to move, but not resize: two standard characteristics of dialog boxes that adhere to the Microsoft Windows Guidelines.
- A title bar. We will include a title bar in all of our screens to guide the user. The title bar for this screen also will include a control-menu box for moving and closing the dialog box.
- Static text. The static texts in this screen will identify the purpose of each area and the information needed for the data entry boxes. While we have not included help for the user to assist with, say, the required format for information to be entered in a data field, you could do so. In this way, you would be helping the user to satisfy the validity checking demands for a particular field. (Often, a user manual provided during training also would do the trick because it would present the standard operating procedures of a company. Some prefer this information to be online either as part of a Help application associated with the main application or as information displayed in a message bar or status bar along the bottom of a screen.)

- Data-entry boxes or fields. These are areas into which a user would type the information needed to complete the "form" being displayed.
- Command buttons. These are buttons—here OK and Cancel—that perform commands that either accept the information as entered by the user or end the process without any data being added to the database; here the CUSTOMER table.

These elements, all used to complete the fields from the CUSTOMER table, are built using the Resource Workshop provided with Pascal with Objects, version 7. All of the elements of our dialog box are simply a set of controls available from the Resource Workshop. The controls we use include: static text, edit text, groups of buttons, and a series of child windows as groups with shading and captions to identify the purpose of the group.

Creating a dialog box in the Borland Resource Workshop Again, we use the Resource Workshop to design the look and feel of the user interface elements, here a dialog box. With it, we determine the size of the dialog box; its esthetic appearance; the size, location, and types of the various controls that we need; and so on. With the exception of how some of the controls work when used in a group, the resources for the dialog box do not actually "do" anything: that's what the program code does. Every element in each resource that you create must have a corresponding element in the Pascal program itself. So, each dialog box must have a corresponding object type descended from **TDialog** that contains fields for the dialog box controls and methods to process the data from these fields. We also will be redefining what the Ok and Cancel buttons do when their commands are called as part of a **TDialog** style operation. Chapter 5 will cover these program elements. For now, we'll breeze through what you'll need to do to create the "New Customer" dialog box, our first and simplest foundation screen.

Creating the "New Customer" dialog box To create a dialog box, you launch the Resource Workshop from the Pascal program group, select Open project from the File menu option, and choose the .RES file that you created when you made the menu. Click Ok, and the full Resource menu will appear with a window listing the resources you have already created. From the Resource menu bar option, select New, then choose DIALOG as the type of resource you will be creating. The dialog editor will open as shown in FIG. 3-6, and a dialog box as well as the toolboxes for the control, alignment, and other tools also will be there for you to work with. You now are ready to build the dialog box.

The window style. To caption the dialog window, click twice on the dialog frame where it now says DIALOG_1. The Window style dialog box will open. Fill in or check off the various areas of the Window style dialog box as follows to create a dialog box like the one shown in FIG. 3-5:

Caption: New Customer
Class: BORDLG

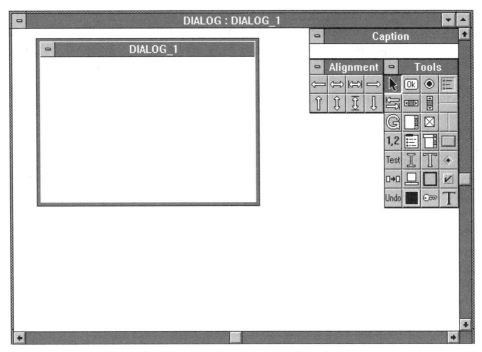

3-6 The Resource Workshop's dialog editor window with editing toolboxes and a generic dialog box.

This class from the BWCC.DLL, the Borland Windows Custom Controls DLL, produces the "chiseled steel" background and sets up the coordinated color scheme and controls for a "Borland-style" dialog box that, as you will see, includes the Ok push button with the green check mark, and so on:

Window type	Popup
Frame style	Caption
Font	Leave blank. We'll take the default.
Dialog style	System menu.

This includes the button on the upper left corner with the usual system commands in its menu.

Modal frame.

This allows a user to move the frame around; however, the dialog box cannot be resized.

Group box. This tool from the resource editor puts a shaded box around a group of controls to group them visually. You can include a caption in this box as well. This group box is one of the tools available as an element from the Borland Windows Custom Control DLL. After you size this box, click twice on it with the mouse and a dialog box for defining the style elements of the group box will appear. Here's what we used to produce the box you see for the "Name" grouping.

Caption   Name:
Control ID   101

This Control ID will differ for each element in the dialog box. You'll use the ID later to bind the code, as needed, to the controls in the dialog box. While you won't need this ID (a shaded box isn't going to perform any action), you will need to keep track of the ID numbers and the purposes of the control for others, such as a button or Edit text box.

Shade type   Group shade

This makes the box appear to be recessed into the chiseled steel background of the dialog box itself.

Alignment for caption   Left
Attributes   Visible
Caption   Above

This choice also adds in a horizontal gray line below the caption to make it appear as it if were a labeled ribbon.

Static text. This allows us to insert static text into the dialog box as identifiers for the data entry fields. (You can use the menu bar or the toolbox to access this and other controls.) Here's the style definitions for the Last: static text:

Caption   Last:
Control ID   102
Attributes   Visible

If you do not choose the "border" style, then the grayed area of this control's window will blend in with the gray of the group box.

Control type   Left text

If you want to align the static text so that it butts up against the edit boxes for data entry, then use the "Right text" option.

Edit text. This allows us to create a data entry box. For this control, we will want to make it stand out against the gray background, so we'll use a border and leave the interior of the box white. Here's the style definitions we used.

Caption   None. Leave the Text button depressed.
Control ID   104

This control ID and others from these edit boxes are going to be needed later on when we hook this resource to our code. Keep track of each control ID as a constant for later reference.

Attributes   Tab stop

Check this so the user can move from field to field with the Tab key on the keyboard.

Visible.	
Border.	
Justification	Left
Scroll bar	None. This is only one line of text.
Case insensitive.	This allows a user to enter upper and lower case letters, etc.
Single line.	We want the user to enter information for only one field.
Password, Convert OEM, Keep none.	None checked off.
Automatic scroll	

Horizontal. This choice means that we don't have to worry if the user enters information that is longer than the edit text box but shorter than the field length. Generally, we make the box big enough to contain the entire field of the table, but this is simply a matter of convenience and not required.

Win 3.1 Styles None.

Buttons. The buttons shown are from the BWCC library of custom controls. To use them instead of the standard Windows buttons, select the "Control ¦ Custom" menu option, then scroll down to select "Pushbutton." Both the Ok and Cancel buttons are custom push buttons. If you want to use a Windows-style button here, then simply select the "Control ¦ Push button" option. Unlike the Borland-style buttons, you will have to enter the caption that you want to appear within the button. Here are the style elements that you should enter in the "Borland button style" dialog box:

Caption Button.

Use this caption because the Control ID will reference the type of Borland-style button to appear here.

Control ID 1.

A control ID of one (1) will reference the Borland-style Ok button. Similarly, when you create the Cancel button, a control ID of two (2) will reference the Borland-style Cancel button.

Attributes Tab stop.

This allows a user to use the Tab key to move to this button and activate it.

Visible.
Button type Pushbutton.

To complete this dialog box, you'll need to mouse around with the various controls so that they align with each other and appear pleasing to the eye as well as practical to move through when a user works with the dialog.

Foundation screen two: select customer

When a user selects the Sale option, the user interface screen that first appears is a dialog box that allows the user to select an existing customer or add a new customer to the database. The first foundation screen, "New Customer," is the dialog box that appears when the user clicks on the Add . . . button. Our second foundation screen is, as FIG. 3-7 illustrates, a simple variation on most of the controls that we presented in FIG. 3-5, the "New Customer" dialog.

3-7 The Select Customer dialog box.

We have added some controls to this dialog that allow the user to scroll through a list of all existing employees using a set of scrolling buttons: First, Last, Next, and Prev (Previous). This scrolling feature defines our second foundation screen's technique. Whenever we need to select or view something from a collection of items (customers, inventory, and items for a sale), a variation of this foundation screen will appear. Additionally, this screen also incorporates a type of status bar at the top to indicate the total number of records in the table and the number of the record from that table currently displayed. Finally, the Add button issues a command to display another dialog box, the "New Customer" dialog, our first foundation screen.

To create this dialog box, simply begin by making a copy of the "New Customer" resource, creating a new dialog resource, enlarging it to leave room for the new controls, then pasting the "New Customer" controls inside the new dialog's frame. Once the controls are in place, you might need to tweak their positions before you continue. The major change that you will need to make to the controls that you just pasted in place is to change all of the edit boxes to a read only style so that a user will not then be able to access the boxes. They won't need to do so anyway because this screen is simply a display screen so that a user can verify that they have the correct customer for the sale they are about to write.

To make a data box read only, click twice on it, check off the Read only button in the Win 3.1 Styles choice, and click Ok to save the change. Do this for each one of the data boxes for this new dialog box.

The interesting controls for this dialog box focus on the "status bar" that tops off the dialog. After all, the buttons in the "Scrolling" group are simply the default Windows style buttons. The control ID's assigned to them will be of interest later when we write the code to perform the actions that they describe because we will be using them to navigate a table. Keeping track of the location of that cursor and displaying the key for each record is the purpose of the status bar. Creating it is not a complex matter, but we will be using a number of the BWCC controls available to us to dress it up.

The shaded box itself is, once again, a group box with a caption. Into that box, we place first a Borland style static text box that is large enough to contain the key field (12 spaces +1) from the customer record using the following style attributes:

Caption	Leave this blank and the "Text" box checked.
Control ID	115. This happens to be the one we ended up with. Yours might be different, but keep track of this ID because it will be how we inject the contents of the record's key into this static text box.
Attributes	Visible. If you do not choose the "border" style, then the grayed area of this control's window will blend in with the gray of the group box.
Control type	Left text.

By way of dressing up this status bar, we include a "dip" to separate the record's key from the next set of information, the current number and total number of records in the table. To do this, you will need to use the "vertical dip" from the Borland custom controls and these style choices:

Caption	Leave this blank.
Control ID	120. This happens to be the one we ended up with. Yours might be different.
Shade type	Vertical dip.
Attributes	Visible.
Alignment for caption	Left.

The remaining static text boxes will label and display the current record number and total number of records in the table. Creating them follows the same procedures that you use for any static text box, remembering to keep track of the control ID for the empty boxes where we will later insert the appropriate information gleaned for us by the Engine from the table and its record count.

When you have created a dialog box, you really should check to make sure that the controls are grouped or sequenced properly so that, when you tab from one to the next, the cursor follows the correct sequence. To accomplish this, choose Set order from the Options menu. Your cursor will change to a "1,2" icon, allowing you to rearrange the numbering sequence. If all is well, then leave the sequencing as it is.

Just about the last thing that you'll want to do before you close out your resource session is to make sure that you rename the default names for the dialogs that you create. You can do this with the "Resource | Rename" menu option. Save the resource with a name that you'll easily remember when you add it to the beginning of the main program's file as a compiler directive. Check the compiler's "Options | Directories" choice to make sure that you have included the path for this resource in the "Resources" path statement.

Foundation screen three: new sale

This final foundation screen uses several techniques not explored in the other two types of user interface screens—namely, a document window. We have chosen this technique so that you can see how it is done and so that you can allow for a user who might want to have several sales open at the same time and move between them. Because this third foundation screen also is the basis for the "History" screen that can display all of the previous sales by a particular customer, a user could have both the "New Sale" screen and a history of purchases for the same customer open at the same time using this document window method. In addition, the New Sale window also will spawn a child window to allow the user to select the merchandise to be sold from the INVENTORY table. This New Sale window then will create the necessary record on the SALE table and the records for each item in that sale on the SALE ITEMS table. To accomplish this, we will need to rely on our own linking facility to maintain the referential integrity of the system.

As you can see in FIG. 3-8, this final user interface element presents some intriguing coding challenges. When completed, this final foundation screen for the user interface also is used as the basis for the Purchasing History option on the main menu bar.

Unlike the other two screens, this screen is not a Resource Workshop product. Instead, we code it from scratch because it contains several concepts that we want to demonstrate with it. Basically, we'll be showing how to create a user interface that relies on linked tables. After all, the normalizing process for this application has left us with the situation that requires the New Sale entry to create a record in the SALE table and the SALE ITEMS table as well. To accomplish this, we will need to conceive of the window here as a desktop onto which we will be placing two separate window units each one referencing a table from the database. To coordinate this operation, we will rely on the sale number window in the group of fields connected to the SALE table. This sale number will be used as a foreign key for the SALE ITEMS table so that both tables use the sale num-

3-8 The New Sale window for this application, which uses a series of child windows to display and manage data.

ber properly as the shared reference which will allow us to maintain referential integrity.

We get to the "New Sale" screen by first selecting an existing customer or adding a new customer, in which case we move to an input screen to create a customer record. That completed, an Ok moves a user on to the "New Sale" screen itself.

Whenever an item is added to the order, the application offers a series of prompts to ensure that the correct item identification number is located by moving a user through scrolling box lists and input line screens. Having located the item, the application gathers the necessary item information, prompts the user for the quantity to be ordered, then fills in the box properly on the "New Sale" window.

When a user clicks the "New Sale" screen's Ok button, the entire order is written away to the proper database tables.

Figure 3-9 is an exploded view of the "New Sale" table illustrating the groups of windows we are using to complete a sale.

When we get down to writing the code for this Sale Window, we're going to create a Chinese puzzle box of windows on top of windows. We begin with a window that will form the foundation for all of the other windows. Onto it, we'll position static text, edit controls, combo boxes, and buttons. We also will be grouping these windows so that we can attach them to the various tables we'll want them to use data from or write data to.

The main window object for this data entry screen is called **TSaleWindow**, and we inherit **TCursorWindow** to do it. **TCursorWindow** is one of the object types that we have written that, as a descendant of **TWindow**, allows you to associate a Database Framework cursor object and an interface or window or dialog object so that you can access Paradox tables. The next chapter covers all of the special objects that we wrote as reusable code in detail; therefore, when you look at the code here realize that the ObjectWindows objects such as **TWindow**, **TDialog**, **TStatic**, **TEdit**, **TButton**, and others will be the ancestors for the objects that you'll encounter here to place edit boxes, combo boxes, and buttons that give them the functionality this application requires.

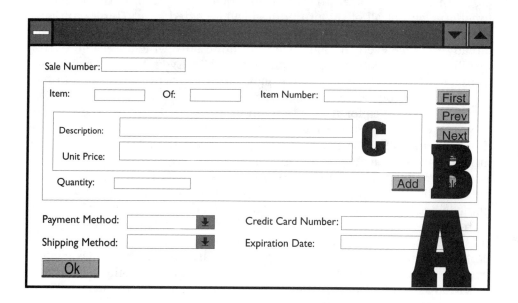

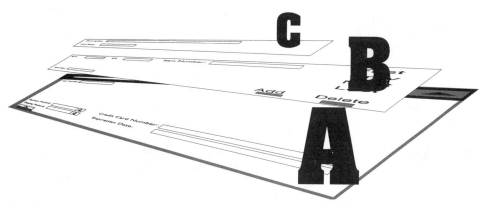

3-9 An exploded view of the various groups of windows and how they are layered on top of the New Sale window's frame. The window's frame (A) contains data from the SALE table and is generated by the object **TSaleWindow**; the first inner group (B), generated by **TItemsWindow**, contains data from the SALES ITEMS table; and the innermost group (C), generated by **TInventoryWindow**, contains data from the IN-VENTORY table.

The unit containing all of the code to accomplish this **TSaleWindow** is found in the file TSALWIN.PAS. The code here is not fully listed, but there's enough to show you the principles for constructing such a complex data entry screen. Further, the code that shows how to implement all of the Engine's functions will not show up here—it'd be a distraction—but realize that all of the later chapters will show you just how to incorporate the Engine. For now, the main interest is only the code that positions and prepares these windows and controls for incorporation with the Engine's functions, so not all of the procedures will be listed here. Think of it as a stripped down chassis with some of the brackets and wiring for later use already in place even though you're not quite sure which wires go to the headlights and which ones to the air-conditioner. Even though it won't run in this condition, the chassis does look fine and sparkly and you can begin to feel how it'll ride on the open road.

The object types for the three main windows for this third foundation screen are called **TSaleWindow**, **TItemsWindow**, and **TInventoryWindow**. The first, **TSaleWindow**, is the bottom layer onto which the two other groupings and their respective controls are placed. (See FIG. 3-9 where this is the window labeled A.) **TSaleWindow** itself contains windows as edit fields, combo boxes, and a button. The edit controls in this window are all going to be associated with the SALE table and each control will be hooked to the proper field in the SALE table using the specialized objects you'll find in the next chapter. The **TItemsWindow** similarly contains static text, edit boxes, scrolling buttons and so on that are all, naturally, associated with the SALES ITEMS table (labeled as B in FIG. 3-9). Finally, **TInventoryWindow**, groups controls that display information from the INVENTORY table (labeled as C in FIG. 3-9).

The task of coordinating how each of these tables gets the right information when we create this sale is the function of our referential integrity unit that offers us the opportunities to provide the necessary master/detail or parent/child relations between the tables as anticipated by the relational scheme that we devised for this application in chapter 2. The code for accomplishing these links and maintaining them is the subject of chapter 7.

Figure 3-10 displays the constructor for the Sale Window onto which all controls and other groupings will be placed. During this routine, we also will place the Sales Items window within this Sale window.

3-10 This code excerpt from TSALWIN.PAS excerpts moments from the constructor for the sale window show how to size and position the various controls, combo boxes, static text, and a command button.

```
(*****************************************************************************
* CLASS:        TSaleWindow
*
* MEMBER:       Init    (Constructor)
*
* DESCRIPTION:  Creates an object of this type.
*
*****************************************************************************
```

```
constructor TSaleWindow.Init(AParent: PWindowsObject; AName: PChar;
                        ACursor: PCursor);
var
  dummyPtr : PWindow;
  dummyEd  : PEdit;
begin
.
.
.
{ Call constructor of the base object. }
  inherited Init(AParent, AName, ACursor);
.
.
.
{ Create static text label that says 'Sale Number:' }
  dummyPtr := new(PStatic, Init(@Self, -1, 'Sale Number:', 10, 10, 100,
25,20));

{ Create a static field object for the sale number. WE MUST GIVE IT AN }
{ ID NUMBER SO THAT wm_DisplayField GETS SENT TO IT.                   }
  dummyPtr := new(PFieldStatic, Init(@Self, id_sale_number, 110, 10, 110, 20,
         getCursor, SALE_SALE_NUMBER));

{ Center the text and put a border around it. }
  dummyPtr^.Attr.style := dummyPtr^.Attr.style or ws_Border or es_Center;



{ Create the Items window. }
  dummyPtr := new(PItemsWindow, Init(@Self, 'Items', itemsCursor));

{ Set the coordinates for the Items window. }
  dummyPtr^.Attr.X := 10;
  dummyPtr^.Attr.Y := 40;
  dummyPtr^.Attr.W := 600;
  dummyPtr^.Attr.H := 150;

{ Put a border around the box. }

  dummyPtr^.Attr.Style := dummyPtr^.Attr.Style or ws_Border or ws_Visible or
      ws_Child;

{ Place the credit card number static text and edit field. }
  dummyPtr := new(PStatic, Init(@Self, -1, 'Credit Card Number:', 270, 200,
       150, 20, 50));
  dummyEd := new(PFieldEdit, Init(@Self, id_Card_Number, 410, 200, 200,
       25, CARD_NUMBER_LEN + 1, FALSE, getCursor, SALE_CARD_NUMBER));
```

```
{ Place the expiration date static text and edit field. }
  dummyPtr := new(PStatic, Init(@Self, -1, 'Expiration Date:', 270, 230,
       150, 20, 50));
  dummyEd := new(PFieldEdit, Init(@Self, id_Card_Date, 410, 230, 200, 25,
       DATE_LEN + 1, FALSE, getCursor, SALE_CARD_DATE));

{ Place the payment method static text and combo box. }
  dummyPtr := new(PStatic, Init(@Self, -1, 'Payment Method:', 10, 200,
       150, 20, 50));
  PayMethod := new(PFieldListBox, Init(@Self, id_pay_method, 130, 200,
       100, 100, getCursor, SALE_PAYMENT_METHOD));

{ Place the ship method static text and combo box. }
  dummyPtr := new(PStatic, Init(@Self, -1, 'Shipping Method:', 10, 230,
       150, 20, 50));
  ShipMethod := new(PFieldListBox, Init(@Self, id_ship_method, 130, 230,
       100, 100, getCursor, SALE_SHIP_METHOD));

{ Place the OK button. }
  dummyPtr := new(PRButton, Init(@Self, IDOK, '&Ok', 10, 265, 70, 25, True));

{ Have the window come up this big all the time. }
  Attr.H := 323;
  Attr.W := 627;

end;
```

As you can see, there is quite a bit to do to get the boxes and text to appear in their proper positions. As long as we're at it, we'll give you one more code snippet. Figure 3-11 will show you how to place the text within the combo boxes. This code comes from a method that uses the *SetupWindow* method to ensure that this window is loaded with the proper texts and data. Here, we're interested only in how to get the selections that we want to offer for the shipping method and payment method.

The remaining windows for this data-entry screen all continue the same principles found previously. The clever part, as you will read, is how we message around the needed calls to keep the window's display current and manage referential integrity throughout this data-entry screen. After all, our relational scheme requires that we use information from the tables mentioned earlier—SALE, SALES ITEMS, INVENTORY—plus one more: CUSTOMER. These later discussions will show how this code also decrements the INVENTORY table properly. Our "History" option uses the principles from this third foundation screen to show all the items within each sale for a particular customer. So, we do get some mileage out of this par-

3-11 This code from TSALWIN.PAS shows how to place text within a combo box so that a user can click on a selection.

```
(**********************************************************************
* CLASS:        TSaleWindow
*
* MEMBER:       SetupWindow
*
* DESCRIPTION:  This procedure is called so the window can initialize
*                          its state before it is shown to the user.
*
**********************************************************************)
procedure TSaleWindow.SetupWindow;
begin

{ Call the base object. }

  inherited SetupWindow;
.
.
.
{ Add the payment methods to the payment method combo box. }
  PayMethod^.addString('AMEX');
  PayMethod^.addString('Visa');
  PayMethod^.addString('Master Card');
  PayMethod^.addString('C.O.D.');

{ Add the shipping methods to the shipping method combo box }
  ShipMethod^.addString('Ground');
  ShipMethod^.addString('3-day Air');
  ShipMethod^.addString('Next Day');

end;
```

ticular coding strategy. After you take a look at all of the code for the Sale window, you probably will be grateful that the sale dialog boxes and their objects already were written.

Conclusion

By the end of the planning process for the tables and their data entry screens, you should have a thorough outline of the high-level structure of the complete application and some details for specifying the construction of the screens. With a sense of what tables are active for any screen, you also will be able to plan on the validity checking for each operation and which operations require you to maintain referential integrity.

4
The objects of our application

When we planned the menu and other user interface elements for this application, we mentioned that, because these resources did not actually "do" anything, each resource would need a corresponding object and the appropriate Pascal code to implement the choices expressed there. By way of analogy, the controls within each of the dialog boxes must at some point connect to the data in our tables. The link to that data, the Engine, now becomes central to our planning for the application. This chapter first will look at the unit **OOPXENG**, which contains all of the object types for the Paradox Engine 3.0 Pascal Database Framework. You should check out the conventions for pointers and other programming concepts found in the Engine's Database Framework Reference manual before you rummage around in this chapter.

We already have encountered two elements of the Engine in our discussion of defining the tables for this application—the type **PTableDesc** and the arrays of **TFieldDesc** objects first mentioned in chapter 2 discussion of TABLEDIC.PAS. Now, we'll cover the object types that comprise the Engine itself.

With the Engine's objects in hand, we can contemplate how we'll use them to provide access to the application's tables from the user interface. As with any Windows application, we'll need to be sending and receiving messages as we do these operations, so we'll begin there once we cover the Engine. We'll look at topics such as how to make sure that the First button moves the record cursor to the first record on a table, provide the means for polling all of the data entry fields in a dialog box to check if anything has changed, and more.

Once we have covered the objects that we will need to use throughout the application's various dialogs and document windows, we'll be ready to see how we integrate them with the user interface, the main interest of chapter 5. Before we pop the hood to show how the Engine powers this application, let's quickly leaf through the shop manual's exploded view of the Engine's hierarchy of object types and their purposes.

The Pascal database framework hierarchy

Borland now has provided an object layer that encapsulates the functions of the Engine and allows us to develop this application using the OOP techniques inherent in Pascal with Objects. The old, procedural functions defined in the Pascal Engine still are provided, but the Engine's new Database Framework, shown in FIG. 4-1, continues to extend Borland's commitment to the OOP environment.

Pascal Database Framework

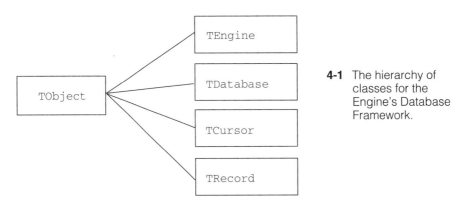

4-1 The hierarchy of classes for the Engine's Database Framework.

TObject

The object type **TObject** is the base object type for all of Pascal's Library Objects, including the Database Framework Objects. Because we are creating a Windows application, we will be using the definition of this object as found in the unit WOBJECTS. For this reason, the unit **OOPXENG**, the Paradox Engine 3.0 Database Framework, "uses" this unit.

TEngine

The first derived object, **TEngine**, encapsulates information related to the Engine and its environment. All Database Framework applications need only one **TEngine** object and must begin by creating and opening a **TEngine** object in one of the Engine's three environmental modes: a local, standalone environment (DOS); a networked environment; or a Windows environment that includes both standalone and networked situations. In addition to defining the application's environment, the **TEngine** fields also establish that the Engine is running and, using the field *lastError*, handle the return of an Engine error return code after each **TEngine** member function call. The **TEngine** methods perform the following:

- Open and close the Engine.
- Enter or remove a password from the system.
- Return information such as the current environment setting, a network user name, or an error message.
- Set the environment defaults for the Engine, the maximum table size, whether the tables will be Paradox 4.0 or 3.5 compatible, and whether or not the internal hardware error handler is set.

TDatabase

Using **TEngine** to establish an instance of the Engine and get it up and running, or rather idling, the Engine now naturally needs objects to work with. **TDatabase**, derived from **TObject**, encapsulates the concept of a database as a collection of related tables and the access structures needed to manipulate their data. This class provides functions that operate on a set of persistent Paradox objects, such as tables, indexes, locks, and so on. This object type, then, provides means necessary for creating, renaming or copying tables; reporting on their structures; and setting up the Paradox's primary and secondary indexes.

As expected, a listing of the member functions for **TDatabase** includes all of the operations necessary to interact with a table and its generalized structure. These methods for **TDatabase** perform the following tasks:

- Open and close the database.
- Create a table or establish that one exists already; append the records from another table; copy, delete, or rename a table and its family of files; upgrade a table's format from Paradox 3.5 to 4.0; and clear all records from a table.
- Protect a table with a password, check to see if it's protected, and remove the protection.
- Perform locking routines on a table to control access by another user; find the user who is causing a locking error.
- Create and delete primary and secondary indexes, including those defined as simple, composite or case-sensitive.
- Determine the structure of a table including the number and structure of its fields, the number of fields in a primary key and the structure of a secondary index; that is, the fields used to define the secondary index.
- Flush any changed record buffers.

TCursor

Moving toward more precise control over a database, the **TCursor** object type encapsulates a system for accessing, navigating, and manipulating the records of a table by allowing a programmer to access a table's records randomly or sequentially whether or not the table is indexed. This cursor object type manages functions such as locating, accessing, appending, and deleting records. When you use **TCursor** to manipulate records, its constructor calls a **TRecord** constructor to create a generic record object that automatically mirrors the actual field structure of that table by using the definitions established whenever you create any Paradox table. You thus can invoke **TRecord**'s many methods for reading and writing fields without explicitly creating a **TRecord** object.

The means for manipulating data in even more specific ways is available through custom records, a feature of the Engine that we will not be using in this application.

The complete range of data members and member functions for **TCursor** provides the following:

- Point to the generic record for this cursor so that you can perform record operations on this cursor's current generic record. It also is used internally for custom record transfer operations.
- Open and close the cursor.
- Append, insert, update, or delete the current record in conjunction with the cursor's status.
- Clone the cursor so that you can open a table more than once on the same index or resynchronize two cursors open on the same table but on different indexes. Then, by moving the cursor to match a key value, resynchronize the match with the primary index view.
- Read the current record, return the current record number, or return the number of records in the table.
- Move the cursor to the beginning and end of a table, move forward and backward one record, or move to a specific record number.
- Perform record and table locking and unlocking.
- Determine if someone else has changed the table, then refresh or resynchronize the table.

TRecord

This final object type in the Engine's hierarchy, **TRecord**, encapsulates the properties of a *generic* record. The field structure for this generic record is not determined until the Database Framework application is run. Therefore, a **TRecord** object always is created in the context of an existing **TCursor** object that determines the table and field structure from the definitions of the table.

TRecord provides you with methods for reading and writing the fields of a record, including BLOBs.

A summary of the functions of **TRecord** includes the following functions:

- Attach and detach a record from a given cursor.
- Clear a record's buffer.
- Handle BLOB fields.
- Read a value from a given field or write a given value to a field or set a given field to blank.
- Establish various place holders for custom records.
- Determine information such as the number of fields in a record, the field type for a field number, the field number from the field name, the field number of a custom record from a generic field number, and if a field is blank.
- Copy a given record from or to a given record.

Our own objects

Those were the Engine's five object types that the Database Framework hierarchy provides. In addition to these object types, there are some others that are needed for various operations. A partial listing of these defined types, records, and the object type **TFieldDesc** are listed in TABLE 4-1. The following is a list of our own objects.

**Table 4-1   A partial listing of the defined
types, records, and the object type** TFieldDesc.

Object	Description
PTableDesc	**PTableDesc** is a collection of **TFieldDesc** objects used to define the record structure of a table
Daterec	**Daterec** is the default Date record used to convert dates between the internal Paradox date structure and formats such as *mm*/*dd*/*yyyy* or others. Paradox calculates dates internally by counting the number of days elapsed since January 1, 1 A.D.
TFieldDesc	An object that defines a field descriptor. An array of these structures can define both generic and custom records.

TMDIDBFWindow   TFieldEdit
TCursorWindow   TFieldListBox

TCursorButton	TFieldStatic
TCursorButtonDown	TCurRecStatic
TCursorButtonUp	TTotRecStatic
TCursorButtonFirst	TCursorDialog
TCursorButtonLast	TQueryBuilder
TRButton	

To handle the hooks between the user interface and the Paradox Engine, we have assembled a set of our own objects. In addition, there is an object (**TR-Button**, found in TCURBTN.PAS) that clears up a minor confusion between a Borland-style button and Windows-style button that crops up because we're using the Borland Windows Custom Controls (BWCC). Using inheritance, our new objects integrate Engine functions and ObjectWindows objects.

To arrive at these new objects, we analyzed the types of actions and displays needed for our application and arrived at these general categories:

- Connect the application window (an MDI window) with the Paradox Database Framework so that we could access the Engine's functions and the tables.
- Make sure that the buttons performed the actions that they described such as moving from record to record, or creating and deleting records.
- Make sure that the data entry boxes displayed information and allowed a user to view, enter, or edit information that would meet the required validity checks before the data was written to a record. Make sure that the combo boxes displayed the correct choices and wrote these choices to the correct field in a record.
- Make sure that various other controls such as a static text control displayed the correct information from a table or record.
- Make sure that you could query a table.
- Make sure that tables were linked properly.
- Make sure that we validated data using rules established during our planning sessions. (For this last one only, we used the ObjectWindows **TValidator** now available with Pascal with Objects, version 7.0, and did not create our own object type.)

With this outline, we realized that we needed to handle several types of actions:

- Associating the Database Framework with a Multiple Document Window.
- Associating a table's cursor with a dialog or a window.
- Associating controls such as the Ok and Cancel buttons with actions that update a record. (To accomplish this, we will be overriding the commands already available through ObjectWindows and thus do not need to create a new object.)

- Associating a control such as a button with a table's cursor to move the cursor and display data.
- Associating controls such as edit boxes, combo boxes, and static text boxes with fields in a table.
- Building a query.
- Linking tables.

Finally, a survey of the objects available with ObjectWindows led us to settle in on creating objects that inherited characteristics primarily from **TWindow** and **TDialog**. Further, we determined that we would need to create objects that inherited **TControl** and **TMDIWindow** to complete our set of new objects. We need **TDialog** because we designed several dialog boxes, and we need **TWindow** because we have designed several windows for our needs. Because we loaded both the dialog boxes and windows with controls, we knew that we also needed to inherit elements of **TControl**, in particular **TListBox**, **TStatic**, and **TButton**. Lastly, the application itself was an MDI Window, and thus we needed to work with **TMDIWindow** to accomplish this last facet.

While not a part of the user interface (UI) design, we also had to account for data validation, so **TValidator** became the logical candidate, especially because **TEdit** includes **Validator** as a field. We did not need to write any further objects but simply used two objects, **TRangeValidator** and **TPXPictureValidator**, to accomplish the types of data validation we needed to do. You can read more on this aspect of the application in the chapter 6 discussion of validity checking.

The new objects and their ancestors

As a result of our analysis, we created the following reusable objects to manage the links between the Engine and the UI. The other objects that we need for this program perform tasks associated with each of the dialog boxes and windows that we have created for the UI. Each of them inherits

Ancestors						New Object	
TWindow	→	TMDIWindow			→	TMDIDBFWindow	
TWindow					→	TCursorWindow	
TWindow	→	TControl	→	TButton	→	TCursorButton →	...Down
							...Up
							...First
							...Last
TWindow	→	TControl	→	TButton	→	TRButton	
TWindow	→	TControl	→	TListBox	→	TComboBox →	TFieldListBox
TWindow	→	TControl	→	TStatic	→	TEdit →	TFieldEdit
TWindow	→	TControl	→	TStatic	→	TFieldStatic →	TCurRecStatic
							TTotRecStatic
TDialog					→	TCursorDialog	
TDialog					→	TQueryBuilder	

aspects of the objects described here and implements them to do more specialized tasks associated with their dialog boxes or windows.

TMDIDBFWindow

This object associates a **TMDIWindow** with the Paradox Database Framework (DBF). It logs in to the database and starts the Engine. Source module: TMDIDBF.PAS.

TCursorWindow

This object implements a window associated to a **TCursor**. It inherits **TWindow**. Source module: TCURWIN.PAS.

TCursorDialog

This object implements a dialog that is associated to a **TCursor**. It inherits **TDialog** and not **TWindow**. Basically, the **TCursorWindow** and **TCursorDialog** objects are identical, except that one is designed for a dialog box and the other a document window. Source module: TCURDLG.PAS.

TCursorButton

This object implements a button that performs some action using a **TCursor**. The action performed when it is pressed is to send *haveValuesChanged* to the parent window, DO some ACTION, load the generic record buffer, and tell its parent window to display the fields. (See source module: TCURBTN .PAS, **TCursorButton.BNClicked**, approximately line 218.)

TCursorButtonDown, TCursorButtonUp, TCursorButtonFirst, and TCursorButtonLast

These objects implement the *doMove* virtual function of **TCursorButton**, which moves a cursor open on with a table. Source module: TCURBTN.PAS.

TRButton

When using BWCC, OWL assumes all **TButtons** are Borland-style buttons. This object, **TRButton**, implements the regular Windows-style button and contains only the function *getClassName*. Source module: TCURBTN.PAS.

TFieldEdit

This implements an edit box control that associates a field in a table with an edit control on a window or dialog. Source module: TFEDIT.PAS.

TFieldListBox

This object implements a combo box control that associates a table's fields or the contents of a field with a combo box on a window or dialog. Source module: TFLIST.PAS.

TFieldStatic

This object resembles **TFieldEdit** except that it associates a static control with a field in a table. It is used for output only because it merely displays information about the table to a user. Check back to the POS.RES file and you will see that the SELECT_CUST dialog uses a status bar to display a Customer's ID number. This static control is simply a static text box with no text in it. **TFieldStatic** provides that text. Source module: TFSTAT.PAS.

TCurRecStatic and TTotRecStatic

These objects are like the **TFieldStatic** object; however, instead of being associated with a field in a table, they display the current record number and the total number of records in a table respectively. Source module: TFSTAT.PAS.

TQueryBuilder

This dialog builds a query for a given table. Source module: TQBUILD.PAS.

Messages and the new objects

Before we start to explain the code for these new objects, we need to cover one last topic, the bane of all Windows programmers: messages. Fortunately, we're going to be passing around only a few messages, so don't despair. We need these messages to provide the means for displaying data, saving data, and checking to see if data has changed in a window or dialog: a total of three messages. As expected, none of these messages are generated by any of the generic objects in ObjectWindows; they're all produced by the objects that we have created for the application to handle the procedures we need to work with the Engine and the application's tables.

The three messages

The three types of messages are wm_DisplayFields, wm_SaveFields, and wm_HaveValuesChanged.

wm_DisplayFields

This message is sent to our descendants of **TDialog** or **TWindow** objects. It tells the object that it should tell the field type controls to display the field values.

wm_SaveFields

This message is sent to our descendants of **TDialog** or **TWindow** objects. It tells the object that it should tell the field type controls to save the field values.

wm_HaveValuesChanged

This message is sent to our descendants of **TDialog** or **TWindow** objects. It tells the object that it should ask the field type controls if the value has been modified by the user.

These are the three messages; the next section will explain how they work.

How the messages work

TCursorDialog and **TCursorWindow** send the messages wm_SaveFields, wm_DisplayFields, and wm_HaveValuesChanged to every control on its client area. This includes buttons, scroll bars, and every other control (say, a group box, a control that only performs a cosmetic purpose for us) and not just the special ones. The dialog or window does not know which control will respond to the message or how it will respond.

When a message is received by such a control, the control that is associated with an object that we have devised uses its methods that handle the message to perform an appropriate action or actions.

wm_SaveFields and wm_DisplayFields These two messages work similarly. The **TCursorDialog** and **TCursorWindow** objects each have procedures named *WMSaveFields* and *WMDisplayFields* that, in turn, call the *Save-Fields* and *DisplayFields* methods.

SaveFields uses the *ForEach* method from **TWindowsObject** to dispatch the wm_SaveFields message to all the controls on the window or dialog. There is a local procedure, called *SaveField*, which is used by *ForEach*, to send the wm_SaveFields message to each control. *DisplayFields* works the same way.

Figure 4-2 provides a quick look at how the code for the wm_SaveFields is used in the **TCursorWindow** object. The full code for these messages will appear later in the chapter when we present the code for all of our new objects.

wm_HaveValuesChanged This message resembles the operations of wm_SaveFields and wm_DisplayFields, except that it uses the *FirstThat* method of **TObjectWindows** rather than the *ForEach* method. We use the *FirstThat* method because we are not interested in sending a message to each and every control but only in sending a message until a control responds that it has changed. Once any control in the dialog or window indicates that its value has changed, that's enough for us to want to do something about the entire window or dialog, usually save the record or display a new one.

4-2 This excerpt from TCURWIN.PAS introduces one of the Windows messages used in this application.

```
(*********************************************************************
* TYPE: TCursorWindow
*
* METHOD:      WMSaveFields
*
* DESCRIPTION:  Responds to the wm_SaveFields message.
*
********************************************************************)
procedure TCursorWindow.WMSaveFields(var Msg: TMessage);
begin
  SaveFields;
end;

(*********************************************************************
* TYPE: TCursorWindow
*
* METHOD:      SaveFields
*
* DESCRIPTION:  Saves the fields into the table's record buffer.
*
********************************************************************)
procedure TCursorWindow.SaveFields;

  { This local function is used to send the message to every }
  { control on the Window.                                   }
  procedure SaveField(AWindowsObject: PWindowsObject); far;
  var
    controlID: Integer;
  begin

    controlID := AWindowsObject^.getId;

    if controlID <> -1 then
      sendMessage(AWindowsObject^.HWindow, wm_SaveFields, 0, 0);

  end;

begin

{ Use the ForEach function of TWindowsObject to send the message   }
{ wm_SaveFields to every control on the Window.  Only those controls }
{ that know how to handle that message will perform some action.    }

  ForEach(@SaveField);
end;
```

When a control responds TRUE to the wm_HaveValuesChanged message, then the local method *AskField* will return TRUE.

The scroll buttons (First, Last, Next, and Prev) help send these messages to the dialog or window. You can check this out when you look at the code in TCURBTN.PAS. For example, **TCursorButton.BNClicked** sends the messages to the parent window. It sends a wm_HaveValuesChanged first, moves the table's cursor appropriately using one of the Engine's **TCursor** methods such as *gotoNext*, loads the record buffer with the new values, and concludes by sending the wm_DisplayFields to initiate the actions needed to display the data in a control.

A wm_SaveFields type of message is never generated by any of the generic ObjectWindows controls. It and our other messages are generated only by dialogs and windows that we have created in this application.

Take a look at **TInventoryDialog.WMHaveValuesChanged** in FIG. 4-3, which processes a wm_HaveValuesChanged message. You will be able to trace out that it calls the method *UpdateRecord*. This function then calls **TCursorDialog.HaveValuesChanged**. If the function returns TRUE, then it will send the call *SaveFields*, a method from the base object **TCursorDialog**, to all of the controls to update the record with the new values.

The objects **TFieldEdit** and **TFieldStatic**, including the **TCurRecStatic** and **TTotRecStatic**, also use the three messages wm_DisplayFields, wm_SaveFields, and wm_HaveValuesChanged.

4-3 This excerpt from TINVDLG.PAS shows how to use a method to respond to a Windows message written for this application.

```
(*******************************************************************
* OBJECT TYPE:   TInventoryDialog
*
* METHOD:        WMHaveValuesChanged
*
* DESCRIPTION:   This procedure gives the dialog a chance to see if the
*                field values have been changed by the user.
*******************************************************************)
procedure TInventoryDialog.WMHaveValuesChanged(var Msg: TMessage);
begin
  UpdateRecord;
end;


(*******************************************************************
* OBJECT TYPE:   TInventoryDialog
*
* METHOD:        UpdateRecord
*
* DESCRIPTION:   This function checks to see if the user has changed the
*                fields and it will save them.
*******************************************************************)
```

```
procedure TInventoryDialog.UpdateRecord;
var
  msgReturn: Integer;
begin
  if(HaveValuesChanged) then
  begin
    msgReturn := MessageBox(HWindow,
      'The field values of the current record have been changed.
       Do you want to save?',
      'Update Record',   mb_yesno or mb_iconquestion);

    if(msgReturn = IDYES) then
    begin
      SaveFields;

{ Update the record in the table. }

      ERROR(getCursor^.updateRec(getCursor^.genericRec),
        'Updating the record');
    end;
  end

end;
```

wm_DisplayFields All of the previous objects have a member procedure called *WMDisplayField* that responds to the wm_DisplayField message. Depending on the type of object, the proper information is shown. Notice that, because these messages are processed by objects that are being iterated over by **TCursorDialog.DisplayFields** or **TCursorWindow.Display-Fields**, they each process the message for only the one control that they are associated with. The same follows for wm_SaveFields when its message is received by the control objects listed earlier.

wm_SaveFields Only the **TFieldEdit** and **TFieldList** controls use this message. The procedure *WMSaveField* will respond to this message and store the current contents of the edit box in the generic record buffer. For an explanation of the generic record buffer, check out the Paradox Engine Database Framework manual or simply realize that the **TCursor** object always knows the structure of the records that it works with and stores information in a generic record buffer corresponding to a record's structure.

wm_HaveValuesChanged This message asks a **TFieldEdit** control if the value in an edit box has changed. The procedure *WMHasValueChanged* calls the *IsModified* method of **TEdit** (**TEdit.IsModified**). The result of this method (*IsModified*) is returned in the **TMessage.result** variable. If **TMessage.result** is TRUE, then the caller knows that the value in the edit box has been modified.

Message code

The code necessary to define the constants for the messages that we send is found in the file WMDBF.PAS, which is listed in FIG. 4-4. To avoid conflicts with the standard Windows messages, this file follows the convention for defining our own messages suggested in the *ObjectWindows Programming Guide*. There, the top of the message range Windows uses is defined by the constant wm_User. So, to define a message for our own application, we define a message ID based on wm_User that falls in the range wm_User...wm_User+31,744.

4-4 This file illustrates how to define the constants used for the Windows messages developed for this application.

```
(* * * * * * * * * * * * * * * * * * * * * * * * * * * * * * * * * * * * * * * * * * * * * * * * * * * * * * * * * * * * * * * * * * * * * * * * * * * * * *
* FILE:          WMDBF.PAS
*
* DESCRIPTION:  This file contains the message numbers that the DBF-OWL
*               objects pass between each other.
* * * * * * * * * * * * * * * * * * * * * * * * * * * * * * * * * * * * * * * * * * * * * * * * * * * * * * * * * * * * * * * * * * * * * * * * * * * * *)
unit  WMDBF; {Unit name }

{ This section defines what other Pascal programs may use from this unit. }

interface

uses  WinTypes,
      WinProcs,
      Objects,
      OWindows;

const
  wm_DisplayFields = wm_User + 100;
  wm_SaveFields     = wm_User + 101;
  wm_HaveValuesChanged = wm_User + 102;

{ private section }
implementation

{ startup code }
begin
end.
```

The new objects and their code

Unit: TMDIDBF

This unit defines an object that associates a **TMDIWindow** object (here, an application window) with the **TEngine** and **TDatabase** objects of the Paradox Engine's Database Framework. Hence, the name, TMDIDBF. When an instance of this type of application starts, this object will initialize the single instance of **TEngine** and **TDatabase** needed from these Engine objects.

Object type: TMDIDBFWindow
   Inherits: TMDIWindow

Fields
eng eng: PEngine; **private**

A pointer to the **TEngine** class being used by the instance.

db db: PDatabase; **private**

A pointer to the instance **TDatabase**.

Methods
Init constructor Init(ATitle: PChar; AMenu: HMenu);

Creates an instance of the **TEngine** and **TDatabase** objects. We need only one instance of **TEngine** object, which we will open as a Windows type Engine using the *engineType* value *pxWin*.

    Similarly, we need only one instance of **TDatabase**. Although **TDatabase** does create, rename, and copy tables and reports on their structures, by reference to a table name, we nevertheless have to create a cursor (a **TCursor** object) to access and navigate that table. (See **TCursorWindow** and **TCursorDialog**, and others that follow.)

Done destructor Done; virtual;

Disposes of the MDI frame object window, the **TEngine** and **TDatabase** objects.

getEngine function getEngine: PEngine;

This function returns the **TEngine** associated with this frame.

getDatabase function getDatabase: PDatabase;

This function returns the **TDatabase** associated with this frame.

Figure 4-5, which follows, contains the complete code for creating a **TMDIDBFWindow** object type and its related methods.

4-5 This file, TMDIDBF.PAS, contains the complete code for establishing a Multiple Document Interface Window object, **TMDIWindow**, that is associated with the **TEngine** and **TDatabase** objects of the Paradox Engine Database Framework. This object is called a **TMDIDBFWindow**.

```
(***************************************************************************
 *
 * FILE:          TMDIDBF.PAS
 *
 * DESCRIPTION:   This unit defines an object that incorporates a TMDIWindow
 *                object with DBF classes BEngine and BDatabase.  When an
 *                instance of this type of application starts, it will init
 *                these needed engine classes.
 *
 ***************************************************************************)
Unit TMDIDBF; { Unit name }

{ This section defines what other pascal Programs may use from this unit. }

interface

{ Tell the compiler what units are needed. }

uses    WinTypes,
        WinProcs,
        OWindows,
        OopXEng;            { The Database Framework (DBF) unit }


{ The new types defined in this unit. }

type

(***************************************************************************
 * OBJECT TYPE:  TMDIDBFWindow
 *
 * INHERITS: TMDIWindow
 *
 * DESCRIPTION:   This object overrides TMDIWindow to create
 *                instances of TEngine and TDatabase.  It also overrides
 *                the destructor to close and free these objects.
 *
 ***************************************************************************)
  PMDIDBFWindow = ^TMDIDBFWindow;
  TMDIDBFWindow = object(TMDIWindow)

{ Override the constructor to also create TDatabase and TEngine.}

  constructor Init(ATitle: PChar; AMenu: HMenu);
```

```
{ The destructor should close the database and the engine. }

  destructor Done; virtual;

{ Declare accessor functions that allow other object types }
{ to access the pointers. }

{ The private section contains routines and data needed by TDBFApplication }
{ only.  Other classes can not access this data or call these procedures.  }

  private

{ A pointer the TEngine object being used by the instance. }

  eng: PEngine;

{ A pointer to the instances TDatabase.                                    }

  db: PDatabase;

{ Define some functions that return data members. }

  public

  function getDatabase: PDatabase;

  function getEngine: PEngine;

  end; { object TMDIDBFWindow }

{ end type section }


{ This section contains the code necessary to make the object type work. }

implementation

(*********************************************************************
* OBJECT TYPE:   TMDIDBFWindow
*
* METHOD:        Init   (CONSTRUCTOR)
*
* DESCRIPTION:  This is called for every instance of the program that is
*               run.  We will turn on the Engine here.
*********************************************************************)
constructor TMDIDBFWindow.Init(ATitle: PChar; AMenu: HMenu);
begin
{ Call TMDIWindow.Init (constructor) }
```

```
TMDIWindow.Init(ATitle, AMenu);

{ Create an instance of TDatabase and TEngine for this instance. }

eng := New (PEngine, defInit(pxWin));

{ Check to see that the Engine object was created ok. }

  if((eng <> nil) and (eng^.lastError = PXSUCCESS))then
  begin

{ Create the database object. }

    db := New (PDatabase, Init(eng));

{ Did it work? }

      if((db = nil) or (db^.lastError <> PXSUCCESS))then
      begin

{ No? Then show an error. }

      MessageBox(0, 'Could not Initialize Database', 'Init Error',
        MB_OK or MB_ICONSTOP);

      PostAppMessage(GetCurrentTask, WM_QUIT, 0, 0);
      end;
  end
  else begin

{ No? Then show an error. }

      MessageBox(0, 'Could not Initialize Engine', 'Init Error',
        MB_OK or MB_ICONSTOP);

      PostAppMessage(GetCurrentTask, WM_QUIT, 0, 0);
  end;

end;

(*********************************************************************
* OBJECT TYPE:  TMDIDBFWindow
*
* METHOD:       done    (DESTRUCTOR)
*
* DESCRIPTION:  The destructor will dispose of the BEngine and the BDatabase.
*********************************************************************)
```

```
destructor TMDIDBFWindow.Done;
begin

{ Dispose of the database if it was allocated. }

  if(db <> nil) then
  begin
    dispose(db, done);
  end;

{ Dispose of the Engine also. }

  if(eng <> nil) then
  begin
    dispose(eng, done);
  end;

  inherited Done;

end;

(*************************************************************************
 * OBJECT TYPE:  TMDIDBFWindow
 *
 * METHOD:        getDatabase
 *
 * DESCRIPTION:  This function returns the TDatabase associated to this frame.
 *************************************************************************)
function TMDIDBFWindow.getDatabase: PDatabase;
begin
  getDatabase := db;
end;


(*************************************************************************
 * OBJECT TYPE:  TMDIDBFWindow
 *
 * METHOD:        getEngine
 *
 * DESCRIPTION:  This function returns the TEngine associated to this frame.
 *************************************************************************)
function TMDIDBFWindow.getEngine: PEngine;
begin
  getEngine := eng;
end;

{ Units can have start up code.  There is none for this unit. }
begin
end.
```

Unit: TCurWin

This unit defines the object type **TCursorWindow**, which associates a **TWindow** object and a **TCursor** object from the Paradox Engine Database Framework to provide access to the functions that operate a cursor open on a table in the application.

Object type: TCursorWindow
  Inherits: TWindow

Field

tablesCursor tablesCursor: PCursor; **private**

A field to store the associated cursor.

Methods

Init constructor Init(AParent: PWindowsObject; AName: PChar; ACursor: PCursor);

Creates a **TCursorWindow** object of this type and associates a table's cursor with this object that allows us to access the Database Framework **TCursor** functions.

Done destructor Done; virtual;

Closes the cursor if it's open. Destroys the cursor object and detaches it from the database. Disposes of the **TScroller** object in **Scroller**, if any, before calling the *Done* destructor inherited from **TWindowsObject** to dispose of the entire object.

getCursor function getCursor: PCursor;

Returns the pointer to the embedded cursor object.

HaveValuesChanged function HaveValuesChanged: Boolean;

This function checks to see if a user has changed the value of a field. Within this function, there is a local function *AskField*, which the *FirstThat* function uses to send the message wm_HaveValuesChanged to every control on the Window. If the function ever returns True, then *FirstThat* will return a pointer to the first control that returned True.

WMDisplayFields procedure WMDisplayFields(var Msg: TMessage);
                    virtual wm_First + wm_DisplayFields;

This procedure responds to the wm_DisplayFields message.

DisplayFields procedure DisplayFields;

This procedure displays the contents of the fields of a table in the **TField...** type controls.

WMSaveFields procedure WMSaveFields(var Msg: TMessage);
                    virtual wm_First + wm_SaveFields;

This procedure responds to the wm_SaveFields message.

SaveFields procedure SaveFields;

This procedure saves the data in the fields from **TField...** type controls into the table's generic record buffer. Within this procedure, there is a local procedure that uses the **TWindowsObject** method *ForEach* to send the wm_SaveFields message to each control on the window.

When a control that knows how to handle such a message receives it, the *WMSaveFields* method in that control will respond by calling its *Save-*

Field method to save the data to the generic record buffer using the **TRecord** methods *setNull* (for blank fields) or *putString*.

Figure 4-6 is the complete listing of the file TCURWIN.PAS, which defines the unit **TCurWin** for the **TCursorWindow** object type.

4-6 This complete file, TCURWIN.PAS, demonstrates how to create a **TWindow** type object that is associated with a **TCursor** object from the Engine's Database Framework.

```
(*****************************************************************
*
* FILE:          TCURWIN.PAS
*
* DESCRIPTION:  This file defines the object TCursorWindow.  This object
*               combines a TWindow and a DBF TCursor.
*****************************************************************)
unit TCURWin; { Unit name }

{This section defines what other Pascal programs may use from this unit.
}

interface

{ Tell the compiler what units are needed. }

uses    WinTypes,
        WinProcs,
        OWindows,
        ODialogs,
        OopXEng,         { The Database Framework (DBF) unit      }
        WmDbf;           { Messages supported by our new objects }


{ The new types defined in this unit. }

type

(*****************************************************************
* OBJECT TYPE:  TCursorWindow
*
* INHERITS: TWindow
*
* DESCRIPTION:  This object defines some new properties for a Window.  The
*               Window encapuslates a TCursor and can control special
*               controls on the Window that contain fields from the
*               TCursor.
*****************************************************************)
  PCursorWindow = ^TCursorWindow;
  TCursorWindow = object(TWindow)

{ A constructor for the object }

    constructor Init(AParent: PWindowsObject; AName: PChar;
```

```
                        ACursor: PCursor);

{ A destructor }

    destructor Done; virtual;

{ A function that checks to see if the user has changed any field values. }

    function HaveValuesChanged: Boolean;

{ A procedure that will respond to the wm_DisplayFields message. }

    procedure WMDisplayFields(var Msg: TMessage);
      virtual wm_First + wm_DisplayFields;

{ A procedure to display the fields of the table in TField controls. }

    procedure DisplayFields; virtual;

{ A procedure that takes the values from the current control }
{ and places them in the record buffer.                      }

    procedure SaveFields;

{ A procedure to respond to the wm_SaveField message }

    procedure WMSaveFields(var Msg: TMessage);
      virtual wm_First + wm_SaveFields;

{ Private data members and functions}

  private

{ A member to store the associated cursor }

    tablesCursor: PCursor;

{ Accessor functions to private data }
  public

{ Returns the associated cursor. }

    function getCursor: PCursor;

  end; { TCursorWindow }

implementation
```

```
(***********************************************************************
 * TYPE: TCursorWindow
 *
 * METHOD:        Init     (Constructor)
 *
 * DESCRIPTION:  Creates an object of this type.
 *
 ***********************************************************************)
constructor TCursorWindow.Init(AParent: PWindowsObject; AName: PChar;
      ACursor: PCursor);
begin

{ Call constructor of the base object. }

   inherited Init(AParent, AName);

{ Save the data member tablesCursor. }

   tablesCursor := ACursor;

end;

(***********************************************************************
 * TYPE: TCursorWindow
 *
 * METHOD:        Done     (Destructor)
 *
 * DESCRIPTION:  Frees an object of this type.
 *
 ***********************************************************************)
destructor TCursorWindow.Done;
begin

   tablesCursor^.close;

{ Dispose of the cursor. }

   dispose(tablesCursor, Done);

   inherited Done;

end;

(***********************************************************************
 * TYPE: TCursorWindow
 *
 * METHOD:        getCursor
```

```
*
* DESCRIPTION:  Returns the pointer to the embedded cursor object.
*
******************************************************************)
function TCursorWindow.getCursor: PCursor;
begin

{ Returns the pointer to the cursor }

  getCursor := tablesCursor;
end;

(*****************************************************************
* TYPE: TCursorWindow
*
* METHOD:       MWDisplayFields
*
* DESCRIPTION:  Responds to the wm_DisplayFields message.
*
******************************************************************)
procedure TCursorWindow.WMDisplayFields(var Msg: TMessage);
begin
  DisplayFields;
end;

(*****************************************************************
* TYPE: TCursorWindow
*
* METHOD:       DisplayFields
*
* DESCRIPTION:  Displays the fields of the table in TField controls.
*
******************************************************************)
procedure TCursorWindow.DisplayFields;

  { This local function is used to send the message to every }
  { control on the Window.                                   }
  procedure DisplayField(AWindowsObject: PWindowsObject); far;
  var
    controlID: Integer;
    begin

      controlID := AWindowsObject^.getId;

      if controlID <> -1 then
        sendMessage(AWindowsObject^.HWindow, wm_displayfields, 0, 0);
    end;

begin
```

```
{ Use the ForEach function of TWindowsObject to send the message
{ wm_DisplayField to every control on the Window.  Only those controls
{ that know how to handle that message will perform some action.

  ForEach(@DisplayField);
end;

(*********************************************************************
* TYPE: TCursorWindow
*
* METHOD:        MWSaveFields
*
* DESCRIPTION:  Responds to the wm_SaveFields message.
*
**********************************************************************
procedure TCursorWindow.WMSaveFields(var Msg: TMessage);
begin
  SaveFields;
end;

(*********************************************************************
* TYPE: TCursorWindow
*
* METHOD:        SaveFields
*
* DESCRIPTION:  Saves the fields into the table's record buffer.
*
**********************************************************************
procedure TCursorWindow.SaveFields;

  { This local function is used to send the message to every }
  { control on the Window.                                   }
  procedure SaveField(AWindowsObject: PWindowsObject); far;
  var
  controlID: Integer;
  begin

      controlID := AWindowsObject^.getId;

      if controlID <> -1 then
        sendMessage(AWindowsObject^.HWindow, wm_SaveFields, 0, 0);

  end;

begin
{ Use the ForEach function of TWindowsObject to send the message
{ wm_SaveFields to every control on the Window.  Only those controls
{ that know how to handle that message will perform some action.
```

```
  ForEach(@SaveField);
end;

(*****************************************************************************
 * TYPE: TCursorWindow
 *
 * METHOD:        HaveValuesChanged
 *
 * DESCRIPTION:  This function checks to see if a user has changed the value
 *                of a field.
 *****************************************************************************)
function TCursorWindow.HaveValuesChanged: Boolean;

  { This local function is used to send the message to every }
  { control on the Window.                                   }
  function AskField(AWindowsObject: PWindowsObject): Boolean; far;
  var
  controlID: Integer;
    result: Longint;
  begin

      controlID := AWindowsObject^.getId;

      if controlID <> -then
      begin
        result := sendMessage(AWindowsObject^.HWindow, wm_HaveValuesChanged,
          0, 0);

{ Return what the control did. }

        AskField := Boolean(result);
      end
      else

{ Return false. }

        AskField := False;

  end;

begin

{ Use the FirstThat function of TWindowsObject to send the message          }
{ wm_HaveValueChanged to every control on the Window.  Only those controls}
{ that know how to handle that message will perform some action.            }
{ If the function EVER returns true, then FirstThat will return a pointer }
{ to the control that returned TRUE.                                        }

  if(FirstThat(@AskField) <> nil) then
  HaveValuesChanged := True
```

```
  else
    HaveValuesChanged := False;

end;

{ startup }
begin
end.
```

Unit: TCURBTN

This unit defines the abstract object type **TCursorButton**, which associates a **TButton** object (inherits **TWindow**, **TControl**) and a **TCursor** object from the Paradox Engine Database Framework to provide access to the functions that operate a cursor open on a table in the application and, using buttons descended from this abstract object type, move the cursor, or record pointer, as needed. The objects which inherit **TCursorButton** are: **TCursorButtonDown**, **TCursorButtonUp**, **TCursorButtonFirst**, and **TCursorButtonLast**. Because we also are using the BWCC.DLL, we need to make sure that we can create Windows style buttons as well as Borland style buttons; hence, the **TRButton** object that makes sure that we get a regular button when we want one.

Object type: TCursorButton
  Inherits: TButton

This is an abstract object type. It will define some common functions that all of the cursor buttons perform. It is, of course, associated with a **TCursor** object so that we can navigate a table.

Field

tableCursor tableCursor: PCursor; **private**

A field that points to the associated cursor object.

Methods

Init constructor Init(AParent: PWindowsObject; AnId: Integer; AText: PChar; X, Y, W, H: Integer; IsDefault: Boolean; ACursor: PCursor);

Constructs a button object with the usual associated parameters, including a **TCursor** object. We will use this constructor when we are working with document windows.

InitResource constructor InitResource(AParent: PWindowsObject; ResourceID: Word; ACursor: PCursor);

Constructs a button object with arguments that associate it with a windows resource (*ResourceID*) and with a **TCursor** object so that we can access the database. We will use this constructor when we are working with dialog windows.

BNClicked procedure BNClicked(var Msg: TMessage); virtual nf_First +bn_Clicked;

This button down function will respond to the user pressing the button on the dialog or window. Using the wm_HaveValuesChanged message, it gives the parent the opportunity to see if the user has changed any of the values. It then will use an overloaded *doMove* procedure to move the cursor, reload the generic record buffer with the current field values, and tell the parent to display the record.

doMove   procedure doMove; virtual;

This procedure moves the record pointer (cursor) and must be overloaded so that the movement is made explicit.

getCursor   function getCursor: PCursor;

This function returns the associated cursor.

Object type: TCursorButtonDown
  Inherits: TCursorButton

Method
doMove   procedure doMove; virtual;

When this *doMove* function is overloaded, it will move the cursor to the appropriate record on the table using the **TCursor** function *gotoNext*.

Object type: TCursorButtonUp
  Inherits: TCursorButton

Method
doMove   procedure doMove; virtual;

This function will move the cursor to the appropriate record on the table using the **TCursor** function *gotoPrev*.

Object type: TCursorButtonFirst
  Inherits: TCursorButton

Method
doMove   procedure doMove; virtual;

This function will move the cursor to the first record on the table using the **TCursor** functions *gotoBegin* and *gotoNext*. These two functions are necessary because of the "virtual" record that begins each Paradox 4.0 table.

Object type: TCursorButtonLast
  Inherits: TCursorButton

Method
doMove   procedure doMove; virtual;

This function will move the cursor to the last record on the table using the **TCursor** functions *gotoEnd* and *gotoPrev*. These two functions are necessary because of the "virtual" record that ends each Paradox 4.0 table.

Object type: TRButton
  Inherits: TButton

Method
getClassName   function getClassName: PChar; virtual;

 While we are using BWCC controls, we also want to be able to use the regular Windows style buttons. Because of the BWCC.DLL, *getClassName* returns a 'BorBtn' class, so we simply make *getClassName* return the window button class name, "Button".

Figure 4-7 is the complete listing for the various **TCursorButton** objects that we have created to associate a button object with a cursor object.

4-7 This file, TCURBTN.PAS, demonstrates how to create the **TCursorButton** object types which associate a **TButton** object (Inherits **TWindow**, **TControl**) and a **TCursor** object from the Paradox Engine Database Framework.

```
(**********************************************************************
*
* FILE:          TCURBTN.PAS
*
* DESCRIPTION:   This file defines button object move the current record
*                of a TCursor.  There is a button for First, Last, Next and
*                Prev.
**********************************************************************)
unit TCURBTN; { Unit name }

{ This section defines what other Pascal programs may use from this unit. }

interface

{ Tell the compiler what units are needed. }

uses    WinTypes,
        WinProcs,
        OWindows,
        ODialogs,
        OopXEng,          { The Database Framework (DBF) unit      }
        WmDbf;            { Messages supported by our new objects  }

{  The new types defined in this unit. }

type

(*********************************************************************
* OBJECT TYPE:  TRButton
*
* INHERITS: TButton
*
* DESCRIPTION:  Since we are using BWCC controls, OWL thinks that all
*               TButtons we create should be BorBtn.  The cursor buttons
*               uses regular buttons.  To change this we will create a
*               new button whose type name is "Button".
*********************************************************************)
  PRButton = ^TRButton;
  TRButton = object(TButton)

  function getClassName: PChar; virtual;

  end; { TRButton }
```

4-7 Continued.

```
(********************************************************************:
* OBJECT TYPE:   TCursorButton
*
* INHERITS: TButton
*
* DESCRIPTION:   This is an abstract type.  It will define some common
*                functions that all of the cursor buttons perform.
********************************************************************)
  PCursorButton = ^TCursorButton;
  TCursorButton = object(TRButton)

{ A constructor for the object }

    constructor Init(AParent: PWindowsObject; AnId: Integer; AText: PChar;
      X, Y, W, H: Integer; IsDefault: Boolean; ACursor: PCursor);

{ A dialog resource item constructor }

    constructor InitResource(AParent: PWindowsObject; ResourceID: Word;
      ACursor: PCursor);

{ The button down function will respond to the user pressing the button. }

    procedure BNClicked(var Msg: TMessage); virtual nf_First + bn_Clicked;

{ This is the function that performs the movement. THIS FUNCTION MUST BE }
{ OVERLOADED.                                                           }

    procedure doMove; virtual;

  private

{ The associated cursor }

    tableCursor: PCursor;

{ Accessor functions }

  public

{ Return the associated cursor. }

  function getCursor: PCursor;

  end; { TCursorButton }
```

```
(*******************************************************************
* OBJECT TYPE:  TCursorButtonDown
*
* INHERITS: TCursorButton
*
* DESCRIPTION:  This object moves the record pointer down one record when
*               the user clicks on the button.
*******************************************************************)
  PCursorButtonDown = ^TCursorButtonDown;
  TCursorButtonDown = object(TCursorButton)

{ Overload the doMove function to move down. }

    procedure doMove; virtual;

  end; { TCursorButtonDown }

(*******************************************************************
* OBJECT TYPE:  TCursorButtonUp
*
* INHERITS: TCursorButton
*
* DESCRIPTION:  This object moves the record pointer up one record when
*               the user clicks on the button.
*******************************************************************)
  PCursorButtonUp = ^TCursorButtonUp;
  TCursorButtonUp = object(TCursorButton)

{ Overload the doMove function to move up. }

  procedure doMove; virtual;

  end; { TCursorButtonUp }

(*******************************************************************
* OBJECT TYPE:  TCursorButtonFirst
*
* INHERITS: TCursorButton
*
* DESCRIPTION:  This object moves the record pointer to the first record.
*******************************************************************)
  PCursorButtonFirst = ^TCursorButtonFirst;
  TCursorButtonFirst = object(TCursorButton)

{ Overload the doMove function to move to the first record. }
```

```
    procedure doMove; virtual;

  end; { TCursorButtonFirst }
(********************************************************************
* OBJECT TYPE:  TCursorButtonLast
*
* INHERITS: TCursorButton
*
* DESCRIPTION:  This object moves the record pointer to the last record.
********************************************************************)
  PCursorButtonLast = ^TCursorButtonLast;
  TCursorButtonLast = object(TCursorButton)

{ Overload the doMove function to move to thelast record. }

    procedure doMove; virtual;

  end; { TCursorButtonLast }


{ This section contains the code necessary to make the object work. }

implementation

(********************************************************************
* OBJECT TYPE:  TCursorButton
*
* METHOD:       Init     (Constructor)
*
* DESCRIPTION:  Creates an object of this type.
*
********************************************************************)
constructor TCursorButton.Init(AParent: PWindowsObject; AnId: Integer;
AText: PChar; X, Y, W, H: Integer; IsDefault: Boolean; ACursor: PCursor);
begin

{ Call the base object. }

  inherited Init(AParent, AnId, AText, X, Y, W, H, IsDefault);

{ Save the cursor. }

  tableCursor := ACursor;

end;
```

```
(*********************************************************************
* OBJECT TYPE:   TCursorButton
*
* METHOD:        InitResource     (Constructor)
*
* DESCRIPTION:   Creates an object of this type.
*
*********************************************************************)
constructor TCursorButton.InitResource(AParent: PWindowsObject;
  ResourceID: Word;  ACursor: PCursor);
begin

{ Call the inherited constructor. }

  inherited InitResource(AParent, ResourceID);

{ Save the cursor. }

  tableCursor := ACursor;

end;

(*********************************************************************
* OBJECT TYPE:   TCursorButton
*
* METHOD:        BNClicked
*
* DESCRIPTION:   This function will respond to the user pressing the button.
*                It will reload the generic record with the current field
*                values and then tell the parent to display the record again.
*********************************************************************)
procedure TCursorButton.BNClicked(var Msg: TMessage);
begin

{ Give the parent the opportunity to see if the user has changed any of the }
{ field values.                                                             }

  sendMessage(Parent^.HWindow, wm_HaveValuesChanged, 0, 0);

{ Do the movement. }

  doMove;

{ Get the current record's field values and put them in the generic record. }

  tableCursor^.getRecord(tableCursor^.genericRec);
```

```
{ Tell the parent to reload the fields. }

  sendMessage(Parent^.HWindow, wm_DisplayFields, 0, MAKELONG(0,

end;

(*******************************************************************
* OBJECT TYPE:   TCursorButton
*
* METHOD:        doMove
*
* DESCRIPTION:   This function preforms the movement.  It does nothing
*                here; and so, descendant objects must overload it.
*
*******************************************************************)
procedure TCursorButton.doMove;
begin
end;

(*******************************************************************
* OBJECT TYPE:   TCursorButton
*
* METHOD:        getCursor
*
* DESCRIPTION:   Returns the pointer to the embedded cursor object.
*
*******************************************************************)
function TCursorButton.getCursor: PCursor;
begin

{ Return the pointer to the cursor. }

  getCursor := tableCursor;
end;

(*******************************************************************
* OBJECT TYPE:   TCursorButtonDown
*
* METHOD:        doMove
*
* DESCRIPTION:   This function will move to the next record.
*******************************************************************)
procedure TCursorButtonDown.doMove;
begin

{ Move to the next record in the table. }

  tableCursor^.gotoNext;
```

```
end;

(****************************************************************
 * OBJECT TYPE:   TCursorButtonUp
 *
 * METHOD:        doMove
 *
 * DESCRIPTION:  This function will move to the previous record.
 ***********************************************************)
procedure TCursorButtonUp.doMove;
begin

{ Move to the previous record in the table. }

  tableCursor^.gotoPrev;

end;

(****************************************************************
 * OBJECT TYPE:   TCursorButtonFirst
 *
 * METHOD:        doMove
 *
 * DESCRIPTION:  This function will move to the first record.
 ***********************************************************)
procedure TCursorButtonFirst.doMove;
begin

{ Move to the first record in the table. }

  tableCursor^.gotoBegin;
  tableCursor^.gotoNext;

end;

(****************************************************************
 * OBJECT TYPE:   TCursorButtonLast
 *
 * METHOD:        doMove
 *
 * DESCRIPTION:  This function will move to the last record.
 ***********************************************************)
procedure TCursorButtonLast.doMove;
begin

{ Move to the last record in the table. }
```

4-7 Continued.

```
    tableCursor^.gotoEnd;

    tableCursor^.gotoPrev;

end;

(***********************************************************************
 * OBJECT TYPE:   TRButton
 *
 * METHOD:        getClassName
 *
 * DESCRIPTION:  We do not want to use BorBtn's on the sale window, so this
 *               object must return the regular window button object name.
 *
 ***********************************************************************)
function TRButton.getClassName: PChar;
begin
  getClassName := 'button';
end;

{ start up }

begin
end.
```

Unit: TFEDIT

This unit defines the object type **TFieldEdit**, which associates a **TEdit** object with a field in a table using **TCursor** and the **TRecord** object, which the **TCursor** constructor calls to create a generic record object for the given open cursor. With **TFieldEdit**, we can save and display the data in any field from a table. This object uses our three Windows messages and their related procedures to poll the objects on a window or dialog box as necessary.

Object type: TFieldEdit
  Inherits: TStatic, TEdit

Fields
tablesCursor tablesCursor: PCursor; **private**

A field that points to the associated cursor object.

tablesField tablesField: FieldNumber; **private**

A field to save the field number of the record in the table on which the cursor is open.

Methods

Init constructor Init(AParent: PWindowsObject; AnId: Integer; X, Y, W, H: Integer;
  ATextLen: Word; Multiline: Boolean; ACursor: PCursor; AField: FieldNumber);

Constructs an interface object that represents a corresponding edit control element and also associates this control with a **TCursor** object so that we can access the database. Most of the methods inherited from **TEdit** manage the edit control's text, and there are two important methods inherited from **TEdit's** ancestor, **TStatic**: *GetText* and *SetText*. These last two methods are used to retrieve the control's text and store it in the *ATextString* argument and set the control's text to be the string passed in *ATextString*. *GetText* returns the size of the retrieved string.

Because the **TEdit** object includes **Validator** as a field, we also will be able to use its validity checking procedures later when we want to test the validity of an edit control's data.

We will use this constructor when we are working with a document window.

InitResource constructor InitResource(AParent: PWindowsObject; ResourceID,
  ATextLen: Word; ACursor: PCursor; AField: FieldNumber);

Constructs an edit control object with arguments that associate it with a windows resource (*ResourceID*) and with a **TCursor** object so that we can access the database. Otherwise, this constructor performs like the *Init* constructor. We will use this *InitResource* constructor when we are working with dialog windows.

getCursor function getCursor: PCursor;

Returns the pointer to the embedded cursor object.

getFieldNumber function getFieldNumber: FieldNumber;

Returns the field number associated to this control. We need this field number so that we can correctly read from and write to the proper field in a record.

WMHasValueChanged procedure WMHasValueChanged(Var Msg: TMessage);
  virtual wm_First + wm_HaveValuesChanged;

This procedure checks to see if a user has changed the value of a field.

Throughout this application the Windows messages are expressed in the plural because we will be sending them to all controls within a dialog or window. Each control, however, individually reacts to the message in some way. Because the procedure acts only for that one control, the procedure's variable uses a singular verb. This naming convention of ours applies also to **WMDisplayField** and **WMSaveField** described later. We use the **ForEach** and **FirstThat** iterators to ensure that the message is sent to all controls appropriately, and the various **WM...** procedures to respond to that message as it applies to each single control within a dialog or child window.

WMDisplayField procedure WMDisplayField(var Msg: TMessage); **virtual**
wm_First + wm_DisplayFields;

This procedure responds to a wm_DisplayFields message.

DisplayField procedure DisplayField;

This procedure displays the contents of the field of a table in a **TEdit** type control. If the field is of the type double, then we use the *GetDouble* procedure from **TRecord**. If it is a string, then we use *getString* but also must copy this Pascal string to a null-terminated string using *StrPCopy* (hence: uses Strings in this unit's header). We need to do this because Windows works with null-terminated and not Pascal-style strings. If we don't use *StrPCopy*, then we are likely to get buggy output when we display the data in a window or dialog box.

WMSaveField procedure WMSaveField(var Msg: TMessage); virtual wm_First + wm_SaveFields;

This procedure responds to a wm_SaveFields message.

SaveField procedure SaveField;

This procedure saves the data from **TEdit** type control and puts it into the table's generic record buffer. In this procedure, we also will have to convert our null-terminated string back to a Pascal string using *StrPas* (hence: uses Strings in this unit).

Figure 4-8 is the complete listing for the various **TFieldEdit** objects that we have created to associate an edit object with a cursor object.

4-8 This file, TFEDIT.PAS, demonstrates how to create a **TFieldEdit** object and its related methods that associate a **TCursor** object with **TEdit** type objects.

```
(*****************************************************************************
 *
 * FILE:         TFEDIT.PAS
 *
 * DESCRIPTION:  This file defines the object TFieldEdit.  This object
 *               combines a TEdit and a field in a Paradox Table.
 *****************************************************************************)
unit TFEDIT; { Unit name }
{$N+}
```

```pascal
{ This section defines what other Pascal programs may use from this unit. }

interface

{ Tell the compiler what units are needed. }

uses    WinTypes,
                    WinProcs,
                    OWindows,
        ODialogs,
                    OopXEng,         { The Database Framework (DBF) unit }
        strings,
        WmDbf;               { Messages for our DBF objects like this one }


{   The new types defined in this unit. }

type

(******************************************************************************
* OBJECT TYPE:  TFieldEdit
*
* INHERITS:     TEdit
*
* DESCRIPTION: This object lets a TEdit control display the value of a
*              field in a Paradox table.  The field value is taken from the
*              record buffer within a TCursor.
******************************************************************************)
        PFieldEdit = ^TFieldEdit;
        TFieldEdit = object(TEdit)

{ This constructor allows the edit control to be placed on any windows }
{ object like a window.                                                 }

                constructor Init(AParent: PWindowsObject; AnId: Integer;
                     X, Y, W, H: Integer; ATextLen: Word; Multiline: Boolean;
                        ACursor: PCursor; AField: FieldNumber);

{ This constructor is used when the object represents a control on a }
{ dialog box.                                                         }

                constructor InitResource(AParent: PWindowsObject;
                        ResourceID, ATextLen: Word; ACursor: PCursor; AField:
FieldNumber);

{ The  DisplayField gets the value of the field out of the record buffer }
{ and displays the value in the control                                   }
```

```
            procedure DisplayField;

{ A function to respond to the wm_DisplayFields message }

            procedure WMDisplayField(var Msg: TMessage);
                    virtual wm_First + wm_DisplayFields;

{ The SaveField function will take the current value in a control and place }
{ it in the record buffer.                                                  }

        procedure SaveField;

{ A function to respond to the wm_SaveFields message }

            procedure WMSaveField(var Msg: TMessage);
                    virtual wm_First + wm_SaveFields;

{ A procedure to respond to a wm_HaveValuesChanged message. }

            procedure WMHaveValueChanged(var Msg: TMessage);
                    virtual wm_First + wm_HaveValuesChanged;

{ Private data members and functions}

        private

{ A member to store the associated cursor }

            tablesCursor: PCursor;

{ A member to save the field }

    tablesField: FieldNumber;

{ A member to store the old value }

            oldValue: array [0..255] of char;

{ Accessor functions to private data }

        public

{ Return the associated cursor }

            function getCursor: PCursor;

{ Return the field }
```

```
            function getFieldNumber: FieldNumber;

  end; { TFieldEdit }

{ end type section }

{ This section contains the code necessary to make the object work. }

implementation

(***********************************************************************
 * OBJECT TYPE:   TFieldEdit
 *
 * METHOD:        Init     (Constructor)
 *
 * DESCRIPTION:   Creates an object of this type.
 *
 ***********************************************************************)
constructor TFieldEdit.Init(AParent: PWindowsObject; AnId: Integer;
        X, Y, W, H: Integer; ATextLen: Word;
  Multiline: Boolean; ACursor: PCursor; AField: FieldNumber);
begin

{ Construct the base object. }

        inherited Init(AParent, AnId, '', X, Y, W, H, ATextLen, Multiline);

{ Save the cursor pointer and the field that this control is associated to. }

        tablesCursor := ACursor;
  tablesField := AField;
end;
(***********************************************************************
 * OBJECT TYPE:   TFieldEdit
 *
 * METHOD:        InitResource     (Constructor)
 *
 * DESCRIPTION:   Creates an object of this type that is on a dialog box.
 *
 ***********************************************************************)
constructor TFieldEdit.InitResource(AParent: PWindowsObject;
        ResourceID, ATextLen: Word; ACursor: PCursor; AField: FieldNumber);
begin

{ Construct the base object. }

  inherited InitResource(AParent, ResourceID, ATextLen);

{ Save the field and cursor info. }
```

```
{ Save the field and cursor info. }

  tablesCursor := ACursor;
  tablesField := AField;
end;

(***********************************************************************
* OBJECT TYPE:  TFieldEdit
*
* METHOD:       getCursor
*
* DESCRIPTION:  Returns the pointer to the embeded cursor object.
*
***********************************************************************)
function TFieldEdit.getCursor: PCursor;
begin

{ Return the pointer to the cursor. }

  getCursor := tablesCursor;
end;

(***********************************************************************
* OBJECT TYPE:  TFieldEdit
*
* METHOD:       getFieldNumber
*
* DESCRIPTION:  Returns the field number associated to this control.
*
***********************************************************************)
function TFieldEdit.getFieldNumber: FieldNumber;
begin

{ Return the pointer to the cursor. }

        getFieldNumber := tablesField;
end;

(***********************************************************************
* OBJECT TYPE:  TFieldEdit
*
* METHOD:       DisplayField
*
* DESCRIPTION:  This method will get the value of the field out
*               of the record buffer and display the value in the control.
***********************************************************************)
```

```
procedure TFieldEdit.DisplayField;
var
  recordBuffer: PRecord;   { A pointer to the record buffer in the cursor }
  isNull: Boolean;
  valAsString: String;
  valAsPChar: array[0..256] of char;
  fldType: PXFieldType;
  subType: PXFieldSubType;
  length: Integer;
  ValAsDoub: Double;
begin

{ Get the record buffer. }

  recordBuffer := tablesCursor^.genericRec;

{ What type is the field? }

  recordBuffer^.getFieldType(tablesField, fldType, subType, length);

{ If the type is a double, then get it as a double. }

  if(fldType = fldDouble) then
  begin
  recordBuffer^.getDouble(tablesField, valAsDoub, isNull);

    if(not isNull) then
        Str(valAsDoub:0:2, valAsString);
  end
  else
{ Get the field's value as a string. }
  recordBuffer^.getString(tablesField, valAsString, isNull);

{ Was the value blank? }

  if(isNull) then
  valAsString := '';

{ Convert the pascal style string to a null-terminated string (NTS). }

  strPCopy(valAsPChar, valAsString);

{ Display this value. }

  SetText(valAsPChar);

{ save the value in the old value data member }
```

```
  GetText(oldValue, 255);
end;

(*************************************************************************
* OBJECT TYPE:  TFieldEdit
*
* METHOD:       WMDisplayField
*
* DESCRIPTION: This function responds to the wm_DisplayField message.
*************************************************************************)
procedure TFieldEdit.WMDisplayField(var Msg: TMessage);
begin
  displayField;
end;

(*************************************************************************
* OBJECT TYPE:  TFieldEdit
*
* METHOD:       SaveField
*
* DESCRIPTION: The SaveField function will take the current value in the
*              control and place it in the record buffer.
*************************************************************************)
procedure TFieldEdit.SaveField;
var
  recordBuffer: PRecord;  { A pointer to the record buffer in the cursor }
  valAsString: String;
  valAsPChar: array[0..256] of char;
begin

{ Get the value from the control. }

  GetText(valAsPChar, 255);
  valAsString := strPas(valAsPChar);

{ Get a pointer to the record buffer. }

  recordBuffer := tablesCursor^.genericRec;

{ Is the value blank? }

    if valAsString = '' then
    begin

{ Yes, then store a blank. }

      recordBuffer^.setNull(tablesField);
```

```
      end
      else
      begin

{ Store the value in the record buffer. }

      recordBuffer^.putString(tablesField, valAsString);

      end;

{ Save the value in the old value data member. }

  GetText(oldValue, 255);

end;

(*****************************************************************************
 * OBJECT TYPE:  TFieldEdit
 *
 * METHOD:       WMSaveField
 *
 * DESCRIPTION: This function responds to the wm_SaveFields message.
 *****************************************************************************)
procedure TFieldEdit.WMSaveField(var Msg: TMessage);
begin
  SaveField;
end;

(*****************************************************************************
 * OBJECT TYPE:  TFieldEdit
 *
 * METHOD:       WMHaveValueChanged
 *
 * DESCRIPTION: This function responds to the wm_HaveValuesChanged message.
 *****************************************************************************)
procedure TFieldEdit.WMHaveValueChanged(var Msg: TMessage);
var
  currentValue: array [0..255] of char;
begin

{ Get the current value. }

  GetText(currentValue, 255);

{ Compare it to the old value data member. }

  if(strComp(oldValue, currentValue) <> 0) then
    Msg.result := Longint(TRUE)
  else
```

4-8 Continued.

```
    Msg.Result := Longint(FALSE);

end;

{ unit startup code }
begin
end.
```

Unit: TFLIST

Object type: TFieldListBox
  Inherits: TComboBox

This object defines a **TFieldListBox** that associates a **TComboBox** control with a **TCursor** object so that we can display a field's data in a list box control.

The methods for this object type resemble those for **TStatic**. Except for pointing out any relevant differences, consult **TFieldEdit** if you need to.

Fields

originalValue originalValue: Integer; **private**

A field that stores the original value of a field when it is gotten out of a table's record.

tablesCursor tablesCursor: PCursor; **private**

A field that points to the associated cursor object.

tablesField tablesField: FieldNumber; **private**

A field to save the field number of the record in the table on which the cursor is open.

Methods

Init constructor Init(AParent: PWindowsObject; AnId: Integer; X, Y, W, H: Integer; ACursor: PCursor; AField: FieldNumber);

InitResource constructor InitResource(AParent: PWindowsObject; ResourceID: Integer; ACursor: PCursor; AField: FieldNumber);

getCursor function getCursor: PCursor;

Returns the pointer to the embedded cursor object.

getFieldNumber function getFieldNumber: FieldNumber;

Returns the field number associated to this control. We need this field number so that we can correctly read from and write to the proper field in a record.

WMHasValueChanged procedure WMHasValueChanged(var Msg: TMessage); virtual wm_First + wm_HaveValuesChanged;

This procedure checks to see if a user has changed the value of a field.

WMDisplayField procedure WMDisplayField(var Msg: TMessage); virtual wm_First + wm_DisplayFields;

This procedure responds to a wm_DisplayFields message.

DisplayField **procedure** DisplayField;

This procedure displays the contents of the field of a table in a **TComboBox** type control.

WMSaveField procedure WMSaveField(var Msg: TMessage); virtual wm_First + wm_SaveFields;

This procedure responds to a wm_SaveFields message.

SaveField procedure SaveField;

This procedure saves the data from **TComboBox** type control and puts it into the table's generic record buffer.

The listing in FIG. 4-9 of TFLIST.PAS shows how to associate a cursor object and a control object to manage the display of data from a table in a combo box. If you want to see how to list a table's field names in a combo box, consult the *Init* (constructor) method in the TQBUILD.PAS module listed in FIG. 4-12 later in this chapter.

4-9 This file, TFLIST.PAS, demonstrates how to associate a table's field names or the contents of a field with a combo box control on a Windows-type window or dialog.

```
(*******************************************************************
*
* FILE:          TFLIST.PAS
*
* DESCRIPTION:  This file defines the object TFieldListBoxt.  This object
*               combines a TComboBox and a field in a Paradox Table.
*******************************************************************)
unit TFLIST; { Unit name }

{ This section defines what other Pascal programs may use from this unit. }

interface

{ Tell the compiler what units are needed. }

uses    WinTypes,
        WinProcs,
        OWindows,
        ODialogs,
```

4-9 Continued.

```
        OopXEng,          { The Database Framework (DBF) unit }
        strings,
        WmDbf;            { Messages for our DBF objects like this one }


{ The new types defined in this unit. }

type

(*************************************************************************
 * OBJECT TYPE:  TFieldListBox
 *
 * INHERITS:     TComboBox
 *
 * DESCRIPTION: This object lets a TComboBox control display the value of a
 *              field in a Paradox table.  The field value is taken
 *              from the record buffer within a TCursor.
 *************************************************************************)
  PFieldListBox = ^TFieldListBox;
  TFieldListBox = object(TComboBox)

{ This constructor allows the edit control to be placed on any windows }
{ object like a window.                                                }

    constructor Init(AParent: PWindowsObject; AnId: Integer;
       X, Y, W, H: Integer; ACursor: PCursor; AField: FieldNumber);

{ This constructor is used when the object represents a control on a }
{ dialog box.                                                        }

    constructor InitResource(AParent: PWindowsObject;
       ResourceID: Integer; ACursor: PCursor; AField: FieldNumber);

{ The DisplayField gets the value of the field out of the record buffer }
{ and displays the value in the control.                                }

    procedure DisplayField;

{ A procedure to respond to the wm_DisplayField message }

    procedure WMDisplayField(var Msg: TMessage);
      virtual wm_First + wm_DisplayFields;

{ The SaveField procedure will take the current value in the control and }
{ place it in the record buffer.                                         }

    procedure SaveField;
```

```
{ A procedure to respond to the wm_SaveField message }

   procedure WMSaveField(var Msg: TMessage);
     virtual wm_First + wm_SaveFields;

{ A procedure to respond to a has value changed message }

   procedure WMHasValueChanged(var Msg: TMessage);
     virtual wm_First + wm_HaveValuesChanged;

{ Private data members and functions}

  private

{ A member to store the associated cursor }

    tablesCursor: PCursor;

{ A member to save the field }

    tablesField: FieldNumber;

{ A member that remembers the original value }

    originalValue: Integer;

{ Accessor functions to private data }

  public

{ Return the associated cursor. }

    function getCursor: PCursor;

{ Return the field }

    function getFieldNumber: FieldNumber;

  end; { TFieldListBox }

{ end type section }

{ This section contains the code necessary to make the object work. }

implementation

(*********************************************************************
* OBJECT TYPE:  TFieldListBox
```

4-9 Continued.

```
*
* METHOD:        Init     (Constructor)
*
* DESCRIPTION:   Creates an object of this type.
*
********************************************************************************)
constructor TFieldListBox.Init(AParent: PWindowsObject; AnId: Integer;
  X, Y, W, H: Integer; ACursor: PCursor; AField: FieldNumber);
begin

{ Construct the base object.}

  inherited Init(AParent, AnId, X, Y, W, H, cbs_DropDownList, 255);

{ Save the cursor pointer and the field that this control is associated to. }

  tablesCursor := ACursor;
  tablesField := AField;

  originalValue := -1;

end;

(******************************************************************************
* OBJECT TYPE:  TFieldListBox
*
* METHOD:        InitResource     (Constructor)
*
* DESCRIPTION:   Creates an object of this type that is on a dialog box.
*
(******************************************************************************
constructor TFieldListBox.InitResource(AParent: PWindowsObject;
  ResourceID: Integer; ACursor: PCursor; AField: FieldNumber);
begin

{ Construct the base object. }

  inherited InitResource(AParent,  ResourceID, 255);

{ Save the field and cursor info. }

  tablesCursor := ACursor;
  tablesField := AField;

  originalValue := -1;

end;
```

```
(**********************************************************************
* OBJECT TYPE:   TFieldListBox
*
* METHOD:        getCursor
*
* DESCRIPTION:   Returns the pointer to the embedded cursor object.
*
**********************************************************************)
function TFieldListBox.getCursor: PCursor;
begin

{ Return the pointer to the cursor. }

  getCursor := tablesCursor;
end;

(**********************************************************************
* OBJECT TYPE:   TFieldListBox
*
* METHOD:        getFieldNumber
*
* DESCRIPTION:   Returns the field number associated to this control.
*
**********************************************************************)
function TFieldListBox.getFieldNumber: FieldNumber;
begin

{ Return the pointer to the cursor. }

  getFieldNumber := tablesField;
end;

(**********************************************************************
* OBJECT TYPE:   TFieldListBox
*
* METHOD:        DisplayField
*
* DESCRIPTION:   This member will get the value of the field out
*                of the record buffer and display the value in the control.
**********************************************************************)
procedure TFieldListBox.DisplayField;
var
  recordBuffer: PRecord;        { A pointer to the record buffer in the cursor }
  isNull: Boolean;
  valAsInt: Integer;
begin

{ Get the record buffer. }
```

```
  recordBuffer := tablesCursor^.genericRec;

{ Get the field's value as a short. }

  recordBuffer^.getInteger(tablesField, valAsInt, isNull);

{ Was the value blank? }

  if isNull = true then
     valAsInt := -1;

{ Display this value. }

  SetSelIndex(valAsInt);

{ Save this value in the original value member }

   originalValue := valAsInt;

end;

(***************************************************************************
* OBJECT TYPE:  TFieldListBox
*
* METHOD:       WMDisplayField
*
* DESCRIPTION: This function responds to the wm_DisplayField message.
***************************************************************************)
procedure TFieldListBox.WMDisplayField(var Msg: TMessage);
begin
  displayField;
end;

(***************************************************************************
* OBJECT TYPE:  TFieldListBox
*
* METHOD:       SaveField
*
* DESCRIPTION:  The SaveField function will take the current value in the
*               control and place it in the record buffer
***************************************************************************)
procedure TFieldListBox.SaveField;
var
  recordBuffer: PRecord;        { A pointer to the record buffer in the cursor
  valAsInt: Integer;
begin

{ Get the value from the control. }
```

```
  valAsInt := GetSelIndex;


{ Get a pointer to the record buffer. }

  recordBuffer := tablesCursor^.genericRec;

{ Is the value blank? }

  if valAsInt < 0 then
  begin

{ Yes, then store a blank. }

    recordBuffer^.setNull(tablesField);
  end
  else
  begin

{ Store the value in the record buffer. }

    recordBuffer^.putInteger(tablesField, valAsInt);

  end;
end;

(**********************************************************************
* OBJECT TYPE:  TFieldListBox
*
* METHOD:       WMSaveField
*
* DESCRIPTION: This function responds to the wm_SaveField message.
**********************************************************************)
procedure TFieldListBox.WMSaveField(var Msg: TMessage);
begin
  SaveField;
end;

(**********************************************************************
*
* OBJECT TYPE:  TFieldListBox
*
* METHOD:       WMHasValueChanged
*
* DESCRIPTION: This function responds to the wm_HasValueChanged message.
**********************************************************************)
procedure TFieldListBox.WMHasValueChanged(var Msg: TMessage);
begin
```

```
{ If the value has been changed, then set the result field in the message }
{ to True.                                                                 }

    Msg.result := LongInt(GetSelIndex <> originalValue);

end;

{ unit startup code }
begin
end.
```

Unit: TFSTAT

Object type: **TFieldStatic**
Inherits: **TStatic**

This object defines a **TFieldStatic** that associates a **TStatic** control with a **TCursor** object so that we can display a field in a static text control.

Unlike the usual static text controls, this object and its two descendants display anything but static text because we are using them as parts of a "status bar" to display information from the database, which here is the key field from a table as well as the current record number and total number of records in the table. Nevertheless, because this object and **TFieldEdit** both inherit **TStatic**, the methods we define here are the same. Except for pointing out any relevant differences, consult **TFieldEdit** if you need to.

The objects **TCurRecStatic** and **TTotRecStatic** inherit **TFieldStatic** and each change the *SaveField* method so that the object displays the current record number or the total number of records in the table on which the cursor currently is open.

Because these three objects are intended only to display information, there is no need to save any of this information, so the *SaveField* methods in all three objects do nothing.

Fields
tablesCursor tablesCursor: PCursor; **private**

tablesField tablesField: FieldNumber; **private**
Methods
Init	constructor
InitResource	constructor
WMDisplayField	procedure
DisplayField	procedure
WMSaveField	procedure
SaveField	procedure
getCursor	function
getFieldNumber	function

Object type: **TCurRecStatic**
TTotRecStatic
Inherits: **TFieldStatic**

Methods

Init   constructor

InitResource   constructor

WMDisplayField procedure

DisplayField   procedure

For the **TCurRecStatic** object, *DisplayField* uses **TCursor's** *GetCurRec-Number* method to get the number of the record that the cursor is currently on. Similarly, *DisplayField* in **TTotRecStatic** uses the **TCursor** method *GetRecCount* to display the total number of records in the table that the cursor is currently open on.

WMSaveField procedure

SaveField   procedure

In neither case do we need to save anything, so this method does nothing.

The following listing in FIG. 4-10 of TFSTAT.PAS shows how to associate a cursor object and a static text control object to manage the display of data from a table in a static text window. The two types here are specialized implementation that display either the current record number or the total number of records in a table.

4-10 This file, TFSTAT.PAS, demonstrates how to associate a static object such as **TStatic** and a **TCursor** object to display data in a static control on a dialog.

```
(***********************************************************************
*
* FILE:         TFSTAT.PAS
*
* DESCRIPTION:  This file defines the object TFieldStatic.  This object
*               combines a TStatic and a field in a Paradox Table.
***********************************************************************)
unit TFSTAT; { Unit name }
{$N+}
{ This section defines what other Pascal programs may use from this unit. }

interface

{ Tell the compiler what units are needed. }

uses    WinTypes,
        WinProcs,
        OWindows,
```

```
        ODialogs,
        PXENGWIN,
        OopXEng,          { The Database Framework (DBF) unit }
        strings,
        WmDbf;            { Messages for our DBF objects like this one }


{ The new types defined in this unit. }

type

(***********************************************************************
 * OBJECT TYPE:  TFieldStatic
 *
 * INHERITS:     TStatic
 *
 * DESCRIPTION:  This object lets a TStatic control display the value of a
 *               field in a Paradox table.  The field value is taken from
 *               the record buffer within a TCursor.
 ***********************************************************************)
  PFieldStatic = ^TFieldStatic;
  TFieldStatic = object(TStatic)

{ This constructor allows the static control to be placed on any windows }
{ object like a window.                                                  }

    constructor Init(AParent: PWindowsObject; AnId: Integer;
       X, Y, W, H: Integer; ACursor: PCursor; AField: FieldNumber);

{ This constructor is used when the object represents a control on a }
{ dialog box.                                                        }

    constructor InitResource(AParent: PWindowsObject;
       ResourceID, ATextLen: Word; ACursor: PCursor; AField: FieldNumber);

{ The DisplayField gets the value of the field out of the record buffer }
{ and displays the value in the control.                                }

    procedure DisplayField; virtual;

{ A function to respond to the wm_DisplayField message }

    procedure WMDisplayField(var Msg: TMessage);
       virtual wm_First + wm_DisplayFields;

{ Private data members and functions}

  private
```

```
{ A member to store the associated cursor }

    tablesCursor: PCursor;

{ A member to save the field }

    tablesField: FieldNumber;

{ Accessor functions to private data }

  public

{ Return the associated cursor. }

    function getCursor: PCursor;

{ Return the field. }

    function getFieldNumber: FieldNumber;

  end; { TFieldStatic }

(***********************************************************************
 * OBJECT TYPE:  TCurRecStatic
 *
 * INHERITS: TFieldStatic
 *
 * DESCRIPTION:  This object is like a TFieldStatic, but it displays
 *               the current record number of the record.
 ***********************************************************************)
  PCurRecStatic = ^TCurRecStatic;
  TCurRecStatic = object(TFieldStatic)

{ Constructors }
    constructor Init(AParent: PWindowsObject; AnId: Integer;
      X, Y, W, H: Integer; ACursor: PCursor);

    constructor InitResource(AParent: PWindowsObject;
      ResourceID: Word; ACursor: PCursor);

{ The DisplayField gets the current record number and displays the value }
{ in the control.                                                         }

    procedure DisplayField; virtual;

{ The SaveField function does nothing. }

    procedure SaveField; virtual;

  end; { TCurRecStatic }
```

```
(************************************************************************
 * OBJECT TYPE:  TTotRecStatic
 *
 * INHERITS: TFieldStatic
 *
 * DESCRIPTION:  This object is like a TFieldStatic, but it displays
 *               the total number of records in a cursor.
 ***********************************************************************)
  PTotRecStatic = ^TTotRecStatic;
  TTotRecStatic = object(TFieldStatic)

{ Constructors }
    constructor Init(AParent: PWindowsObject; AnId: Integer;
      X, Y, W, H: Integer; ACursor: PCursor);

    constructor InitResource(AParent: PWindowsObject;
      ResourceID: Word; ACursor: PCursor);

{ The DisplayField gets the total number of records and displays the  }
{ value in the control.                                                }

  procedure DisplayField; virtual;

{ The SaveField function does nothing. }

  procedure SaveField; virtual;

  end; { TTotRecStatic }

{ end type section }

{ This section contains the code necessary to make the object work. }

implementation

(************************************************************************
 * OBJECT TYPE:  TFieldStatic
 *
 * METHOD:       Init     (Constructor)
 *
 * DESCRIPTION:  Creates an object of this type.
 *
 ***********************************************************************)
constructor TFieldStatic.Init(AParent: PWindowsObject; AnId: Integer;
  X, Y, W, H: Integer; ACursor: PCursor; AField: FieldNumber);
begin
```

```
{ Construct the base object. }

   inherited Init(AParent, AnId, '', X, Y, W, H, 255);

{ Save the cursor pointer and the field that this control is associated to. }

   tablesCursor := ACursor;
   tablesField := AField;
end;

(**********************************************************************
 * OBJECT TYPE:  TFieldStatic
 *
 * METHOD:       InitResource     (Constructor)
 *
 * DESCRIPTION:  Creates an object of this type that is on a dialog box.
 *
 **********************************************************************)
constructor TFieldStatic.InitResource(AParent: PWindowsObject;
   ResourceID, ATextLen: Word; ACursor: PCursor; AField: FieldNumber);
begin

{ Construct the base object. }

   inherited InitResource(AParent, ResourceID, ATextLen);

{ Save the field and cursor info. }

   tablesCursor := ACursor;
   tablesField := AField;
end;

(**********************************************************************
 * OBJECT TYPE:  TFieldStatic
 *
 * METHOD:       getCursor
 *
 * DESCRIPTION:  Returns the pointer to the embedded cursor object.
 *
 **********************************************************************)
function TFieldStatic.getCursor: PCursor;
begin

{ Return the pointer to the cursor. }

   getCursor := tablesCursor;
end;
```

4-10 Continued.

```
(**********************************************************************
* OBJECT TYPE:  TFieldStatic
*
* METHOD:        getFieldNumber
*
* DESCRIPTION: Returns the field number associated to this control.
*
**********************************************************************)
function TFieldStatic.getFieldNumber: FieldNumber;
begin

{ Return the pointer to the cursor. }

  getFieldNumber := tablesField;
end;

(**********************************************************************
* OBJECT TYPE:  TFieldStatic
*
* METHOD:        DisplayField
*
* DESCRIPTION:  This procedure will get the value of the field out
*               of the record buffer and display the value in the control.
**********************************************************************)
procedure TFieldStatic.DisplayField;
var
  recordBuffer: PRecord;  {  A pointer to the record buffer in the cursor }
  isNull: Boolean;
  valAsString: String;
  valAsPChar: array[0..256] of char;
  fldType: PXFieldType;
  subType: PXFieldSubType;
  length: Integer;
  ValAsDoub: Double;
begin

{ Get the record buffer. }

  recordBuffer := tablesCursor^.genericRec;

{ What type is the field? }

  recordBuffer^.getFieldType(tablesField, fldType, subType, length);
```

```
{ If the type is a double, then get it as a double. }

  if(fldType = fldDouble) then
  begin
    recordBuffer^.getDouble(tablesField, valAsDoub, isNull);

    if(not isNull) then
        Str(valAsDoub:5:2, valAsString);
  end
  else
{ Get the field's value as a string. }
    recordBuffer^.getString(tablesField, valAsString, isNull);

{ Was the value blank? }

  if isNull = true then
    valAsString := '';

{ Convert the Pascal style string to a null terminated string (NTS). }

  strPCopy(valAsPChar, valAsString);

{ Display this value. }

  SetText(valAsPChar);

end;


(*********************************************************************
 * OBJECT TYPE:  TFieldStatic
 *
 * METHOD:        WMDisplayField
 *
 * DESCRIPTION: This procedure responds to the wm_DisplayField message.
 *********************************************************************)
procedure TFieldStatic.WMDisplayField(var Msg: TMessage);
begin
  displayField;
end;


(*********************************************************************
 * OBJECT TYPE:  TCurRecStatic
 *
```

4-10 Continued.

```
* METHOD:        Init    (Constructor)
*
* DESCRIPTION:  Creates an object of this type.
*
*********************************************************************)
constructor TCurRecStatic.Init(AParent: PWindowsObject; AnId: Integer;
  X, Y, W, H: Integer;  ACursor: PCursor);
begin

{ Construct the base object. }

  inherited Init(AParent, AnId, X, Y, W, H, ACursor, 0);
end;

(*********************************************************************
* OBJECT TYPE:  TCurRecStatic
*
* METHOD:        InitResource    (Constructor)
*
* DESCRIPTION:  Creates an object of this type that is on a dialog box.
*
*********************************************************************)
constructor TCurRecStatic.InitResource(AParent: PWindowsObject;
  ResourceID: Word; ACursor: PCursor);
begin

{ Construct the base object. }

  inherited InitResource(AParent, ResourceID, 10, ACursor, 0);

end;

(*********************************************************************
* OBJECT TYPE:  TCurRecStatic
*
* METHOD:        DisplayField
*
* DESCRIPTION:  This procedure will get the current record number and
*               display it.
*********************************************************************)
procedure TCurRecStatic.DisplayField;
var
  curRecNum: RecordNumber;
  valAsString: String;
  valAsPChar: array[0..256] of char;
begin

{ Get the record number. }
```

```
   curRecNum := tablesCursor^.getCurRecNum;

{ Convert this to a string. }

   Str(curRecNum, valAsString);

{ Convert that to a PChar. }

   strPCopy(valAsPChar, valAsString);

{ Display this value. }

   SetText(valAsPChar);

end;

(*********************************************************************
 * OBJECT TYPE:  TCurRecStatic
 *
 * METHOD:       SaveField
 *
 * DESCRIPTION:  This function does nothing. There is no place to save
 *               the value.
 *********************************************************************)
procedure TCurRecStatic.SaveField;
begin
end;

(*********************************************************************
 * OBJECT TYPE:  TTotRecStatic
 *
 * METHOD:       Init     (Constructor)
 *
 * DESCRIPTION:  Creates an object of this type.
 *
 *********************************************************************)
constructor TTotRecStatic.Init(AParent: PWindowsObject; AnId: Integer;
  X, Y, W, H: Integer; ACursor: PCursor);
begin

{ Construct the base object. }

   inherited Init(AParent, AnId, X, Y, W, H, ACursor, 0);
end;

(*********************************************************************
 * OBJECT TYPE:  TTotRecStatic
 *
 * METHOD:       InitResource     (Constructor)
```

4-10 Continued.

```
*
* DESCRIPTION:  Creates an object of this type that is on a dialog box.
*
********************************************************************)
constructor TTotRecStatic.InitResource(AParent: PWindowsObject;
  ResourceID: Word; ACursor: PCursor);
begin

{ Construct the base object. }

  inherited InitResource(AParent, ResourceID, 10, ACursor, 0);

end;

(********************************************************************
* OBJECT TYPE:  TTotRecStatic
*
* METHOD:       DisplayField
*
* DESCRIPTION:  This member will get the total number of records and
*               will display this total.
********************************************************************)
procedure TTotRecStatic.DisplayField;
var
  totRecs: RecordNumber;
  valAsString: String;
  valAsPChar: array[0..256] of char;
begin

{ Get the total number of records. }

  totRecs := tablesCursor^.getRecCount;

{ Convert this to a string. }

  Str(totRecs, valAsString);

{ Convert that to a PChar. }

  strPCopy(valAsPChar, valAsString);

{ Display this value. }

  SetText(valAsPChar);

end;
```

```
(**********************************************************************
* OBJECT TYPE:  TTotRecStatic
*
* METHOD:       SaveField
*
* DESCRIPTION:  This function does nothing. There is no place to save
*               the value.
***********************************************************************)
procedure TTotRecStatic.SaveField;
begin
end;

{ Unit startup code }
begin
end.
```

Unit: TCURDLG

This unit defines the object type **TCursorDialog**, which associates a **TDialog** object and a **TCursor** object from the Paradox Engine Database Framework to provide access to the functions that operate a cursor open on a table in the application.

Object type: TCursorDialog
   Inherits: TDialog

Field

tablesCursor   tablesCursor: PCursor;   **private**

A field that points to the associated cursor object.

Methods

Init   constructor Init(AParent: PWindowsObject; AName: PChar; ACursor: PCursor);

Creates a **TCursorDialog** object of this type and associates a table's cursor with this object that allows us to access the Database Framework *TCursor* functions.

Done   destructor Done; virtual;

Disposes of the **TScroller** object in **Scroller**, if any, before calling the *Done* destructor inherited from **TWindowsObject** to dispose of the entire object.

WMDisplayFields   procedure WMDisplayFields(var Msg: TMessage); **virtual**
   wm_First + wm_DisplayFields;

This procedure responds to a wm_DisplayFields message.

DisplayFields   procedure DisplayFields;

This procedure displays the contents of the fields of a table in the **TField...** type controls.

WMSaveFields procedure WMSaveFields(var Msg: TMessage); virtual wm_First + wm_SaveFields;

This procedure responds to a wm_SaveFields message.

SaveFields procedure SaveFields;

This procedure saves the data in the fields from **TField...** type controls into the table's generic record buffer. Within this procedure, there is a local procedure that uses the **TWindowsObject** method *ForEach* to send the wm_SaveFields message to each control on the dialog.

When a control that knows how to handle such a message receives it, the *WMSaveFields* method in that control will respond by calling its *SaveField* method to save the data to the generic record buffer using the **TRecord** methods *setNull* (for blank fields) or *putString*.

HaveValuesChanged function HaveValuesChanged: Boolean;

This function checks to see if a user has changed the value of a field. Within this function, there is a local function *AskField* that the *FirstThat* function uses to send the message wm_HaveValuesChanged to every control on the Window. Within this function, there is a local function *AskField* that the *FirstThat* function uses to send the message wm_HaveValuesChanged to every control on the Window. If the function ever returns True, then *FirstThat* will return a pointer to the first control that returned True.

getCursor function getCursor: PCursor;

Returns the pointer to the embedded cursor object.

The file listed in FIG. 4-11 shows how to associate a cursor object and a dialog object to manage the display of data from a table.

4-11 This file, TCURDLG.PAS, demonstrates how to associate a cursor object and a dialog object.

```
(************************************************************************
*
* FILE:          TCURDLG.PAS
*
* DESCRIPTION:   This file defines the object TCursorDialog.  This object
*                combines TDialog and a DBF TCursor object types.
*************************************************************************)
unit TCURDLG; { Unit name }

{ This section defines what other Pascal programs may use from this unit. }

interface

{ Tell the compiler what units are needed. }

uses    WinTypes,
        WinProcs,
```

```
        OWindows,
        ODialogs,
        OopXEng,          { The Database Framework (DBF) unit      }
        WmDbf;            { Messages supported by our new objects }

{ The new types defined in this unit. }

type

(************************************************************************
 * OBJECT TYPE:  TCursorDialog
 *
 * INHERITS: TDialog
 *
 * DESCRIPTION:  This object defines some new properties for a TDialog.  The
 *               dialog encapsulates a TCursor and can control special
 *               controls on the dialog that contain fields from the
 *               TCursor.
 ************************************************************************)
  PCursorDialog = ^TCursorDialog;
  TCursorDialog = object(TDialog)

{ A constructor for the object }

    constructor Init(AParent: PWindowsObject; AName: PChar;
      ACursor: PCursor);

{ Destructor }

    destructor Done; virtual;

{ A function that checks to see if the user has changed any field values }

    function HaveValuesChanged: Boolean;

{ A function that will respond to the wm_DisplayFields message }

    procedure WMDisplayFields(var Msg: TMessage);
      virtual wm_First + wm_DisplayFields;

{ A function to display the fields of the table in TField controls }

    procedure DisplayFields;

{ A function to take the values from the current control }
{ and place them in the record buffer.                    }

    procedure SaveFields;

{ A function to respond to the wm_SaveField message }
```

```
    procedure WMSaveFields(var Msg: TMessage);
      virtual wm_First + wm_SaveFields;

{ Private data members and functions }

  private

{ A member to store the associated cursor }

    tablesCursor: PCursor;

{ Accessor functions to private data }
  public

{ Returns the associated cursor }

    function getCursor: PCursor;

  end; { TCursorDialog }


{ end type section }

{ This section contains the code necessary to make the objects work. }

implementation

(*********************************************************************
 * OBJECT TYPE:  TCursorDialog
 *
 * METHOD:       Init    (Constructor)
 *
 * DESCRIPTION:  Creates an object of this type.
 *
 *********************************************************************)
constructor TCursorDialog.Init(AParent: PWindowsObject; AName: PChar;
  ACursor: PCursor);
begin

{ Call constructor of the base object. }

  inherited Init(AParent, AName);

{ Save the data member tablesCursor. }

  tablesCursor := ACursor;

end;
```

```
(**********************************************************************
 * OBJECT TYPE:   TCursorDialog
 *
 * METHOD:        Done      (Destructor)
 *
 * DESCRIPTION:   Destroys an object of this type.
 *
 **********************************************************************)
destructor TCursorDialog.Done;
begin
  inherited Done;
end;

(**********************************************************************
 * OBJECT TYPE:   TCursorDialog
 *
 * METHOD:        getCursor
 *
 * DESCRIPTION:   Returns the pointer to the embedded cursor object.
 *
 **********************************************************************)
function TCursorDialog.getCursor: PCursor;
begin

{ Return the pointer to the cursor. }

  getCursor := tablesCursor;
end;

(**********************************************************************
 * OBJECT TYPE:   TCursorDialog
 *
 * METHOD:        MWDisplayFields
 *
 * DESCRIPTION:   Responds to the wm_DisplayFields message.
 *
 **********************************************************************)
procedure TCursorDialog.WMDisplayFields(var Msg: TMessage);
begin
  DisplayFields;
end;

(**********************************************************************
 * OBJECT TYPE:   TCursorDialog
 *
 * METHOD:        DisplayFields
 *
 * DESCRIPTION:   Displays the fields of the table in TField controls.
 *
 **********************************************************************)
```

4-11 Continued.

```
procedure TCursorDialog.DisplayFields;

  { This local function is used to send the message to every }
  { control on the dialog.                                   }
  procedure DisplayField(AWindowsObject: PWindowsObject); far;
  var
    controlID: Integer;
    begin

      controlID := AWindowsObject^.getId;

      if controlID <> -1 then
          sendDlgItemMsg(controlID, wm_DisplayFields, 0, 0);
  end;

begin

{ Use the ForEach function of TWindowsObject to send the message        }
{ wm_DisplayField to every control on the dialog.  Only those controls  }
{ that know how to handle that message will perform some action.        }

  ForEach(@DisplayField);
end;
(**********************************************************************
* OBJECT TYPE:  TCursorDialog
*
* METHOD:       MWSaveFields
*
* DESCRIPTION:  Responds to the wm_SaveFields message.
*
***********************************************************************)
procedure TCursorDialog.WMSaveFields(var Msg: TMessage);
begin
  SaveFields;
end;

(**********************************************************************
* OBJECT TYPE:  TCursorDialog
*
* METHOD:       SaveFields
*
* DESCRIPTION:  Saves the fields into the table's record buffer.
*
***********************************************************************)
procedure TCursorDialog.SaveFields;

  { This local function is used to send the message to every }
```

```
{ control on the dialog.                                                  }
  procedure SaveField(AWindowsObject: PWindowsObject); far;
  var
    controlID: Integer;
    begin

      controlID := AWindowsObject^.getId;

      if controlID <> -1 then
        sendDlgItemMsg(controlID, wm_SaveFields, 0, 0);

  end;

begin

{ Use the ForEach function of TWindowsObject to send the message          }
{ wm_DisplayField to every control on the dialog.  Only those controls    }
{ that know how to handle that message will perform some action.          }

  ForEach(@SaveField);
end;

(**************************************************************************
* OBJECT TYPE:  TCursorDialog
*
* METHOD:       HaveValuesChanged
*
* DESCRIPTION:  This function checks to see if a user has changed the value
*               of a field.
**************************************************************************)
function TCursorDialog.HaveValuesChanged: Boolean;

  { This local function is used to send the message to every }
  { control on the dialog.                                   }
  function AskField(AWindowsObject: PWindowsObject): Boolean; far;
  var
    controlID: Integer;
    result: Longint;
    begin

      controlID := AWindowsObject^.getId;

      if controlID <> -1 then
      begin
        result := sendDlgItemMsg(controlID, wm_HaveValuesChanged, 0, 0);

{ Return what the control said. }

        AskField := Boolean(result);
```

```
      end
      else
```

{ Return false. }

```
        AskField := False;

   end;

begin
```

{ Use the FirstThat function of TWindowsObject to send the message   }
{ wm_HaveValueChanged to every control on the dialog. Only those controls}
{ that know how to handle that message will perform some action.   }
{ If the function EVER returns true, then FirstThat will return a pointer }
{ to the control that returned TRUE.   }

```
   if(FirstThat(@AskField) <> nil) then
     HaveValuesChanged := True
   else
     HaveValuesChanged := False;

end;
```

{ unit startup code }
```
begin
end.
```

Unit: TQBUILD

This unit implements the query builder dialog box. We use it to assemble the query that we then submit to the query object itself that manages a single table query.

Object type: TQueryBuilder
  Inherits: TDialog

Fields

fieldNames fieldNames: PComboBox; **private**

A pointer to the combo box object containing the list of field names for the open table.

value value: PEdit; **private**

A pointer to the edit control containing the value to be matched as a restriction for the query.

restrictions restrictions: PListBox; **private**

A pointer to the list box object containing the list of restrictions for this query.

isEqual	isEqual
isNotEqual	isNotEqual
isLess	isLess
isLessOrEqual	isLessOrEqual
isGreater	isGreater
isGreaterOrEqual	isGreaterOrEqual: PRadioButton; **private**

Pointers to the set of radio buttons in the **TRadioButton** control used with this dialog.

tablesCursor tablesCursor: PCursor; **private**

A field that points to the associated cursor object.

theQuery theQuery: PQuery; **private**

A pointer to the **TQuery** object.

Methods

Init constructor Init(AParent: PWindowsObject; ACursor: PCursor; AQuery: Query);

Constructs an object of this type using the Windows resource QUERY _BUILDER, which combines a combo box for listing the names of the field in the table to be queried, a group of radio buttons for selecting an operator for a restriction, an edit box for the value of the restriction, and a list box to hold the restrictions for that query.

setUpWindow procedure setUpWindow; virtual;

This procedure is called so that the dialog can initialize its state before being shown to the user.

IDAdd procedure IDAdd(var Msg: TMessage); virtual id_First + id_add_ restriction;

This procedure adds a restriction to the query by assembling a string to be passed to the query object from the field name found in the combo box control, an operator found in the control forming group of radio buttons, and the value found in the edit box control.

addRestrictionToQuery function addRestrictionToQuery(fieldName: PChar; query Op: opType; aValue: PChar): Boolean; **private**

This private function adds a restriction consisting of a field's name, *field-Name*, an operator type, *queryOp* (see the operators' fields list previously), and a value to be compared, *aValue*. If the restriction was successfully added to the lists of restrictions, then the function returns TRUE; if not, it returns FALSE.

The file that follows in FIG. 4-12 provides the necessary objects for the resources we use in the dialog box for assembling a query.

4-12 This file, TQBUILD.PAS, demonstrates how to provide the objects for Windows resources that we use to build a query.

```
(*************************************************************************
 *
 * FILE:          TQBUILD.PAS
 *
 * DESCRIPTION:   This file implements the query builder Dialog.
 *************************************************************************)
unit  TQBUILD; {Unit name }
{$N+}

{ This section defines what other Pascal programs may use from this unit. }

interface

uses     WinTypes,
         WinProcs,
         OWindows,
         ODialogs,
         OopXEng,          { The Database Framework (DBF) unit }
         PXQUERY,          { The TQuery unit which performs queries }
         Strings,
         POSUTILS,
         PXEngWin;

const

{ Control id numbers for the controls on the TQueryBuilder dialog. }

     id_field_names      =  101;
     id_values           =  111;
     id_add_restriction  =  113;
     id_restrictions     =  114;
     id_equal            =  104;
     id_notequal         =  105;
     id_less             =  106;
     id_lessorequal      =  107;
     id_greater          =  108;
     id_greaterorequal   =  109;

type

(*************************************************************************
 * OBJECT TYPE:  TQueryBuilder
 *
 * INHERITS: TDialog
 *
 * DESCRIPTION:  This object type implements the query builder dialog.
 *************************************************************************)
```

```
        PQueryBuilder = ^TQueryBuilder;
        TQueryBuilder = object(TDialog)

{ A constructor for the object. }

        constructor Init(AParent: PWindowsObject; ACursor: PCursor;
          AQuery: PQuery);


{ Set up the dialog when it comes up. }

        procedure SetupWindow; virtual;

{ A procedure to handle the pressing of the Add restriction button }

        procedure IDAdd(var Msg: TMessage);
          virtual id_First + id_add_restriction;

{ Private data and members }

      private

{ The Fields' list box }

        fieldNames : PComboBox;

{ Value box }

        value : PEdit;

{ Restrictions box }

        restrictions:  PListBox;

{ Radio buttons }

        isEqual,
        isNotEqual,
        isLess,
        isLessOrEqual,
        isGreater,
        isGreaterOrEqual: PRadioButton;

{ Remember the table's cursor. }

        tablesCursor:  PCursor;

{ Remember the query object. }

        theQuery: PQuery;
```

{ A function to add the restriction to the TQuery object. }

```
    function addRestrictionToQuery(fieldName: PChar;
      queryOp: opType; aValue: PChar): Boolean;

  end; { TQueryBuilder }

implementation

(************************************************************************
* OBJECT TYPE:  TQueryBuilder
*
* METHOD:        Init    (Constructor)
*
* DESCRIPTION: Ccreates an object of this type.
*
************************************************************************)
constructor TQueryBuilder.Init(AParent: PWindowsObject; ACursor: PCursor;
  AQuery: PQuery);
begin

{ Call constructor of the base object. }

    inherited Init(AParent, 'QUERY_BUILDER');

{ Remember the cursor. }

    tablesCursor := ACursor;

{ Remember the query. }

    theQuery := AQuery;

{ Construct the field names' combo box. }

    fieldNames := new(PComboBox, InitResource(@Self, id_field_names, 26));

{ Construct the restrictions list box. }

    restrictions := new(PListBox, InitResource(@Self, id_restrictions));

{ Construct the value edit box. }

    value := new(PEdit, InitResource(@Self, id_values, 255));

{ Construct the objects for the operators as radio buttons. }
```

```
    isEqual := new(PRadioButton, InitResource(@Self, id_equal));
    isNotEqual := new(PRadioButton, InitResource(@Self, id_notequal));
    isLess := new(PRadioButton, InitResource(@Self, id_less));
    isLessOrEqual := new(PRadioButton, InitResource(@Self, id_lessorequal));
    isGreater := new(PRadioButton, InitResource(@Self, id_greater));
    isGreaterOrEqual := new(PRadioButton, InitResource(@Self, id_greaterorequal))

end;

(***************************************************************************
 * OBJECT TYPE:   TQueryBuilder
 *
 * METHOD:        SetupWindow
 *
 * DESCRIPTION:   This procedure is called so the dialog can initialize
 *                its state before it is shown to the user.
 *
 ***************************************************************************)
procedure TQueryBuilder.SetupWindow;
var
  fieldCount: Integer;
  curRec: PRecord;
  desc: TFieldDesc;
  asChar: array[0..26] of char;
begin

{ Call the constructor for the field descriptor array for the table. }

  desc.Init;

{ Call the base object. }

  inherited SetupWindow;

{ Get the generic record. }

  curRec := tablesCursor^.genericRec;

{ Load the combo box with the field names from the table. }

  for fieldCount := 1 to curRec^.getFieldCount do
  begin
    curRec^.getFieldDesc(fieldCount, @desc);
    strPCopy(asChar, desc.fldName);
    fieldNames^.addString(asChar);
  end;

  desc.Done;
```

```
end;

(**********************************************************************
* OBJECT TYPE:  TQueryBuilder
*
* METHOD:        IDadd
*
* DESCRIPTION:  This procedure adds a restriction to the query.
*
**********************************************************************)
procedure TQueryBuilder.IDAdd(var Msg: TMessage);
var
  restString: array [0..300] of char;
  aField: array [0..25] of char;
  anOp: pchar;
  aValue: array [0..255] of char;
  queryOp: opType;
begin

{ Get the field name. }

  if( fieldNames^.getSelString(aField, 26) <= 0) then
  begin
    messageBox(Hwindow, 'You must select a field name', 'Error',
    MB_ICONHAND or MB_OK);
    exit;
  end;

{ Get the operator. }

  if(isEqual^.getCheck = bf_checked) then
  begin
    queryOp := OP_EQ;
    anOP := '=';
    isEqual^.Toggle;
  end
  else if(isNotEqual^.getCheck = bf_checked) then
  begin
    queryOp := OP_NOT_EQ;
    anOP := '<>';
    isNotEqual^.Toggle;
  end
  else if(isLess^.getCheck = bf_checked) then
  begin
    queryOp := OP_LT;
    anOP := '<';
```

```
      isLess^.Toggle;
    end
    else if(isLessOrEqual^.getCheck = bf_checked) then
    begin
      queryOp := OP_LE;
      anOP := '<=';
      isLessOREqual^.Toggle;
    end
    else if(isGreater^.getCheck = bf_checked) then
    begin
      queryOp := OP_GT;
      anOP := '>';
      isGreater^.Toggle;
    end
    else if(isGreaterOrEqual^.getCheck = bf_checked) then
    begin
      queryOp := OP_GE;
      anOP := '>=';
      isGreaterOrEqual^.Toggle;
    end
    else
    begin
      messageBox(Hwindow, 'You must select an operator', 'Error',
        MB_ICONHAND or MB_OK);
      exit;
    end;

    fieldNames^.SetSelIndex(-1);

{ Get the value. }

    if(value^.getText(aValue, 255) = 0) then
      strCopy(aValue, '<BLANK>');

    value^.setText('');

{ Now create the restriction and place it in the list box. }

      strCopy(restString,aField);
      strCat(restString,'    ');
      strCat(restString, anOp);
      strCat(restString, '    ');
      strCat(restString, aValue);


{ Add the restriction to the TQuery object type restriction list. }
```

```
  if(addRestrictionToQuery(aField, queryOp, aValue) = TRUE) then
    restrictions^.addString(restString)
  else
    messageBox(HWindow, 'The value does not match the field''s type.',
      'Can not add restriction', mb_ok or mb_iconinformation);

end;

(***********************************************************************
 * OBJECT TYPE:  TQueryBuilder
 *
 * METHOD:       addRestrictionToQuery
 *
 * DESCRIPTION:  This function adds the restriction to the query's
 *               restriction list.  If the restriction could not be added,
 *               then the function will return FALSE.
 *
 ***********************************************************************)
function TQueryBuilder.addRestrictionToQuery(fieldName: PChar;
      queryOp: opType; aValue: PChar): Boolean;
var
  fieldType: PXFieldType;
  fieldSubtype: PXFieldSubtype;
  fieldLen: Integer;
  pToShort: PInteger;
  pToDouble: PDouble;
  pToChar: PChar;
  aShort: Integer;
  aDouble: Double;
  code: integer;
  fldNumber: FIELDNUMBER;
  nameAsString: string;
begin

{ Get the field's type. }

  nameAsString := strPas(fieldName);
  fldNumber := tablesCursor^.genericRec^.getFieldNumber(nameAsString);

  if(ERROR(tablesCursor^.genericRec^.getFieldType(fldNumber, fieldType,
    fieldSubtype, fieldLen), 'Getting field type') = PXSUCCESS) then
  begin

{ Depending on the field type, we must call different addRestriction functions. }

{ A short field }
    if(FieldType = fldShort) then
```

```
      begin
        if(aValue[0] = '') then pToShort := nil
        else
        begin
          Val(aValue, aShort, code);
            if (code <> 0) then
            begin
              addRestrictionToQuery := FALSE;
              exit;
            end;
              pToShort := @aShort;
      end;
          theQuery^.addRestrictionShort( fieldName, queryOp, pToShort);
      end

{ Is it a double type field? }

      else if(fieldType = fldDouble) then
        begin
          if(aValue[0] = '') then pToDouble := nil
          else
          begin
            Val(aValue, aDouble, code);
              if (code <> 0) then
              begin
                addRestrictionToQuery := FALSE;
                exit;
              end;
              pToDouble := @aDouble;
      end;
          theQuery^.addRestrictionDouble( fieldName, queryOp, pToDouble);
        end
        else
        begin

{ A char, date or blob type field. }

          if(aValue[0] = '') then pToChar := nil
          else pToChar := aValue;
          theQuery^.addRestrictionChar( fieldName, queryOp, pToChar);
          end;
    end;
    AddRestrictionToQuery := TRUE;
end;

{ Startup code }

begin
end.
```

Conclusion

We now have all of the concepts and code for the new and reusable objects that we have created to integrate the Engine and the user interface. There still is the specialized code for each one of our windows and dialogs, but we have gone a long way toward orienting the objects of this application to ensure quicker coding for the rest of the application and any other application that we might want to code using the Paradox Engine Database Framework and Windows resources.

5

Integrating the user interface and the Engine

With the flexibility and power that the Paradox Engine allows a programmer to exercise, there also comes the responsibility for handling more precisely the chores that a PAL script or an interactive Paradox data application control more implicitly. The Engine's close relationship with Paradox itself expands the possibilities for dispersing the work of applications between system's work and database work. Similarly, programmers can use the Engine to store data in a format that also is available as regular Paradox objects. Where the Engine reaches its limits are in the areas that we have provided explicit solutions: validity checking, referential integrity, and queries. You will see in the chapters devoted to these topics that, while the Engine itself does not have explicit functions for managing these concepts, we rely on the Engine's functions to accomplish these tasks.

This chapter will demonstrate our implementation of the Engine's Database Framework OOP layer in the order-entry application that we have designed. Additional features such as validity checking, referential integrity, and queries will turbocharge the Engine's functionality and allow us to roll out an application that not only looks good but has an Engine with real power under the hood.

Cranking up the Engine for the first time

To launch this application as an ObjectWindows application, we first create a main program framework for the application. There, as expected, we will derive our own **TApplication** object type, **TPosApplication**, and use it to provide the structure for this application and to construct an application's window. For this main window, we will be constructing an object derived from our **TMDIDBFWindow** object type because **TMDIDBFWindow** inherits the fundamental behavior of the ObjectWindows **TMDIWindow** object type, which serves as the main window of MDI-compliant applications.

The multiple document interface (MDI) allows an application to manage multiple documents, or multiple views of the same document, within the main application window. An example of this implementation with our application features the Salc window for which a user can create more than one simultaneous instance to handle multiple new sales or retain access to the main window's menu bar to perform, say, a query or look up a customer's past purchases. When an instance of this New Sale child window is minimized, its icon appears within the main window's workspace.

Our object type **TMDIDBFWindow** is derived from **TMDIWindow** for this reason and adds in the Engine functions that we want to establish with it. The additional functionality will create the required single instances of **TEngine** and **TDatabase** so that we can properly access and manipulate the tables within our database. We have made the data for these objects private because we do not want other objects to have access to the data **TEngine** and **TDatabase** require for initializing the application because any changes to the opening configuration of the Engine or the database information such as the tables and their indexes would wreak havoc.

The code in FIG. 5-1 is the complete POS.PAS file. This POS.PAS module contains the name for the executable file that we will create, the necessary compiler directives, as well as the units used by the objects in this file. The **Program** statement properly identifies this module as our program type of file, the one containing the "main" program segment.

5-1 The "main" program segment, units the module uses, and related compiler directives for the application: POS.PAS.

```
(**********************************************************************
*
* FILE:          POS.PAS
*
* DESCRIPTION:   This file contains the main program routine for the POS
*                application.
*
*
*
**********************************************************************)
Program Pos; {Program name is POS.EXE }

{$R+}
{$R POS.RES }

{ Tell the compiler what units are needed to link the program. }
```

```
uses      WinTypes,
          WinProcs,
          OWindows,
          OopXEng,
          BWCC,                { Borland Windows Custom Controls }
          TMDIPOS;             { Our MDI frame class specific to POS }


{ Define the new types we are going to use in the program. }

type

(*********************************************************************
* OBJECT TYPE:  TPosApplication
*
* INHERITS: TApplication
*
* DESCRIPTION: This is the main program class for the POS program.
*
*********************************************************************)
  TPosApplication = object(TApplication)

{ InitMainWindow creates the programs main window. This window will be a }
{ MDI or Multiple Document Interface window.                            }

    procedure InitMainWindow; virtual;

  end; { object TPosApplication }
{ end type section }


(*********************************************************************
* OBJECT TYPE:  TPosApplication
*
* METHOD:       InitMainWindow
*
* DESCRIPTION:  This procedure creates the main program window.  For the
*               POS application it is a MDI Window.
*********************************************************************)
procedure TPosApplication.InitMainWindow;
begin

{ Create a TMDIDBFWindow object as the main window for the application.  }
{ The constructor to this TMDIWindow type window takes a handle to a menu.}
{ This is the application's main menu.                                   }

  MainWindow := New (PMDIPOSWindow, Init('Point of Sale',
```

```
    LoadMenu(HInstance, 'Pos_Main_Menu')));

end;

{ Local variables for the main program section }

var
  PosApp: TPosApplication;


{ Main program section }

begin

{ Create an instance of a TPosApplication. }

  PosApp.Init('Point of Sale Program');

{ Run the program. }

  PosApp.Run;

{ Clean up the application object. }

  PosApp.Done;

end.
```

The compiler directives here direct the compiler to include the resource file for our Windows resources (POS.RES) and inform the compiler that any directives specified in this module take precedence over the same compiler directives that you might have set when configuring the Borland IDE. In this particular application, we instruct the compiler to create an executable file that enables linking with a run-time library that emulates the 80×87 numeric coprocessor (**$E+**), generates code that performs all real-type calculations using 80×87 (**$N+**), generates range-checking code (**$R+**), and incorporates the POS.RES Windows resource file to be included in the application ({**$R POS.RES**}).

We also define the units that we will need for this program segment, including those for an ObjectWindows application, the Engine itself, the library of Borland Windows Custom Controls that we will draw on for the buttons and backgrounds that we'll be using to give this application a "Borland" look, and the unit containing the **TMDIPosWindow** object that we have derived for this particular application's main window framework from our own **TMDIDBFWindow** object type.

The remainder of this code follows the usual expectations for creating the main program section and illustrates how to bring in the full resources of the application by creating an instance of the **TMDIPosWindow** to access all of the subroutines that we need for the complete application.

Initializing the Engine

As an object derived from **TMDIDBFWindow**, **TMDIPosWindow** inherits not only the characteristics of a **TMDIWindow** object, but also includes a routine that uses the Engine's Database Framework OOP layer to create instances of the **TEngine** and **TDatabase** objects that we need. As you can see from the code excerpt from TMDIDBF.PAS in FIG. 5-2, we call the **TEngine** and **TDatabase** constructors from within the **TMDIDBFWindow**'s constructor and check to make sure that each creates its object appropriately. We first must open the Engine and use PXSUCCESS to test that it is operating before we open the default universal database and test the success of this initialization similarly.

5-2 An excerpt from TMDIDBF.PAS that shows how to initialize the Engine and create an instance of the **TDatabase** object as the universal database.

```
* * * * * * * * * * * * * * * * * * * * * * * * * * * * * * * * * * * * * * * * * * * * * * * * * * * * * * * * * * * * * * * * * * *
* TYPE:        TMDIDBFWindow
*
* METHOD:      Init   (CONSTRUCTOR)
*
* DESCRIPTION: This is called for every instance of the program that is
*              run.  We will turn on the Engine and open the default
*              Universal database here.
* * * * * * * * * * * * * * * * * * * * * * * * * * * * * * * * * * * * * * * * * * * * * * * * * * * * * * * * * * * * * * * * * *)
constructor TMDIDBFWindow.Init(ATitle: PChar; AMenu: HMenu);
var
  dummy: BOOL;
begin
{ Call TMDIWindow.Init. }

  TMDIWindow.Init(ATitle, AMenu);

{ Create an instance of TDatabase and TEngine for this instance.  }
{ Open the Engine first allowing for use with Windows concurrency }
{ operations.

  eng := New (PEngine, defInit(pxWin));

{ Check to see that the Engine object was created successfully. }

  if((eng <> nil) and (eng^.lastError = PXSUCCESS))then
```

```
   begin

{ Open the default universal database object. }

     db := New (PDatabase, Init(eng));

{ Check to see that the database object was created successfully. }

        if((db = nil) or (db^.lastError <> PXSUCCESS))then
        begin

{ No? Then show an error. }

         MessageBox(HWindow, 'Could not Initialize Database', 'Init Error',
            MB_OK or MB_ICONSTOP);

          dummy := PostAppMessage(GetCurrentTask, WM_QUIT, 0, 0);
        end;
   end
   else begin

{ No? Then show an error. }

   MessageBox(HWindow, 'Could not Initialize Engine', 'Init Error',
     MB_OK or MB_ICONSTOP);

          dummy := PostAppMessage(GetCurrentTask, WM_QUIT, 0, 0);
   end;

end;
```

This initialization routine is called through **TMDIDBFWindow**'s constructor, *Init,* in the inherited object **TMDIPosWindow**. When we create a **TApplication** type instance for this application (**TPosApplication**), we construct the main window frame and load the menu bar by calling **TMDIPosWindow** with the appropriate program title ('Point of Sale') and argument for the menu bar's Windows resources ('Pos_Main_Menu') as shown in this fragment from POS.PAS, our main program module:

```
procedure TPosApplication.InitMainWindow;
begin
  MainWindow := New (PMDIPOSWindow, Init('Point of Sale',
     LoadMenu(HInstance, 'Pos_Main_Menu')));
end;
```

This construction of the **TMDIPosWindow** initializes the Engine and opens the default or Universal database as shown in FIG. 5-2. Once the routine creates the default database object, we can rely on the TMDIDBFWindow method *getDatabase* to point to the **TDatabase** object and save that pointer in a global variable that provides us with the means for maintaining our reference to the application's persistent database objects such as its tables, indexes, and locking files. With this relationship in place, the code found in the **TMDIPosWindow** method *createDatabase* can generate the tables and indexes for this table when the user selects the Create Database menu option from the Tools menu.

Now that we have some idea of how to work with **TEngine** and **TDatabase**, we move on to the heart of the application's use of the Database Framework, **TRecord** and **TCursor**. With these two classes, we will be able to accomplish the remainder of our operations for the application.

Using TRecord and TCursor:
opening a table and positioning a cursor

The first concept to remember here is that this application relies heavily on a generic record to accomplish the tasks of reading and writing a table's fields for any of the simple dialog boxes. While a generic record does not "know" the structure of a table's fields until the application is running, it then can recognize a record's structure completely. Whenever we want to open a particular table for access, we will use the Pascal **new** procedure to construct a cursor object (**PCursor**) with **TCursor**'s second constructor *InitAndOpen*, which points **TCursor.genericRecord** to a **TRecord** object to allow the cursor to "know" the structure of the record for that table.

Arguments within the *InitAndOpen* constructor point to the Universal database through the *getDatabase* method, define the name of the database table, indicate what type of index the table has, and set the *saveEveryChange* argument to TRUE. The code in FIG. 5-3 illustrates how to accomplish this within the routine of the constructor for our **TInventoryDialog** object type. As you can see, we also check that the table was opened successfully using PXSUCCESS. Further, we position the table's open cursor on the first record in the table using the series of cursor methods *gotoBegin* to move the cursor to the "virtual" record that starts a Paradox table and *gotoNext* to move the cursor to the first actual record of the table because we cannot leave the cursor position at the beginning of the table and use *getRecord*. If *curStatus* is *atBegin*, a *getRecord* call fails with a PXERR_INVCURREC error. The call to *gotoNext* positions the cursor so that it sets *curStatus* to *atRecord*. The *getRecord* method copies the current record of this open cursor, here the first one, into *rec^*, which is here a generic record. With the table properly opened and the cursor positioned on the first record, the code then constructs a dialog box, calling the INVENTORY Windows resource, that loads the values from the generic record into the fields and displays them in the dialog box. When the dialog is finished, the remaining code closes the open cursor on the table and calls the **TCursor** destructor *done* to destroy the cursor object and detach it from the database.

5-3 This excerpt from TMDIPOS.PAS presents a constructor for a dialog box that opens a cursor on a database table and places the record in a generic record buffer.

```
(***************************************************************
* TYPE:          TMDIPOSWindow
*
* METHOD:        Inventory
*
* DESCRIPTION:   This procedure responds to the menu selection:
*                Inventory.
***************************************************************)
procedure TMDIPosWindow.Inventory(var Msg: TMessage);
var
  invDialog : PInventoryDialog;
  inventoryCursor : PCursor;
begin

{ open a cursor for the inventory table. }

  inventoryCursor := new(PCursor, InitAndOpen(getDatabase,
        INVENTORY_DB_NAME, 0, TRUE));

{ Check that the table did open. }

  if(ERROR(inventoryCursor^.lastError, 'Opening INVENTORY table') <>
  PXSUCCESS) then
  begin
  dispose(inventoryCursor, Done);
  exit;
  end;

{ Go to the first record and get it. }

  inventoryCursor^.gotoBegin;
  inventoryCursor^.gotoNext;
  inventoryCursor^.getRecord(inventoryCursor^.genericRec);

{ Get an inventory dialog box. }

  invDialog := new(PInventoryDialog,Init(@self, 'INVENTORY',
  inventoryCursor));

  Application^.ExecDialog(invDialog);

{ Close the table. }

  inventoryCursor^.Close;
  dispose(inventoryCursor, Done);

end;
```

TCursor operations

When the code listed in FIG. 5-3 executed the Inventory dialog box to the application's workspace, it set off a series of events to display a dialog box with the first record of the INVENTORY table displayed in the edit controls and the current record number as well as the total number of records in the table displayed in static text fields. While chapter 4 presented the code for the objects that we have written to associate a control with a Paradox table and its records, this discussion will take a closer look at the sequence of events and objects that are created to accomplish the display of the Inventory dialog box and its data.

The call to the **TInventoryDialog** creates the dialog's constructor using as arguments the title, INVENTORY, and a pointer to the *inventoryCursor*, which already is positioned on the first record of the table. (See FIG. 5-3 above.) The **TInventoryDialog** itself is an object derived from the **TSelectItemDialog** with some additional controls that allow us to add new items and delete existing items from the INVENTORY table. The ancestor for this dialog, **TSelectItemDialog**, also forms part of the sequence of events used to create a new sale. There the dialog simply is meant to scroll through the contents of the table until a user selects an item to be added to the list of merchandise in a sale. Because we use **TSelectItem-Dialog** to handle the code for associating a cursor with an edit control, we'll look at it first.

The TSelectItemDialog The **TSelectItemDialog** is a child of our **TCursorDialog** object type, which overrides the ObjectWindows **TDialog** constructor to include an argument that points to a **TCursor** object, which must be open on a database's table. The code in FIG. 5-3 shows you how to open the cursor properly. The code in FIG. 5-4 demonstrates how we inherit **TCursorDialog** and write the routine that will rely on our **TFieldEdit** and **TFieldStatic** objects to associate a windows resource control with a field in the record the cursor is pointing to.

5-4 This excerpt from the **TSelectItemDialog** shows the constructor and routines that connect a control object with a field in a record from a Paradox table.

```
(************************************************************************
* OBJECT TYPE:   TSelectItemDialog
*
* METHOD:        Init      (Constructor)
*
* DESCRIPTION:   Creates an object of this type.
*
*************************************************************************)
constructor TSelectItemDialog.Init(AParent: PWindowsObject; AName: PChar;
      ACursor: PCursor);
var
  edit : PEdit;
```

5-4 Continued.
```
  control : PControl;
begin

{ Call constructor of the base object. }

  inherited Init(AParent, AName, ACursor);

{ Associate a TFieldStatic with the item number on the dialog. }

        control := new(PFieldStatic, InitResource(@Self, id_Item_Number,
                ITEM_NUMBER_LEN + 1, getCursor, INVENTORY_ITEM_NUMBER));

{ Associate a TCurRecStatic with the current record number on the dialog. }

  control := new(PCurRecStatic, InitResource(@Self, id_CurRec, getCursor));

{ Associate a TTotRecStatic with the total records on the dialog. }

  control := new(PTotRecStatic, InitResource(@Self, id_TotalRecs,
    getCursor));

{ Now create TFieldEdit boxes for the entry fields on the dialog. }

{ Description }

  control := new(PFieldEdit, InitResource(@Self, id_Description,
    ITEM_DESC_LEN + 1, getCursor, INVENTORY_DESCRIPTION));

{ Quantity }

  edit := new(PFieldEdit, InitResource(@Self, id_Quantity,
    QUANTITY_LEN + 1, getCursor, INVENTORY_QUANTITY));

{ Unit price }

edit := new(PFieldEdit, InitResource(@Self, id_Unit_Price,
  UNIT_PRICE_LEN + 1, getCursor, INVENTORY_UNIT_PRICE));
```

Each of the statements follows the principles described in the following sections.

control := Uses the variable that points to the ObjectWindows **TControl** object to point this statement at **TControl**, allowing it to inherit its attributes.

new(PFieldStatic This "new" is the Pascal procedure that allows us to construct the **TFieldStatic** object that follows. In other statements, we will call the appropriate object for the control type that we want to construct. In some statements, we will use a dummy pointer to the **TEdit** (dummyEd) object for our objects derived from that ObjectWindows class. A fuller explanation of **TFieldStatic** is found in chapter 4.

InitResource. This **TFieldStatic** method associates a control object with the control element in the POS.RES resource file using the following argument. This method itself overrides the **TControl** method it has inherited to allow us to point to the proper field in a record.

(@Self, A pointer to the parent-window for this control window.

id_Item_Number, The variable that identifies the resource ID for this control.

ITEM_NUMBER_LEN + 1, A constant defined in TABLEDIC.PAS that contains the length of the field to be displayed in this control to which we have added one (+1) to allow for a Paradox-style null-terminated string.

getCursor, This **TFieldStatic** method returns the pointer to the open cursor, here the *inventoryCursor.*

INVENTORY_ITEM_NUMBER)); A constant defined in TABLEDIC.PAS for the field handle that identifies which table and field we are to display. This one identifies the field "Item Number," in the INVENTORY table.

The remaining code in this excerpt repeats this format specifying each control as required by its contents and purpose.

The **TDialog, TFieldEdit** and **TFieldStatic** objects each include virtual methods, *DisplayField* and *SetupWindow* that are each called whenever a window is constructed. We override **TCursorDialog**'s *SetupWindow* to call *DisplayFields,* a method that sends the message wm_DisplayFields to each control on the dialog, calling the appropriate *DisplayField* member in each window as a *SetupWindow* procedure. While the previous code shows how we associate a resource control, its control object, and the **TCursor** object, we still need to illustrate how to load each of these controls with the values from the table. For that, we rely on our *DisplayFields* method inherited from **TCursorDialog,** which calls the *DisplayField* in each control whenever a dialog box is constructed.

The code in FIG. 5-5 for the *DisplayField* method illustrates how the **TRecord** method's *getFldType, getDouble,* and *getString* are used when they are associated with **TCursor**'s generic record as it buffers the records of an open table. Because we need to display the fields' contents as null-terminated strings in Windows applications, we have included a routine to convert the Pascal-type strings before the *SetText* method inherited from **TStatic** displays the text. As you will see when you run the application, this static text is anything but static because it forms a part of the response to the scrolling buttons that move the table's cursor from record to record.

5-5 This excerpt from TFSTAT.PAS illustrates how two of **TRecord**'s methods, *getFldType* and *getString*, are used to display the contents of a field in a static control.

```
(********************************************************************
* TYPE:        TFieldStatic
*
* METHOD:      DisplayField
*
* DESCRIPTION:  This member will get the value of the field out
*               of the record buffer and displays the value in the control.
********************************************************************)
procedure TFieldStatic.DisplayField;
var
  recordBuffer: PRecord;   { A pointer to the record buffer in the cursor. }
  isNull: Boolean;
  valAsString: String;
  valAsPChar: array[0..256] of char;
  fldType: PXFieldType;
  subType: PXFieldSubType;
  length: Integer;
  ValAsDoub: Double;
begin

{ Get the record buffer. }

  recordBuffer := tablesCursor^.genericRec;

{ What type is the field? }

  recordBuffer^.getFieldType(tablesField, fldType, subType, length);

{ If the type is a double, then get it as a double. }

  if(fldType = fldDouble) then
  begin
    recordBuffer^.getDouble(tablesField, valAsDoub, isNull);

    if(not isNull) then
        Str(valAsDoub:5:2, valAsString);
  end
  else
{ Get the field's value as a string. }
  recordBuffer^.getString(tablesField, valAsString, isNull);

{ Was the value blank? }
  if isNull = true then
  valAsString := '';
```

```
{ Convert the pascal style string to a NTS. }

  strPCopy(valAsPChar, valAsString);

{ Display this value. }

  SetText(valAsPChar);

end;
```

Once we have a process for loading and reloading the dialog box's controls, we can use our cursor button objects to move the cursor's position and reload the dialog boxes to reflect the change. For example, the **TCursorButton** object associated with the resource button Last that moves the cursor to the last record in a table uses its *doMove* method to call two **TCursor** methods to accomplish this move as follows:

```
procedure TCursorButtonLast.doMove;
  begin
    tableCursor^.gotoEnd;
    tableCursor^.gotoPrev;
  end;
```

We first use *gotoEnd* to position the cursor on the last record of the table, a "virtual record" that contains nothing, then move the cursor to the previous record, the final record in the table with data.

TCursor operations: Append, Update, and Delete. So far, we have been discussing the operation of the **TSelectItemDialog**, which **TInventoryDialog** inherits. When it does so, it adds three functions to the dialog: updating edits of the dialog's data, adding a new record, and deleting an existing one. When we edit any of the data in an Inventory dialog box and click the Ok button, the **TInventoryDialog** object's *Ok* method responds by first checking to see if the values of any of the controls have changed, then prompting the user to decide if the change or changes should be saved. If the user responds Yes, then the method uses the **TCursor** *updateRec* function to accomplish this.

If the user clicks on the Add button, the *IDNew* method responds and similarly if the user clicks on the Del button to delete the record currently pointed to by the cursor, the *IDDel* method responds. Each of these operations incorporates several Engine functions to complete these tasks. Both the *Ok* and *IDNew* methods for **TInventoryDialog** use the *UpdateRecord* method that is shown in FIG. 5-6. In this method, we rely on the **TCursorDialog** message *WMSaveFields* to load the contents of the dialog box's controls into the generic record buffer, then call *updateRec* to complete the operation. Before updating the record, however, *UpdateRecord* sends the message *wm_HaveValuesChanged* to check on the controls. If this method returns TRUE, it then proceeds on to the *SaveFields* procedure; otherwise, the standard Windows *Ok* disposes of the dialog box without allowing any changes to the record.

5-6 This excerpt from TINVDLG.PAS shows how we use the Engine to update a record.

```
(*******************************************************************
* TYPE:         TInventoryDialog
*
* METHOD:       UpdateRecord
*
* DESCRIPTION:  This function checks to see if the user has changed the
*               fields and it will save them.
*******************************************************************)
procedure TInventoryDialog.UpdateRecord;
var
  msgReturn: Integer;
begin
  if(HaveValuesChanged = True) then
    begin
      msgReturn := MessageBox(HWindow,
      'The field vaules of the current record have been changed. Do you want
              to save?',
      'Update Record', mb_yesno or mb_iconquestion);

    if(msgReturn = IDYES) then
      begin
        SaveFields;

{ Update the record in the table. }

    ERROR(getCursor^.updateRec(getCursor^.genericRec), 'Updating the record');
    end;
  end;
end;
```

SaveFields iterates through all of the controls in the dialog box sending *wm_SaveFields* message to each. Those controls that know how to respond to such a message (any control with an ID constant that is not –1, where –1 indicates a static control that is not modified at runtime), execute the *SaveField* procedure listed in FIG. 5-7. Because we converted all Pascal-type strings to null-terminated strings (NTS) for our Windows application, we now convert any NTS to a Pascal-type string and establish a pointer to the generic record of the open cursor. We either set the field to blank (null) using **TRecord**'s *setNull* function if the edit control is empty or use **TRecord**'s *putString* function to store the data in the generic record buffer. This *SaveField* procedure "knows" which field to put the data into because each resource control is associated with a control object that has as part of its argument a field handle identifying the field associated with the control. (See FIG. 5-4.) After *SaveFields* iterates through the controls loading their contents into the generic record buffer, the *UpdateRecord* procedure, shown in FIG. 5-6, calls **TCursor's** *updateRec* to finish the process.

5-7 This excerpt from the **TFEdit** unit, TFEDIT.PAS, shows how to place the current contents of an edit control into a field in a generic record buffer.

```
************************************************************************
* TYPE: TFieldEdit
*
* METHOD:         SaveField
*
* DESCRIPTION: The SaveField function will take the current in the
*              control and place it in the record buffer.
************************************************************************)
procedure TFieldEdit.SaveField;
var
  recordBuffer: PRecord;    { A pointer to the record buffer in the cursor. }
  valAsString: String;
  valAsPChar: array[0..256] of char;
begin

{ Get the value from the control. }

  GetText(valAsPChar, 255);
  valAsString := strPas(valAsPChar);

{ Get a pointer to the record buffer. }

  recordBuffer := tablesCursor^.genericRec;

{ Is the value blank? }

  if valAsString = '' then
  begin

{ Yes? then store a blank. }

    recordBuffer^.setNull(tablesField);
  end
  else
  begin

{ Store the value in the record buffer. }

    recordBuffer^.putString(tablesField, valAsString);

  end;
end;
```

The *DisplayFields* procedure for a dialog box follows the same principles as *SaveFields* for loading the contents of a generic record buffer into the controls of a dialog by iterating through the controls and calling *DisplayField* for each.

When we click on the Add button in the Inventory dialog box, we call **TInventoryDialog**'s *IDNew* method, which is shown in FIG. 5-8. This procedure first calls the *updateRecord* to check to see if the current record has been changed, offering the user the chance to update it before moving on. After the user's response, the routine clears the generic record buffer of its contents so that we can be sure of starting fresh, creates a new record key using the *createIdNumber* procedure defined in the **PosUtils** unit and listed in FIG. 5-9, uses *PutString* to insert this number into the INVENTORY_ITEM_NUMBER field of the generic record buffer for the cursor currently still open on our INVENTORY table, uses *appendRec* to append this record, and concludes with the method *DisplayFields*, which loads this information into the dialog box. Because we cleared the generic record buffer, only the static field objects will display any changes. They will display the record number and the updated cursor position and total number of records in the table. The remaining field controls will be clear, or empty.

5-8 The method *IDNew* from TINVDLG.PAS shows how to append a new record to a table.

```
(* * * * * * * * * * * * * * * * * * * * * * * * * * * * * * * * * * * * * * * * * * * * * * * * * * * * * * * * * * * * * * * *
* TYPE:        TInventoryDialog
*
* METHOD:      IDNew
*
* DESCRIPTION: This procedure is activated when the user presses the
*              "Add" button.
* * * * * * * * * * * * * * * * * * * * * * * * * * * * * * * * * * * * * * * * * * * * * * * * * * * * * * * * * * * * * * * *)
procedure TInventoryDialog.IDNew(var Msg: TMessage);
var
  newId: String;
begin

{ Call the update record procedure to save the values. }

  UpdateRecord;

{ Blank out the record buffer. }

  getCursor^.genericRec^.clear;

{ Create a new ID number. }

  createIdNumber(newId);
```

```
     { Put this ID Number into the record buffer. }

       getCursor^.genericRec^.putString(INVENTORY_ITEM_NUMBER, newId);

     { Append this record. }

       getCursor^.appendRec(getCursor^.genericRec);

     { Update the fields on the dialog. }

       DisplayFields;

     end;
```

5-9 This procedure creates a 12-digit string for us to use as a record's key by assembling information from DOS's system date and time functions. This procedure returns a string value.

```
(*******************************************************************
*
* METHOD:       createIdNumber
*
* DESCRIPTION:  This function creates a unique 12 digit ID number for
*               various ID's in the system.
*
* RETURNS:      The ID number as a string.
*
*******************************************************************)
procedure createIdNumber(var retString: String);
var
  year, month, day, dayOfWeek,
  hour, min, sec, sec100 : WORD;
  tempString: string;
begin

{ Get the components of the ID number. }

  getDate(year, month, day, dayOfWeek);
  getTime(hour, min, sec, sec100);

{ Take the last two digits of the year and put in into the answer. }

  year := year mod 100;

  str(year, tempString);
  if(Length(tempString) = 1) then insert('0', tempString, 1);
  retString := tempString;

{ Put the month in. }
```

```
  str(month, tempString);
  if(Length(tempString) = 1) then insert('0', tempString, 1);
  retString := retString + tempString;

{ Put the day in. }

  str(day, tempString);
  if(Length(tempString) = 1) then insert('0', tempString, 1);
  retString := retString + tempString;

{Put the hour in. }

  str(hour, tempString);
  if(Length(tempString) = 1) then insert('0', tempString, 1);
  retString := retString + tempString;

{ Put the minute in. }

  str(min, tempString);
  if(Length(tempString) = 1) then insert('0', tempString, 1);
  retString := retString + tempString;

{ Put in the seconds. }

  str(sec, tempString);
  if(Length(tempString) = 1) then insert('0', tempString, 1);
  retString := retString + tempString;
end;
```

When we added a record, we called a routine to create the record's key using *createIdNumber*. This procedure, found in the PosUtils unit (POS-UTILS.PAS), uses the system's date and time resources to create a 12-digit string for the various record keys that we need to generate. Because this Windows application is not designed for a networking environment, we don't need to test the uniqueness of the number by searching the table's index for a match as we attempt to append the record. Figure 5-9 illustrates how to assemble this string.

Finally, when we want to delete a record from a table, here the INVENTORY table, we will use a procedure similar to *IDDel*, which is listed in FIG. 5-10. This routine first prompts a user to ask if the record really is to be deleted. If yes, then the routine simply uses *deleteRec* to do so and moves the cursor off the crack to the next record and reloads the generic record buffer with these values. Because we can be at the last real record when we do this, we also test to make sure that we haven't moved the cursor to the end, or virtual, record by checking for the end of table error and then, if needed, moving the cursor up one record with *gotoPrev* so that we have positioned the cursor on the final actual record of the table. Because we might have inadvertently attempted to load the "virtual record" if we deleted the last record of the table, we blank out the generic record buffer and reload it with the contents of the current record position to make sure we will display the correct data when we conclude this routine with the *DisplayFields* procedure.

5-10 This method, *IDDel* **TInventoryDialog**, shows how to delete a record from a table and make sure that the cursor is not positioned at a crack or at the end of a table when the dialog box's controls are reloaded.

```
(*********************************************************************
* TYPE: TInventoryDialog
*
* METHOD:        IDDel
*
* DESCRIPTION:  This procedure is activated when the user presses the "Del"
*                         Button.
*********************************************************************)
procedure TInventoryDialog.IDDel(var Msg: TMessage);
var
  mbKey: Integer;
  err: Retcode;
begin

{ Ask the user if they really want to delete the current record. }

  mbKey := MessageBox(HWindow,
    'Do you really want to delete this record?', 'Delete',
        mb_yesno or mb_iconquestion);

{ Exit this procedure if they pressed the "No" button. }

  if (mbKey = IDNO) then exit;

{ Delete the record. }

  ERROR(getCursor^.deleteRec, 'Deleting Record');

{ Reload the record buffer. }

  err := getCursor^.gotoNext;

{ Did we delete the table's final, actual record?                      }
{ If we did, then move off the "virtual" record at the end of the table. }
```

```
  if(err = PXERR_ENDOFTABLE) then
    getCursor^.gotoPrev;

{ Blank out the record buffer if the last record was deleted. }

  getCursor^.genericRec^.clear;

{ Get the current record. }

  getCursor^.getRecord(getCursor^.genericRec);

{ Update all of the dialog's windows. }

  DisplayFields;

end;
```

Conclusion

After this run of information, you should have a rudimentary, but thorough, experience of how to associate the Windows resources for a dialog box with the Engine's **TDatabase**, **TRecord**, and **TCursor** objects and navigate your way through a table's records reading, writing, or deleting information with generic records. The next chapter refers again to these objects to show how we can perform validity checking and logically link tables together to maintain the data integrity of the tables in our application. The code for chapter 7 also will demonstrate how to lock a table explicitly when we link tables together.

6
Performing data validity checking with the Engine

A further method for ensuring the integrity of the data stored in a table brings us to the concept of validity checking, which we also can consider as the third of the integrity constraints that also include entity integrity and referential integrity. For a discussion of these last two check out chapter 7. Our variation on a user-defined integrity restraint would implement rules defined by the application's planning process. There, for example, we would specify that the telephone number or social security number for an employee must conform to a particular format or "picture."

The interactive Paradox offers the types of validity checks shown in TABLE 6-1 for its tables and fields.

Table 6-1   The types of validity checks that Paradox offers for its tables and fields.

Validity check	Description
Low Value	Sets the minimum acceptable value for a field.
High Value	Sets the maximum acceptable value for a field.
Default	Sets the standard value for a field.
TableLookup	Requires that the value in a field exist as the first field in another table. Can refer to another table to look up the acceptable values for a field. Automatically copies values from the lookup table to the table you're working in.
Picture	Sets up the requirement that the values in a field match a *picture format.*
Required	Indicates whether a field must have a value, which implies whether or not the field can have a blank value.

While the interactive Paradox allows users to define and clear these rules for data fields, this application hides this capability from a user and uses these validity checking concepts to enforce its own set of rules to ensure that a user has entered data according to criteria established during a planning process.

Several elements of this application already implement aspects of these validity checks. For example, the application requires that each table have a unique key value and supplies that for a user by automatically generating and filling in the value. The application also ensures that a field in one table can, if needed, refer properly to another table. For example, the SALE table's CUSTOMER_ID field uses the CUSTOMER_ID field from the CUSTOMER table. Further, the application can derive an element of a composite key by using the key of another table, as in the case of the SALES ITEMS table's composite key: SALE_SALE_NUMBER, INVENTORY_ITEM_NUMBER. As another form of validity checking, you might consider creating a procedure that fills in a date of sale field automatically as a required element of a sale. When a user selects an existing customer from the CUSTOMER table, we are enforcing a rudimentary type of table lookup validity check because existing and new customers must all have a key field that we then will use as the CUSTOMER_ID field in the SALE table.

The three remaining validity checks from Paradox that we implement in our application—low value, high value, and picture—use the ObjectWindows abstract validator objects.

The TValidator and other validators

With **TValidator** and its related objects, this latest release of ObjectWindows for Pascal offers you three avenues to validate data before a record is created or updated: filtering input as the user types each element of data into a single entry field, validating each field as a whole before moving to the next field, and validating an entire entry screen when an operation is concluded. These possibilities are not mutually exclusive. Because this application already manages some aspects of validity checking, such as ensuring the uniqueness of a record's key, with methods other than those available through the ObjectWindows validator objects, we'll concentrate here on implementing these ObjectWindows validator objects first, then show how to pull in the other types of validity checking not explicitly covered by the validator objects.

Filtering input

The filter validator object **TFilterValidator** provides a generic mechanism for restricting which characters a user can type in a particular edit control. This feature is valuable for ensuring that a user type all numbers in a field requiring numbers and, therefore, cannot substitute a lower case *l* for the number one as many veteran typists who have not relinquished their electric typewriters sometimes still do. Similarly, the filter validator can prevent a user from entering any numbers in a field requiring only letters such as a state field. In addition to **TFilterValidator**, you can rely on the picture validator **TPXPictureValidator** also to filter input by controlling the formatting and types of characters a user can type.

Because the types of data an order-entry application required for a full implementation cover many of the same types of information in various situations, we have decided to rely on the picture validator to assist with the validation of data from the data-entry controls. A picture validator controls data entry by requiring a user to match exactly some format or picture for the information being entered. For example, the picture for a social security number could require that data match exactly the sets of numbers and dashes traditionally used to this data. Similarly, a picture could require that a user enter a phone number with the area code within parentheses, and so on. These pictures assure that all the data within a field will meet the criteria of the picture for that field. Such a validator will not always guarantee the accuracy of the data because a user still might enter a sequence of numbers that matches a picture but still is wrong.

There are some ways around some of these niggling areas, such as a lookup table for all of the states and their zip codes, but we will not be implementing such an extensive array of data validators in this application. Still, this application will give you the tools to do so should you want to extend the implication of some sections of the code to include such a requirement.

For example, while we use a lookup routine to check to make sure that a record exists, you could apply a similar routine to look up some other data. Another possibility would be to use our querying routines to simulate a table lookup that would satisfy a particular match. Further, because we have provided ways to fill in data fields with information existing in some of the application's other tables, we reinforce the validity of that data in any record that uses it. When a user begins a new sale, the first dialog box prompts them to select a customer or create a new one, ensuring that this field in the sale table contains a valid reference to a customer and not a missing or NULL value. This is a natural way to accomplish this validity check because there can be no sale except to some customer and the user cannot skip this step to begin a new sale.

In these ways, we enforce the validity of our data by building in the rules of operation for the application from the start. Once we get beyond these rules, we then rely on our validator objects to complete the checks we need.

TPXPictureValidator also provides us with the additional benefit of being compatible with the pictures that Paradox uses to control data entry, a natural environment for those already familiar with Paradox. Figure 6-1 lists the characters used to create format pictures, and FIG. 6-2 shows some examples of the more common types of pictures that you might need to establish. These pictures are suggestions, and you are free to devise your own pictures, ones that look better to you when you browse your code.

6-1 A list showing the characters you can use in a picture and the meanings for each.

Char	Meaning
#	Any numeric digit
?	Any letter, not case sensitive
&	Any letter, convert to uppercase
@	Any character, not case sensitive
!	Any character, not case sensitive
;	The next character is literal, not a special picture-string character
*	The next character can repeat any number of times. Or, specify the required number of occurrences of the next letter.
[]	Characters inside brackets are optional.
{}	Characters inside braces are grouped.
'	(Comma) Alternative values

6-2 Some examples of picture patterns you might want to use.

Pattern	Meaning
[(*3{#})]*3{#}-*4{#}	Standard telephone number with area code and a space after the area code as an optional requirement
&*?	String of letters with only the first capitalized
*5{#}[-*4#]	Standard five number ZIP code with optional "Plus 4" numbers
###-##-####	Social Security Number
*3{#}-*2{#}-*4{#}	Social Security Number
#[#]/#[#]/##[##]	Date with several options to allow for 1/1/93, etc.
&&	Two capitalized letters. We use this for the State field in an address.
*2{&}	Two capitalized letters.
[*#][.*2#]	Optionally, any number of numeric digits with optional decimal. We use this for money type ($) fields. The two allows us to have numbers less than 1 as decimals or numbers with decimals.

With these concepts in hand, let's take a look at how we have set up the pictures for our implementation of **TPXPictureValidator**. For the sake of convenience, we have grouped all of the various pictures that we might use in the application in one unit, TPOSUTILS.PAS. This allows us to assign variables that all units can access, forestalls duplication of code, and provides for easy management of code revisions. Figure 6-3 excerpts those lines of code from TPOSUTILS.PAS that create the pictures.

6-3 This excerpt from TPOSUTILS.PAS demonstrates how we set up pictures and assign them to the variables that we will use throughout the units, as needed.

```
{ Set up the pictures. }

{ A picture for names, capital first letter, then any character }

  pictureName := '&*@';

{ A picture for telephone numbers }

  picturePhone := '[(*3#) ]*3#-*4#';

{ A picture for dates }

  pictureDate := '#[#]/#[#]/##[##]';

{ A picture for a state. }

  pictureState := '&&';

{ A picture for zip codes }

  pictureZip := '*5#';

{ A picture for money fields }

  pictureMoney := '[*#][.*2#]';

{ A picture for just numbers }

  pictureNumber := '*#';

{ A credit card picture }

  pictureCreditCard := '*{#, }';
```

Validating each field

This method for validating information ensures that a user types valid input for a field before moving on to another field. This methodology often is called "validate on Tab" because using the Tab often is the way that a user moves from one input control to another when entering information. In this application, **TPXPictureValidator** implements such a validation scheme when a user attempts to move off one control object to another and has managed to enter data that does not match the picture required by a field using **TPXPictureValidator**.

For example, imagine a field that requires a picture that matches the standard two decimal positions for currency. We would express this picture as:

```
{ A picture for money fields }
        pictureMoney := '[*#][.*2#]';
```

This picture's format uses the following formatting characters:

Match	*	Repetition count
	[]	Option
Special	#	Accept only a digit

The picture is interpreted to mean that the data must match the following criteria:

[*#] Only digits can be entered, but no restriction has been placed on the number of digits. Because we can presume, for this example, that this field is going to contain the unit price for an item, we have established it as a currency field in the table. The picture validator ensures that we will present the data to the table in the proper format. When we defined this field in the table's descriptors, we specified that it was of type **double** and subtype **money**. Further, we have specified that this segment of the picture is optional because we want to be able to enter a value less than one (1) for items whose value is less than a dollar.

[.2#] This segment of the picture, also optional to allow a user to enter a whole number amount without any decimals, prevents a user from entering anything other than a period as a decimal point and more than two decimal places as a part of the price for some merchandise. If a user does not enter the decimal or only the first of two digits after the point, the definition of this field as a **money ($)** data subtype will act to complete the number by appending a decimal point, if one is not present, and any necessary zeros to fill the number out to two decimals.

While the picture validator will prevent any data other than numbers and a period (decimal point) from being entered, a user might realize that a decimal point is missing and use either the arrow keys or a mouse to locate the cursor in the place where the period ought to go. If, at this point, the user incorrectly enters a comma or some alphabetic letter instead of a period, **TPXPictureValidator** will return an error when the user then "tabs" away from the field or uses a mouse to move the cursor to another input field, or clicks on the "Ok" to update or create the record. In this application, such an error results in a display informing the user of the type of error committed and the repositioning of the data entry cursor on the error. In this way, a user is prevented from leaving the field until its data matches the picture required for that data. When the error is rectified, the user then can "tab" away from the field.

This type of validation also is called "validating on focus change" because moving from one input area or control is accomplished by moving the input focus in such a data screen.

Validating full screens

You can validate full data screens in three ways: validating a modal window, validating on a change of focus (which was covered previously), and validating on demand. When a command closes a modal window, the window automatically validates all its controls or subviews, unless the closing command was *cmCancel*. To validate these subviews when a window is closed, the window includes a call to the *CanCancel* method of each subview. If each returns True, the window can close. If False is returned, the window won't be allowed to close. In such an instance, you have to handle which subview returned the False.

To validate on command, you can call *CanClose* at any time. This call utilizes only the validation process of closing a window and does not obligate you to close the window. Calling *CanClose* initiates calls to all of the window's child windows in the order of insertion and returns True if all of them return True.

While you can validate any window, modal or modeless, whenever you want, only modal windows include an automatic validation process on closing. Consequently, if you use any modeless windows for data entry, you must ensure that the application calls the window's *CanClose* method to validate the subviews in the modeless window.

The ObjectWindows validators

ObjectWindows offers six standard validator object types to accomplish the three data validation schemes described earlier. **TValidator** and **TLookupValidator** are both abstract types, but **TValidator** serves as the base type for all of the validator objects. The remaining validators implement specific types of validation processes.

TValidator

The abstract type **TValidator** is the base type for all of the validator objects, and you never create an instance of **TValidator**. All validators inherit four methods from **TValidator**: *Valid, IsValid, IsValidInput,* and *Error*. By overriding these methods in different ways, each of the other descendant validators implement their own specific type of validation. The **TValidator** is a validator to which all input is always valid: *IsValid* and *IsValidInput* always return True, and *Error* does nothing. The descendant validators therefore override *IsValid* and *IsValidInput* to define the valid values.

TFilterValidator

Filter validators only check input as the user types it. **TFilterValidator** uses *IsValidInput* to ensure that only valid characters make it through the input filter, making the complete string valid by definition. A descendant of **TFilterValidator**, **TRangeValidator**, combines filtering with a check on the range of the completed string to validate the data. While not a descendant of **TFilterValidator**, **TPXPictureValidator** also filters input as established by the picture defining the format and character types (alphabetic, number, etc.) of the string to be validated.

TRangeValidator

TRangeValidator is a descendant of **TFilterValidator** that accepts only numbers and also checks the range of the final result of the input. Because it accepts only numbers, **TRangeValidator** acts as a filter validator, accepting only the digits 0 through 9 and the plus and minus characters. The *IsValidInput* method that this object inherits from **TValidator** ensures that only the correct characters get through the filter and overrides the **TValidator** *IsValid* method to return True only if the entered numbers are a valid integer within a range defined in the constructor. The *Error* method displays a message box to notify a user that the entered numbers are out of the range required for the data to be valid. We will be using this validator to make sure that, when a user enters a number for the quantity ordered, the number does not exceed the inventory quantity for that item.

TLookupValidator

The abstract validator **TLookupValidator** provides the basis for a validator that determines the validity of a value by comparing it with a list of acceptable items. This abstract validator is never used as it stands. It also makes one important change and one addition to **TValidator**.

TLookupValidator changes *IsValid* by overriding it to return True only if *Lookup* returns True. Consequently, descendant validator types do not override *IsValid*; they override *Lookup* instead.

In addition to the usual inherited methods, **TLookupValidator** adds the method *Change* that, by default, returns False. When you derive a descendant lookup validator type, you override *Lookup* to compare the passed string with a list, returning True if the string matches some item in that list.

TStringLookupValidator

TStringLookupValidator is a descendant type of **TLookupValidator** that compares the string passed from the edit control with the items in a string list. This validator type includes a method, *NewStringList*, that allows you to set up a string list and dispose of an old list and install a new list.

TStringLookupValidator overrides *Lookup* appropriately to return True when there is an exact match in the string list and uses *Error* to display an error message box when there isn't.

TPXPictureValidator

TPXPictureValidator compares the string typed by the user with a *picture* or template to determine if the input's format is valid. This particular picture validator allows you to create pictures compatible with those used to control the user input in Paradox. The two parameters for this type's constructor establish the picture and a Boolean value to indicate whether to fill in literal characters in the picture automatically. The various overrides for **TPXPictureValidator** ensure that the string matches the picture defined in the constructor and adds a method *Picture* that, like the *Lookup* method in **TLookupValidator**, allows you to derive new kinds of picture validators by overriding only the *Picture* method and not *IsValid*. *IsValid-Input* operates much like a filter validator checking characters as the user types them, allowing only those which match the picture format and optionally filling in literal characters from the picture. This last method is how we include the decimal point in the string for currency figures.

An application uses these validator object types to manage input from a user as a way of overcoming the chances for randomness inherent in any input box that a user can edit. Without a way of absolutely predicting the reaction of a user, but being able to guide the possibilities through accurate labels in a dialog box or window, these validators further constrain a user's input and increase the chances for properly formatted but not necessarily perfectly accurate information. After all, a user still can type in a correctly formatted but wildly inaccurate price for a record in an inventory table or misspell a customer's name. Granted, the truly obsessive compulsive MIS manager might fantasize ways of eliminating even this, but a clearly written user manual, good training, and a data-entry workstation that resembles something other than a tastefully carpeted, neutral gray Skinner box with a padded wrist rest would go a longer way towards fulfilling these MIS dreams than a programmer ought to be responsible for.

Integrating the validators into a user interface

Validators are not interface objects and thus their constructors require only enough information to establish the validation criteria. For example, the parameters for a picture validator's constructor require only the syntax for the picture and a Boolean value to indicate whether to fill in literal characters in the picture automatically. Also, a numeric range validator object needs to define only two parameters: the minimum and maximum values in the valid range. Once these objects are constructed, you need to point the edit control to a validator object. This is easily done because every control object has a field called *Validator*, set to **nil** by default, that can point to a validator object. Because our edit controls are all descendants of **TEdit**, we can use the **TEdit** method *SetValidator* to assign a validator to an edit control. Once we do this, the edit control automatically checks with the validator when processing keyboard events and when called on to validate itself.

Figure 6-4 shows you how to construct and assign a picture validator in a single statement.

6-4 How to implement a validator.

```
Example from TINVDLG.PAS (the Inventory dialog)

        edit := new(PFieldEdit, InitResource(@Self, id_Quantity,
            QUANTITY_LEN + 1, getCursor, INVENTORY_QUANTITY));
        edit^.SetValidator(new(PPXPictureValidator,
            Init(pictureNumber, FALSE)));
```

The example in FIG. 6-4 constructs an instance of our **TFieldEdit** object using variables we have defined as follows:

- *edit* is our local variable pointing to a *PEdit* object.
- *new(PFieldEdit,...* constructs a new instance of our **PFieldEdit** object to coordinate an edit control with a field in a table.
- *InitResource(@Self, id_Quantity,...* associates our **TFieldEdit** object with a Windows edit control resource. We developed this resource using the Borland Resource Workshop to design our user interface. There, we assigned a constant to each control, and here, we use *id_Quantity* to point to that particular resource.
- *QUANTITY_LEN + 1,...* defines a field length for this edit control using a variable defined in our **TableDic** unit (TABLEDIC.PAS) and adds one to allow for a null-terminated string.
- *getCursor,...* is the **TFieldEdit** member that returns the pointer to the embedded cursor object so that we can use the **TCursor** object to manipulate a particular field from the generic record buffer.
- *INVENTORY_QUANTITY));* the field handle, specifies that we will manipulate the INVENTORY table's QUANTITY field in this edit control. The variable *INVENTORY_QUANTITY* is defined in the **TableDic** unit (TABLEDIC.PAS) and points to a field number in the record's descriptor. This particular field's name also is defined as "Quantity in stock" for the user's ease of understanding.

Once we have accomplished this definition of the edit control's various associations in the previous example, we construct the validator object for this control as follows:

- *edit^.SetValidator(new(...* creates a new instance of a validator and assigns it to the *edit* edit control by calling **TEdit**'s *SetValidator* method, which disposes of any existing validator, then sets the *Validator* field of **TEdit**. By *edit*, we mean that this variable points to a **TEdit** type of control object. Elsewhere, we use *edit* to point to a **TControl** type object such as a static control (*PFieldStatic*) associated with a table's cursor.
- *PXPictureValidator,...* redefines *SetValidator's AValid* argument to indicate that we will be using a picture validator.
- *Init(...* (the **PXPictureValidator** constructor) constructs a picture validator object by first calling the *Init* constructor inherited from **TValidator**, allocates a copy of the template, then sets the Boolean value for the filling in the literal characters in the picture.
- *pictureNumber, FALSE));* completes our statement by using the *pictureNumber* variable defined in the *PosUtils* unit (TPOSUTILS.PAS) to specify the picture for this validator and returning a FALSE to indicate that we will not be filling in any literal characters as an option in this string. The **PosUtils** unit assigns the following picture to *pictureNumber*:

pictureNumber := '*#';

In this picture's syntax, the field will accept any numeric digit. The asterisk indicates that the next character (any digit) can be repeated any number of times. When we define a picture for a dollar amount (as in pictureMoney := '*#[.*2#]';), we can specify that there are to be only two digits by using *2#.

Initiating a validity check

This code selection from the **TAddCustomer** object, the first dialog that we designed in chapter 3, shows how we implement the code necessary for the dialog's resources and add to them the necessary validator objects that we want to use. (See FIG. 6-5.) Even though we haven't completely included a validator for every field in this dialog, this code is an extensive example of how to use the picture validator *in situ*. The variables beginning with *id_* refer to the resource's constants for those controls so that each instance of **TFieldEdit** and the other objects that we need refer to the correct resource in the dialog box's display.

The next example shows how to use a **TRangeValidator** as part of procedure that will add an item ordered to a sale. We'll slide past discussing how we link the SALE and SALES_ITEMS tables to maintain referential integrity within the Sale Window, our most complex window that, as you remember, contains child windows that each display information from different tables simultaneously. We'll need the **TRangeValidator** to make sure that a user does not attempt to place an order that exceeds the current inventory for an item. Because we also want to maintain the entity integrity of

6-5 This excerpt from TINVDLG.PAS illustrates how we construct an instance of the dialog box **TInventory** and incorporate validation checks with the code that unites our Windows resources and their objects.

```
(************************************************************************
* TYPE: TAddCustDialog
*
* MEMBER:        Init     (Constructor)
*
* DESCRIPTION:  Creates an object of this type.
*
************************************************************************)
constructor TAddCustDialog.Init(AParent: PWindowsObject; ACursor: PCursor);
var
   dummyPtr: PEdit;
begin

{ Call constructor of the base class. }
   inherited Init(AParent, 'ADD_CUST', ACursor);


{ Now create TFieldEdit boxes for the entry fields on the dialog }

{ Last name }
   dummyPtr := new(PFieldEdit, InitResource(@Self, id_AddLast,
         CUST_NAME_LEN + 1, getCursor, CUSTOMER_LAST_NAME));
{ Add the name picture to the field. }
   dummyPtr^.setValidator(new(PPXPictureValidator,
         Init(pictureName, TRUE)));

{ First name }
   dummyPtr := new(PFieldEdit, InitResource(@Self, id_AddFirst,
         CUST_NAME_LEN + 1, getCursor, CUSTOMER_FIRST_NAME));
{ Add the name picture to the field.}
   dummyPtr^.setValidator(new(PPXPictureValidator,
         Init(pictureName, TRUE)));

{ Street }
   dummyPtr := new(PFieldEdit, InitResource(@Self, id_AddAddress,
         STREET_LEN + 1, getCursor, CUSTOMER_ADDRESS));

{ City }
   dummyPtr := new(PFieldEdit, InitResource(@Self, id_AddCity,
         CITY_LEN + 1, getCursor, CUSTOMER_CITY));

{ State }
   dummyPtr := new(PFieldEdit, InitResource(@Self, id_AddState,
         STATE_LEN + 1, getCursor, CUSTOMER_STATE));
```

```
{ Add the state picture to the field. }
  dummyPtr^.setValidator(new(PPXPictureValidator,
      Init(pictureState, TRUE)));
{ ZIP }
 dummyPtr := new(PFieldEdit, InitResource(@Self, id_AddZip,
      ZIP_LEN + 1, getCursor, CUSTOMER_ZIP));
{ Add the ZIP picture to the field. }
  dummyPtr^.setValidator(new(PPXPictureValidator,
      Init(pictureZip, TRUE)));

{ Telephone }
  dummyPtr := new(PFieldEdit, InitResource(@Self, id_AddTelephone,
      TELEPHONE_LEN + 1, getCursor, CUSTOMER_TELEPHONE));
{ Add the phone picture to the field. }
  dummyPtr^.setValidator(new(PPXPictureValidator,
      Init(picturePhone, TRUE)));
end;
```

our inventory, we will need to decrement the INVENTORY table should our user input a valid quantity. This complex procedure follows this scenario:

- The user clicks on the Add button in the Sale Window to add an item to the sale.
- This event displays an Inventory dialog box so that the user then can scroll through the INVENTORY table to select the item to be ordered. This dialog shows the user the current inventory quantity for that item, but we're taking no chances here. A click of the Ok button signals that this is the item desired.
- This event displays the "Quantity" dialog box containing only one edit control: an input line to enter the quantity to be ordered. A click of the Ok button signals that this is the quantity to be ordered.
- This event leads the procedure to test whether the input is valid (within the range 1 to the current quantity listed in the INVENTORY table). If not, the user has to enter a lower quantity. A click of the Ok ends this dialog.
- The procedure concludes by appending this item to the SALES_ ITEMS table so that a user can then view or delete it before the sale is completed.

There are moments, however, when you might need to use a range validation routine but do not know what the minimum and maximum are. In our application, we have included such a moment in the Sale Window. There, the **TSaleItems** method *WMItemsAdd*, which responds to the buttons command to add an item to the list of merchandise in a sale, validates the quantity to be ordered by establishing a range from 1 (the minimum amount that we must order of anything) to the current quantity in stock, preventing us from creating a sale that cannot be fulfilled from the current inventory. While we will not show how to deal with an unknown minimum amount because we consider a sale to be an order of at least one of any item, the maximum parameter for a **TRangeValidator** is not knowable before a user decides to create the sale and changes as the inventory changes. Additionally, because we need to maintain the integrity of the field INVENTORY_QUANTITY so that it reflects the real world existence of items in stock for a future sale, we include a routine that decrements the quantity in stock properly.

We'll begin the exploration by taking a look at the object to gather the quantity to be ordered. It is there, in FIG. 6-7, that we will find the **TRangeValidator**. The **TQuantityDialog** object type defined in FIG. 6-6 for this dialog box is an implementation of our **TCursorDialog** and inherits the ability to hook up with a **TCursor** object open on a table. The constructor for this type will point to a quantity from the INVENTORY table, *AMaxQuantity*, which is opened as part of the procedure defined by the **TItemsWindow**'s method *WMAddItems*. There also is an object member *OK* that is called when the user presses the Ok button after entering a quantity to be ordered.

6-6 This excerpt from TSALWIN.PAS shows how we define the constructor for the **TSale-Quantity** object in the interface segment of the **TSalWin** unit so that it includes an argument to determine the maximum number using a range validator.

```
(*********************************************************************
* OBJECT:        TQuantityDialog
*
* INHERITS: TQuantityDialog
*
* DESCRIPTION:   This is an implementation of a cursor dialog defined in
*                TCursorDialog.  It is used to enter the quantity of an
*                item that a customer wants to buy.
*********************************************************************)
  PQuantityDialog = ^TQuantityDialog;
  TQuantityDialog = object(TCursorDialog)

    { A constructor for the class }

    constructor Init(AParent: PWindowsObject; AName: PChar;
              ACursor: PCursor; AMaxQuantity: Integer);

    procedure Ok(var Msg: TMessage); virtual id_first + id_OK;

  end; { TQuantityDialog }

implementation
  .
  .
  .
```

When we implement this **TQuantityDialog** object's constructor, as you can see in FIG. 6-7, the argument for the constructor includes *AMaxQuantity* as a pointer to a **TCursor** object. In the *WMAddItems* method, shown later in FIG. 6-9, we open a cursor on the inventory table and assign the value in the INVENTORY_QUANTITY field to the variable *maxQuantity* so that we can use it here when we display the dialog box for this operation. We then use this quantity as the maximum value for the **TRangeValidator** object. Notice that we are testing whether or not the quantity entered by the user falls within the range that we have set from one to *MaxQuantity* and that this quantity from the user input is referenced as a field in the Sales Items table as the field SALES_ITEMS_QUANTITY. The cursor for this SALES_ITEMS table was opened previously when we first called the Sale Window's constructor (see TSALWIN.PAS, **TSaleWindow.Init** for the code that does this) to display the sale window itself.

TQuantityDialog's *OK* method, shown in FIG. 6-8, is a procedure that calls the base class to dispose of the dialog box. Because the dialog box is

6-7 This code shows how to implement the **TSaleQuantity** Constructor defined in FIG. 6-6.

```
(********************************************************************
* TYPE:        TQuantityDialog
*
* METHOD:      Init     (Constructor)
*
* DESCRIPTION: Creates an object of this type.
*
********************************************************************)
constructor TQuantityDialog.Init(AParent: PWindowsObject; AName: PChar;
                    ACursor: PCursor; AMaxQuantity: Integer);
var
  dummyPtr: PEdit;
begin

{ Call the base constructor. }

  inherited Init(AParent, AName, ACursor);

{ Create an edit box for the quantity field. }

  dummyPtr := new(PFieldEdit, InitResource(@Self, id_quant_field,
    QUANTITY_LEN, ACursor, SALES_ITEMS_QUANTITY));

{ Do not allow the user to enter more than the max quantity. }

  dummyPtr^.SetValidator(new(PRangeValidator, Init( 1, AMaxQuantity)));

end;
```

6-8 This procedure shows how we implement the *Ok* button so that it calls the validator by default and saves the fields from the dialog into the current record buffer.

```
(*********************************************************************
* CLASS:        TQuantityDialog
*
* MEMBER:       OK
*
* DESCRIPTION:  This function is called when the users pressed the OK
*               button.
*
*********************************************************************)
procedure TQuantityDialog.Ok(var Msg: TMessage);
begin

{ Call base class (does the verify). }

  inherited Ok(Msg);

{ Save the field value. }

  SaveFields;

end;
```

a modal window, the base class automatically will validate the data in the edit control before disposing of the dialog box. If the input exceeds the range of the validator, then a message box will inform the user of this and return the user to the place in the dialog where the error occurred. After a successful validation, we call the *SaveFields* method inherited from the **TCursorDialog** base class to ensure that we put all of the data in the edit controls into their proper fields in the generic record buffer (here only one field: SALES_ITEMS_QUANTITY). After this, we continue on through the remainder of the *WMAddItems* procedure described in FIG. 6-9. The balance of *WMAddItems* will use this validated quantity to decrement the "Quantity in stock" field in the INVENTORY table so that it reflects the sale being made.

We have edited the code in FIG. 6-9 from the *WMAddItems* method to emphasize the routine that we use to set the range for our quantity to be ordered. When you browse this code, to be found in TSALWIN.PAS, you will find the complete code for making sure that the Engine is running smoothly.

At the conclusion of this procedure, you will notice that we close only the cursor open on the INVENTORY table (*selectItemCursor.close* where this local variable defines a cursor open on the INVENTORY table). The process of completing a sale after we select a quantity to be ordered reloads the Sale Window, which has a child window on it that displays information from the SALES_ITEMS table for the user. So, we need to keep this cursor open. When the values are reloaded in this child window, the contents of the SALES_ITEMS table for this sale can be accessed through the scrolling buttons within that window.

6-9 This procedure shows how to use validated data to decrement a table to reflect a decrease in inventory as a result of a sale.

```
(*********************************************************************
* TYPE:          TItemsWindow
*
* METHOD:        WMItemsAdd
*
* DESCRIPTION:   This procedure responds when the user presses the
*                        Add Button to add items to the sale.
*
*********************************************************************)
procedure TItemsWindow.WMItemsAdd(var Msg: TMessage);
var
(local variables we user here.}
begin
{ Open the inventory table to select an item. }
{ Check that the table did open.  If not, exit. }
{ Go to the first record and get it. }
{ Get a Select Items dialog box. }
{ Did the user select an item? }
{ Lock this record until we decrease the quantity field. }
        { If we could not lock the record, then wait until we can. }
                { If the reocrd cannot be locked, we exit the procedure. }
                { Close the table. }
{ Get the item number selected. }

  selectItemCursor^.getRecord(selectItemCursor^.genericRec);
  selectItemCursor^.genericRec^.getString(INVENTORY_ITEM_NUMBER,
    SelectedItemNumber, isNull);
{ Get the maximum quantity from the INVENTORY_QUANTITY field and           }
{ place this information into our record buffer if it's not null and > 0. }
{ Exec the TQuantityDialog described above in figures 6-6 through 6-8. }

    selectItemCursor^.genericRec^.getInteger(INVENTORY_QUANTITY,
        maxQuantity, isNull);

    if((not isNull) and (maxQuantity > 0)) then
    begin
      getCursor^.genericRec^.clear;
```

6-9 Continued.

```
    getCursor^.genericRec^.putString(SALES_ITEMS_ITEM_NUMBER,
            selectedItemNumber);
    aDialog := new(PQuantityDialog, Init(@Self, 'QUANTITY',
        getCursor, maxQuantity));
    Application^.ExecDialog(aDialog);

{ Subtract the quantity to buy from the quantity in the inventory table and  }
{ make this the new quantity in the inventory table.                         }
    getCursor^.genericRec^.getInteger(SALES_ITEMS_QUANTITY,
        quantityOrdered, isNull);
    selectItemCursor^.genericRec^.putInteger(INVENTORY_QUANTITY,
            maxQuantity - quantityOrdered);

{ Update the inventory table. }
    ERROR(selectItemCursor^.updateRec(selectItemCursor^.genericRec),
        'Updating the inventory table');

{ Append the new record to the sales items table}
    if(ERROR(getCursor^.appendRec(getCursor^.genericRec), 'Adding new Item')
            = PXSUCCESS) then
        { Display this new value. }
            DisplayFields;
        end
    else
{ Or inform the user that there is insufficient inventory.      }
    messageBox(HWindow, 'Not enough inventory to complete this order.',
        'OUT OF STOCK!', MB_ICONEXCLAMATION or MB_OK);

{ Unlock the record. }
    selectItemCursor^.unlockRecord(itemsLockHandle);
    end;

{ Close the table. }
    selectItemCursor^.close;
    dispose(selectItemCursor, Done);
end;
```

7

Maintaining database
integrity with the Engine

Describing data and referential integrity takes only a few words; how to write the code for it will take us through this chapter. Because this application uses more than one table and must rely on the accuracy of all its tables, maintaining a valid group of tables with valid information falls under the rubrics of data and referential integrity. During the planning process for this application, we established the need for links between several tables. This chapter discusses how we maintain those links within a multi-user environment to ensure the validity of each table's data. The Paradox Engine's Database Framework does not offer an object for us to do this; and so, we wrote one to do it.

Basic integrity constraints

We first will consider two of the three basic integrity restraints that this application uses: entity integrity and referential integrity. A third type of data integrity, user-defined integrity constraints, was discussed earlier in chapter 6.

Entity integrity

By entity *integrity*, we mean that we will implement the standard entity integrity rule summarized as *No key of any row in a table can have a null value.* This means, simply, that the application will guarantee the existence of a primary key for each record in a table. The *CreateDatabase* routine first discussed in chapter 2 demonstrates that each table is created with a primary key to ensure that we have uniquely identified each row and, therefore, each record. The primary key field or fields for each record must completely identify the key's attributes and uniqueness so that, knowing the key's value, we then can locate the value of any entity in a table.

When we create the SALES ITEMS table, we deliberately specify that the composite key for this table must consist of a sale number and an inventory item number. In this way, we ensure that the two fields combined as the record's composite key will both have values that are themselves the primary keys of the SALE and INVENTORY tables respectively. These are called *foreign keys*. Because we first have specified that all tables will have primary keys that are unique and use the *createIdNumber* procedure (in POSUTILS.PAS) to ensure this during the creation of each, then we do have a unique key for the SALES ITEMS table, and neither of its attributes will ever be a null value.

We can hardly avoid entity integrity, and the Paradox database structure that the Engine enforces easily allows us to accomplish this. When we come to referential integrity, however, the Engine's Database Framework does not explicitly encapsulate this concept.

Referential integrity

Simply put, we mean that *referential integrity* guarantees the existence of references to any foreign key. When we construct a relation between or among the tables of an application, we use foreign keys to tie the records on one table to those of another. A foreign key is simply a key from another, or detail, table contained as a field in the master table. To enforce referential integrity, the application must enforce the rule summarized as: *The value of a non-null foreign key must be an actual key value in a specific linked table.* In this application, the SALE table's SALE_NUMBER field, its primary key, also is one of the first two fields in the SALES ITEMS table that the application's design structure has defined as the key for that table. So, the SALE table can point to this composite key for SALES ITEMS when it needs to find the entity or entities that any one sale consists of. Similarly, the CUSTOMER_ID field in the SALE table can point to the primary key of the CUSTOMER table to define fully the customer for each sale. In this way, we have ensured that the SALE table references actual key values in other tables.

For our purposes here, we first will focus on maintaining the data integrity expressed by the references between the SALE table as a master table and the SALES ITEMS table as a detail table. Second, we will show how to link the CUSTOMER table, the master table, to the SALE table, the detail table. We then will use this SALE table as a master table to link to the SALES ITEMS table. This sequence ought to suggest that you can devise a multi-layered hierarchy of links instead of a single master table linked to multiple detail tables.

Figure 7-1 illustrates the two types of links that we will be discussing. In our situation, we are not limited, in a strict sense, to a single master table linked to detail tables. Here, we will use the master table to refer to the source of information from which we will reference the more detailed information (the detail table) that a master table will summarize in the one field needed to reference the details associated with it. The detail table, normally thought of as the repository for the details referenced by a field in a master table, can, in our linking environment, become, itself, the master table that links to another detail table.

Table Links

7-1 A schematic of the two types of logical links that we will demonstrate in the **DCursor** object type.

Each example will link the tables differently. In the first, we will be focusing on a composite key while the second will focus on using a secondary index to facilitate our search of the SALES ITEMS table, remembering that the secondary index maintains a reference to the SALE_NUMBER field so that our cursor will know which record it is pointing to. First, however, the class that does the work of maintaining referential integrity, **DCursor** and its methods.

Introducing the DCursor object type

The **DCursor** object type operates as a child of the Database Framework **TCursor** class, inheriting **TCursor**. We will use our **DCursor** class to do the following tasks related to maintaining referential integrity:

- Establish and maintain a link between tables in a master—detail, or parent-child, relation.
- Synchronize the link between the tables so that the cursor positions in the master and detail tables remain consistent and valid.
- Append, insert, update, or delete records correctly so that the links between the tables remain consistent and valid.

Thus, the linking functions simply establish the necessary identifying data members for a master table and use the table's data structure as the source for linking fields within another table, a detail table. The linking functions also similarly establish the identifying information for a detail table, including the table's data structure so that the master table can locate the detail table's primary key to provide the link for all other operations.

Synchronizing the link means establishing and maintaining the record and record contents of the master and detail tables so that the contents of the linked fields can be compared. The comparison locates the matching record in the detail table using a field in the master table and the key in the detail table.

With the tables linked and the cursor positions synchronized, the various editing operations can be performed, including append, delete, insert, and update.

The **DCursor** object will allow tables to be linked and the cursor on each table to be synchronized for proper referencing of records. The class will track changes to a table so that the links between the tables remain consistent and valid. The source code for the **DCursor** object type is found in FIG. 7-6 at the end of this chapter.

Fields

curStatus curStatus : PXCursorStatus; **private**
Specifies the cursor's internal status. Mimics **TCursor's** *curStatus*.

indexUsed indexUsed : Integer; **private**
Specifies whether the index for the table is a primary index or not.

masterTableName masterTableName : String[MaxNameLen]; **private**
Specifies the name of the master table.

detailTableName detailTableName : String[MaxNameLen]; **private**
Specifies the name of the detail table.

theLinkType theLinkType : LinkType; **private**
Specifies the type of link. See *linkTypeIs* for the types of links available.

masterDesc

detailDesc masterDesc, detailDesc : PFieldDesc; **private**
Used for getting field information about the tables: the field descriptors of
the master and detail tables.

userLinkType userLinkType : LinkType; **private**
Specifies the type of link being used.

linkedFields linkedFields : FieldNumberArray; **private**
Specifies the array of fields to be linked.

numberOfLinks numberOfLinks : FieldNumber; **private**
Specifies the number of fields to be linked.

masterHandle masterHandle : PCursor; **private**
The master **TCursor**. Used to reference the master table.

masterRecord masterRecord : PRecord; **private**
A record buffer pointer to hold the master table's current record.

detailRecord detailRecord : PRecord; **private**
A record buffer pointer to a record in the detail table.

theDatabase theDatabase : PDatabase; **private**
A pointer to the database.

firstRecordInScope firstRecordInScope : RecordNumber; **private**
Record number of the first record in a detail table's scope.

Constructors and destructor

Init constructor Init(masterCursor : PCursor; masterName : String);
This constructor creates a **DCursor** object of the inherited type **TCursor**.
This constructor simply associates a **DCursor** with a master table to which
a detail table can be linked at some time. The **DCursor** is unusable until it
is opened with a given detail table. The *masterCursor* argument specifies
the location of the cursor within the table named by the argument *master-
Name*.

InitWithDetail constructor InitWithDetail(masterCursor : PCursor; db : PDatabase;
detailTblName : String; masterName : String);
The second constructor creates a **DCursor** object and opens it on the specified Paradox table as a detail table that is to be linked to the master table.
The *detailTblName* argument specifies the detail table's name.

done   destructor done; **Virtual;**
Closes the cursor if it's open by freeing up any links and removing the pointers to the master and detail tables (*masterRecord*, *detailRecord*) and their respective field descriptors (*masterDesc*, *detailDesc*).

Methods (public)

open   function open(db : PDatabase; tableName : String; indexID : FieldNumber; saveEveryChange : Boolean) : Retcode; **Virtual;**
Opens this cursor for the specified detail table. *indexID* specifies the index to use. If *saveEveryChange* is set to FALSE, posted records will be buffered; if set to TRUE, records will be posted directly to disk.

close   function close : Retcode ; **Virtual;**
Closes the **DCursor** object's cursor if it's open by closing the inherited **TCursor** object.

linkTypeIs   function linkTypeIs : LINKTYPE;
Returns the current type of link as: NONE, ONE_TO_ONE, ONE_TO_MANY, MANY_TO_ONE, MANY_TO_MANY, or GROUP.

link function link(linkHandles : FieldNumberArray; numberOfHandles : FieldNumber) : Retcode;
Determines if the request to link fields between two tables is valid. If it is, *link* determines the link type and sets its internal variables to establish the link.

sync   function sync : Retcode ;
Makes a copy of the record in the master table's *genericRec* buffer and tries to find a record or records in the detail table with the same linked field values. If found, *firstRecordInScope* is set to this record number; otherwise, *firstRecordInScope* is set to zero. If successful, the **DCursor** cursor for the detail table will be positioned on the first matching record in the detail table's scope.

isEmpty   function isEmpty : Boolean;
Tests if the current scope is empty.

getRealCurRecNum   function getRealCurRecNum : RecordNumber;
Returns the absolute current record number by using the *getCurRecNum* inherited from **TCursor**.

updateLinkedRecs   function updateLinkedRecs : Retcode;
Updates all records within the scope of the detail table. The linked fields' values are associated with the master table's current record.

appendRec   function appendRec(rec : PRecord) : Retcode; **Virtual**;
Appends a record to the end of the detail table.

insertRec   function insertRec(rec : PRecord) : Retcode; **Virtual**;
Inserts a record within the scope of the detail table.

deleteRec   function deleteRec : Retcode; **Virtual**;
Deletes the current record in the detail table's scope and checks if the scope still has any records in it.

updateRec   function updateRec(rec : PRecord) : Retcode; **Virtual**;
Updates a record in the current scope.

gotoBegin   function gotoBegin : Retcode; **Virtual**;
Uses the *gotoBegin* function inherited from **TCursor** to move the cursor to the beginning of the table.

gotoEnd   function gotoEnd : Retcode; **Virtual**;
Uses the *gotoEnd* function inherited from **TCursor** to move the cursor to the end of the table.

gotoRec   function gotoRec(recNum : RecordNumber) : Retcode; **Virtual**;
Moves the cursor to the record number requested. The record number is based on the present scope. If the record number exceeds the number of records in the scope, then PXERR_OUTOFRANGE will be returned.

gotoNext   function gotoNext : Retcode; **Virtual**;
Moves the cursor to the next record within the scope.

gotoPrev   function gotoPrev : Retcode; **Virtual**;
Moves the cursor to the previous record within the scope.

getCurRecNum   function getCurRecNum : RecordNumber; **Virtual**;
Returns the current record number with respect to the present scope.

getRecCount   function getRecCount : RecordNumber; **Virtual**;
Determines the total number of records in the present scope.

searchIndex   function searchIndex(keyRec : PRecord; mode : PXSearchMode; fld-Cnt : Integer) : Retcode; **Virtual**;
Restricts the search of **PXSearchMode** to within the restricted view.

Methods (private)

Initialize   procedure Initialize(masterCursor: PCursor; masterName : String);
Constructs a **TRecord** object that creates a generic record object for the given open cursor to act as a buffer to monitor changes of the cursor open on the master table. Establishes pointers to the **TCursor** for the master table and the name of the table it is open on. Initializes the field descriptor objects for the master and detail tables. The **TFieldDesc** constructor *Init* must be called for these objects or unpredictable results will occur. Initializes the following private variables to these values:

```
theLinkType := NONE;
userLinkType := NONE;
numberOfLinks := 0;
firstRecordInScope := 0;
```

```
indexUsed := 0;
curStatus := atBegin;
detailRecord := Nil;
```

isValidLink   function isValidLink(linkHandles : FieldNumberArray; numberOfHandles : FieldNumber) : Retcode;

determineLinkType   function determineLinkType(linkedHandles : FieldNumberArray) : LinkType;

Determines if the current open link is one of the following types of links:

1-1	One to one
1-M	One to many
M-M	Many to many
M-1	Many to one
NONE	No link exists

updateBufferWithMasterKeys   procedure   updateBufferWithMasterKeys   (current MasterRec : PRecord; recordBuffer : PRecord);

Takes the field values of the *currentMasterRec* in the master table that are linked to a detail table and places them in the appropriate fields of a detail table's generic record buffer.

didMasterChange   function didMasterChange(recordBuffer : PRecord) : Boolean;

Checks if the linked field values of the master table's record have changed by examining the master table's generic record buffer.

findFirstLinkedRecord   function findFirstLinkedRecord : Boolean;

Finds the first record in the detail table whose linked field matches those in the master table's generic record buffer.

getRestrictedRecordCount   function getRestrictedRecCount : RecordNumber;

Determines how many records are in the current scope. Examines the detail table and searches for the linked fields for all records with matching fields and returns the number of matching records.

Using the DCursor with the Engine

The series of screens associated with the Sale choice from the application's main menu all use a composite screen view to display the information for any sale function. The normalizing process for this application has given us the necessary insights into which table needs what information to maintain both the efficiency of storage that we desire and the referential integrity that we must maintain. We cannot create a sale without first creating a primary key for the sale's record, ensuring entity integrity. Our paradigm for the SALES ITEMS table requires that we use a composite primary key there to ensure entity integrity also. With a link between the SALE table's key and the composite key of the SALES ITEMS established by the common field SALE_NUMBER, we then can link the two tables in a master-detail relation to maintain referential integrity also.

Integrating DCursor into the user interface

The Sale option from the main menu bar will call the **TSaleWindow** object, as found in TSALWIN.PAS. The constructor for this class, **TSaleWindow**, initiates the necessary pointers for linking the SALE and the SALES ITEMS tables together to maintain the type of referential integrity between these two tables that FIG. 7-2 illustrates.

Table Links

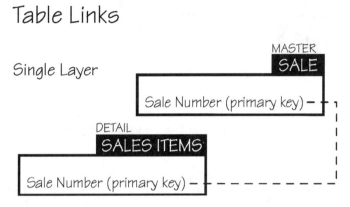

7-2 A schematic of the type of logical link used for a new sale.

The code presented in FIG. 7-3 shows that we first open the SALES ITEMS table using a **DCursor** object. The parameters that we pass to the **DCursor** constructor inform it to establish a link from the SALES_ITEMS table as a detail table to the SALE table as the master table. Having established SALE_NUMBER as our field to link on, we next use **DCursor's** *link* function to attempt to logically link those two fields in each table together.

If this is successful, then we can insert the sales items window into the sale window using **TItemsWindow** and rely on its routines, as shown in FIG. 7-4, to load all the items and, using **DCursor**'s *sync* function, position the cursor in the SALES ITEM table. The *SetupWindow* method is called whenever a window is set up.

As part of our calls to construct the new sale window and its child windows, we repeat the events for the sale's items for the inventory window that is grouped as another window within this frame. In doing so, we establish a link between the INVENTORY table and the SALES ITEMS table so that we can complete the Item number field in that table.

Figure 7-5 shows that whenever we use one of the buttons to move the cursor within the SALES ITEMS table, the display of the INVENTORY table's contents in the window object **TInventoryWindow** are resynchronized to match the "Item number" in the SALES ITEMS table.

7-3 An excerpt from TSALWIN.PAS that shows how to establish a link between two tables using **DCursor**.

```
{ Open the items table as a DETAIL table. }

  itemsCursor := new(PDCursor, InitWithDetail(getCursor, programDatabase,
    SALES_ITEMS_DB_NAME, SALE_DB_NAME));

  if(ERROR(itemsCursor^.lastError,'Opening sale items table') <>
    PXSUCCESS) then exit;

{ Set up the linked fields. }

  itemsLink[1] := SALE_SALE_NUMBER;

{ Link the two tables together. }

  ERROR(itemsCursor^.link(itemsLink, 1), 'Linking the sale items table');

{ Create the item window. }

  dummyPtr := new(PItemsWindow, Init(@Self, 'Items', itemsCursor));
```

7-4 An excerpt from TSALWIN.PAS that shows how to synchronize the position of the cursor on the detail table with that of a foreign key in a link established between two tables using **DCursor**.

```
(*********************************************************************
* TYPE: TItemsWindow
*
* METHOD:       SetupWindow
*
* DESCRIPTION:  This procedure is called so the window can initialize
*               its state before it is shown to the user.
*
*********************************************************************)
procedure TItemsWindow.SetupWindow;
begin

{ Call the base class. }

  inherited SetupWindow;

{  Tell the inventory cursor to sync its view on this new information. }

  inventoryCursor^.sync;

{ Tell the fields to load their values from the record buffer. }

  DisplayFields;

end;
```

7-5 An excerpt from TSALWIN.PAS that shows how to resynchronize the position of the cursor on a detail table when the value of the foreign key in the master table changes.

```
(*********************************************************************
 * TYPE: TItemsWindow
 *
 * METHOD:        DisplayFields
 *
 * DESCRIPTION:   This procedure responds when the window is told
 *                to display the record's field values.
 *
 *********************************************************************)
procedure TItemsWindow.DisplayFields;
begin

{ Resync the INVENTORY table. }

  inventoryCursor^.sync;

{ Blank out its record buffer. }

  inventoryCursor^.genericRec^.clear;

{ Load the record buffer with the information for the item.}

  inventoryCursor^.getRecord(inventoryCursor^.genericRec);

{ Call the base class procedure.}

  inherited DisplayFields;

end;
```

Source code for the DCursor object type

The unit in FIG. 7-6, **TDCursor**, found in the file DCURSOR.PAS, is the complete course code for the **DCursor** object type that this application uses to maintain referential integrity by linking tables together in a master-detail, or parent-child, relationship.

7-6 The complete source code for **DCursor**.

```
(**********************************************************************
*
* UNIT: TDCURSOR          File: TDCURSOR.PAS
*
* DESCRIPTION: This file defines a cursor class that establishes and
*              maintains referential integrity between two tables.
*
*
**********************************************************************)
unit TDCursor;

{$N+} { Turn on 8087 mode. }

interface

uses
    OOPXENG,
    PXOOPMSG,
    PxEngWin,
    STRINGS,
    WINCRT,
    Objects,
    WinDos;

const
{ Set to True for a window of debugging messages to be displayed. }

  debug = False;

  PXERR_NOTENOUGHKEYS               = 600;
  PXERR_FIELDHANDLEOUTOFRANGE       = 601;
  PXERR_INCOMPATABLEFIELDTYPES      = 602;
  PXERR_CANNOTLINKBLOBFIELDS        = 603;
  PXERR_DIFFERENTALPAHFIELDLENGTH   = 604;
  PXERR_EMPTYRESTRICTEDVIEW         = 605;
  PXERR_TOOMANYLINKEDFIELDS         = 606;
  PXERR_INTERNALERROR               = 607;
  PXERR_INVALIDLINK                 = 608;

{ Maximum number of linked fields allowed.  This is an arbitrary      }
{ number of linked fields, but big enough to satisfy any type of link. }

  MAX_LINKEDFIELDS = 64;
  MaxFieldLen = 255;
type
```

```
  Counter = Integer;    { Normal counter definition }

{ Type of links established by two tables.                              }

  LINKTYPE = ( NONE, ONE_TO_ONE, ONE_TO_MANY, MANY_TO_ONE, MANY_TO_MANY,
               GROUP);


(*********************************************************************
*
* OBJECT TYPE: DCursor
*
* DESCRIPTION: This is a cursor class that simulates referential
*              integrity between two tables.
*
*********************************************************************)

  PDCursor = ^DCursor;

  DCursor = object (TCursor)

{ PUBLIC }

{ Constructors.                                                        }

  constructor InitWithDetail(masterCursor : PCursor; db : PDatabase;
    detailTblName : String; masterName : String);
  constructor Init(masterCursor : PCursor; masterName : String);

{ Destructors.                                                         }

  destructor done; Virtual;

{ Opens the Cursor.                                                    }

  function open(db : PDatabase; tableName : String;
    indexID : FieldNumber; saveEveryChange : Boolean) : Retcode; Virtual;

{ Closes the Cursor.                                                   }

  function close : Retcode ; Virtual;

{ Links master and detail tables together.                            }

  function linkTypeIs : LINKTYPE;
  function link(linkHandles : FieldNumberArray; numberOfHandles : FieldNumber)
```

```
    : Retcode;

{ Synchronizes the master and detail table.                                   }

  function sync : Retcode ;

{ Count function.                                                             }

  function isEmpty : Boolean;
  function getRealCurRecNum : RecordNumber;

{ Record update function.                                                     }

  function updateLinkedRecs : Retcode;


{ Append a record to the end of a table's restricted view. Record            }
{ can be a generic or custom record.                                         }

  function appendRec(rec : PRecord) : Retcode; Virtual;

{ Insert a record at the current cursor position. Rec can be a               }
{ generic or custom record.                                                  }

  function insertRec(rec : PRecord) : Retcode; Virtual;

{ Delete the current record of the cursor.                                   }

  function deleteRec : Retcode; Virtual;

{ Update the current record of the cursor. This should not change            }
{ the linked field values. Record can be a generic or custom record.         }

  function updateRec(rec : PRecord) : Retcode; Virtual;

{ Go to beginning of the table.                                              }

  function gotoBegin : Retcode; Virtual;

{ Go to end of the table.                                                    }

  function gotoEnd : Retcode; Virtual;

{ Go to a specific record number in the table restricted view.               }

  function gotoRec(recNum : RecordNumber) : Retcode; Virtual;
```

```
{ Go to the next record of the table's restricted view.                    }

    function gotoNext : Retcode; Virtual;

{ Go to the previous record of the table's restricted view.                }

    function gotoPrev : Retcode; Virtual;

{ Get the record number of the current record based on restricted          }
{ view.                                                                     }

    function getCurRecNum : RecordNumber; Virtual;

{ Find the number of records in the cursor (or table restricted view).     }

    function getRecCount : RecordNumber; Virtual;

{ Search the table for the record that matches key values in keyRec.       }
{ The currently open index determines the order of records for the         }
{ search. Search is restricted to the table's restricted view.             }

    function searchIndex(keyRec : PRecord; mode : PXSearchMode;
      fldCnt : Integer) : Retcode; Virtual;

private

    curStatus : PXCursorStatus;
    indexUsed : Integer;
    masterTableName : String[MaxNameLen];
    detailTableName : String[MaxNameLen];
    theLinkType : LinkType;

{ Used for getting field information about the tables.                      }

    masterDesc, detailDesc : PFieldDesc;

{ Linking information.                                                      }

    userLinkType : LinkType;
    linkedFields : FieldNumberArray;
    numberOfLinks : FieldNumber;

{ The master TCursor. Used to reference the master table.                   }

    masterHandle : PCursor;

{ A record buffer pointer to hold the master table's current record.       }
```

```
  masterRecord : PRecord;

{ A record buffer pointer to a record in the detail table.                    }

  detailRecord : PRecord;

{ A pointer to the database.                                                   }

  theDatabase : PDatabase;

{ Record number of the first record in a detail tables scope.                 }

  firstRecordInScope : RecordNumber;

{ Initializes objects variables.                                              }

  procedure Initialize(masterCursor: PCursor; masterName : String);

{ Link functions.                                                             }

  function isValidLink(linkHandles : FieldNumberArray;
    numberOfHandles : FieldNumber) : Retcode;
  function determineLinkType(linkedHandles : FieldNumberArray)
    : LinkType;

{ Synchronization functions.                                                  }

  procedure updateBufferWithMasterKeys(currentMasterRec : PRecord;
    recordBuffer : PRecord);
  function didMasterChange(recordBuffer : PRecord) : Boolean;
  function findFirstLinkedRecord : Boolean;

{ Count functions.                                                            }

  function getRestrictedRecCount : RecordNumber;

end;  { DCursor object }

implementation

const
  NULL_RECNUM = -1;

(*********************************************************************
*
* TYPE: DCursor
```

```
*
* METHOD: Init
*
* DESCRIPTION: Constructor for the detail table. Initializes private
*              variables and copies TCursor and TDatabase.
*
********************************************************************)
constructor DCursor.Init
   (masterCursor : PCursor; masterName : String);

begin

{ Initialize the private variables and the inherited cursor.            }

   Initialize(masterCursor, masterName);
   TCursor.Init;

end;

(********************************************************************
*
* OBJECT : DCursor
*
* METHOD: InitWithDetail
*
* DESCRIPTION: Constructor for the detail table. Initializes private
*              variables and copies TCursor and TDatabase.
*
********************************************************************)
constructor DCursor.InitWithDetail
   (masterCursor : PCursor; db : PDatabase;
    detailTblName : String; masterName : String);

begin

{ Initialization. Start with private variables, then the inherited      }
{ cursor.                                                                }

   Initialize(masterCursor, masterName);

   TCursor.InitAndOpen(db, detailTblName, 0, False);

   detailTableName := detailTblName;

{ Used exclusively by the class for updating and searching this table.  }
   detailRecord := New (PRecord, Init(@Self));
```

```
{ The database pointer.                                                      }

  theDatabase := db;

end;

(**********************************************************************
*
*
* OBJECT : DCursor
*
* METHOD: Initialize
*
* DESCRIPTION: Initializes private variables.
*
**********************************************************************)
procedure DCursor.Initialize(masterCursor : PCursor; masterName : String);

begin
  theLinkType := NONE;
  userLinkType := NONE;
  numberOfLinks := 0;
  firstRecordInScope := 0;
  indexUsed := 0;
  curStatus := atBegin;
  detailRecord := Nil;

{ The master TCursor.                                                        }

  masterHandle := masterCursor;
  masterTableName := masterName;

{ Acts as a buffer to monitor changes of the master record.                  }

  masterRecord := New(PRecord, Init(masterCursor));
  lastError := masterRecord^.lastError;

{ Initialize the descriptor information objects.                             }
{ Note: This is IMPORTANT.  Init MUST BE CALLED for the objects;             }
{ otherwise, unpredictable results will occur.                               }

  masterDesc := New(PFieldDesc, Init);
  detailDesc := New(PFieldDesc, Init);

end;
```

```
(********************************************************************
*
* TYPE: DCursor
*
* METHOD: open
*
* DESCRIPTION: Opens the Detail table.
*
********************************************************************)
function DCursor.Open
   (db : PDatabase; tableName : String; indexID : FieldNumber;

var
   retval : Retcode;
begin

   retval := TCursor.open(db, tableName, indexID, saveEveryChange);

{ Save the name of the detail table.                              }


   if retval = PXSUCCESS then
   begin

   { Used exclusively by the class for updating and searching this table. }

      detailTableName := tableName;
      detailRecord := New(PRecord, Init(@Self));

   { The database and other variables                             }

      theDataBase := db;

      indexUsed := indexID;

   end;

   curStatus := atBegin;
   Open := retval

end;

(********************************************************************
```

```
*
* TYPE: DCursor
*
* METHOD: Close
*
* DESCRIPTION: Closes the DCursor object.
*
*********************************************************************)
function DCursor.close : Retcode;

begin

  if not isOpen then
  begin
    lastError := PXERR_CURSORNOTOPEN;
    close := lastError;
    exit
  end;

{ Close the inherited cursor.                                       }

  close := TCursor.close;
  curStatus := atEnd;

end;

(*******************************************************************
*
* TYPE: DCursor
*
* METHOD: Done
*
* DESCRIPTION: Destructor for the DCursor object.
*
*********************************************************************)
destructor DCursor.Done;
begin

  if masterRecord <> Nil then
    Dispose(masterRecord, Done);

  if detailRecord <> Nil then
    Dispose(detailRecord, Done);

  if masterDesc <> Nil then
```

```
    Dispose(masterDesc, Done);

  if detailDesc <> Nil then
    Dispose(detailDesc, Done);

  inherited Done;
end;
(************************************************************************
*
* TYPE: DCursor
*
* METHOD: isEmpty
*
* DESCRIPTION: Test if the current scope is empty.
*
*************************************************************************)
function DCursor.isEmpty : Boolean;

begin

  if(getCurRecNum = 0) and (lastError = PXSUCCESS) then
    isEmpty := True
  else
    isEmpty := False

end;

(************************************************************************
*
* TYPE: DCursor
*
* METHOD: getCurRecNum
*
* DESCRIPTION: Returns the current record number of the present scope.
*
*************************************************************************)
function DCursor.getCurRecNum : RecordNumber;

var
  recNum : RecordNumber;

begin
 recNum := 0;
```

```
{ If no link type set up, then simply call the inherited function from   }
{ the TCursor.                                                           }

  if theLinkType = NONE then
    recNum := TCursor.getCurRecNum
  else
  begin

  { If we have the recNum, then synchronize with the master record       }
  { number.                                                              }

    if firstRecordInScope <> 0 then
    begin

      recNum := TCursor.getCurRecNum;

    { If a record was found, then subtract the first record in the       }
    { scope to give us the record number relative to the  detail scope.  }

      if lastError = PXSUCCESS then
        recNum := (recNum-firstRecordInScope)+1;

    end

  { FirstRecordInScope not set, so return table empty.                   }

    else
      lastError := PXERR_TABLEEMPTY;

  end;

  getCurRecNum := recNum

end;

(*************************************************************************
*
* TYPE: DCursor
*
* METHOD: getRealCurRecNum
*
* DESCRIPTION: Returns the absolute current record number.
*
*************************************************************************)
function DCursor.getRealCurRecNum : RecordNumber;
```

```
begin

{ Get the current record number from the inherited Cursor.              }
  getRealCurRecNum := TCursor.getCurRecNum;

end;

(*********************************************************************
*
* TYPE: DCursor
*
* METHOD: getRestrictedRecCount
*
* DESCRIPTION: Determines how many records occupy the current scope.
*
*********************************************************************)
function DCursor.getRestrictedRecCount : RecordNumber;

var
  numRecs, currentRecord : RecordNumber;
  newCursor : PCursor;
  retVal : Retcode;

begin

  if debug then
    writeln('DCursor.getRestrictedRecCount: Enter');

  numRecs := 0;
  newCursor := Nil;

{ If no link, then return the inherited function since the whole table  }
{ is the scope.                                                         }

  if theLinkType = NONE then
  begin
    getRestrictedRecCount := TCursor.getRecCount;
    exit;
  end;

{ Do we have a scope? }

  if firstRecordInScope <> 0 then
  begin

    { Open up a new cursor on the detail table.  This will be used to    }
    { search the table for matching records. The new cursor is simply a  }
```

```
{ clone of the current cursor. The parameter to clone specifies if the }
{ new cursor is to be placed at the same position as the current        }
{ cursor. This operation should work.                                   }

  if debug then
    writeln('DCursor.getRestrictedRecCount: Cloning cursor');

  newCursor := inherited clone(False);

  if (newCursor = nil) or (lastError <> PXSUCCESS) then
  begin
    if debug then
      writeln('DCursor.getRestrictedRecCount: Error cloning Cursor. ',
        'thisCursor Error: ', lastError);

    getRestrictedRecCount := 0;
    exit;
  end;

{ Copy the current contents of the Master record into the detail        }
{ record.                                                                }

    updateBufferWithMasterKeys(masterRecord, detailRecord);

{ Find the first record in the detail table with the contents of the    }
{ linked fields in the master record.                                   }

      retVal  :=  newCursor^.searchIndex(detailRecord,  pxSearchFirst,
numberOfLinks);
    if retVal = PXSUCCESS then
    begin

      numRecs := 1;

        { Count all the records in the table with this key value. }

      while newCursor^.searchIndex(detailRecord, pxSearchNext,
        numberOfLinks)
                            = PXSUCCESS do
        numRecs := numRecs + 1;

    end

{ No records were found.                                                 }

    else
```

```
begin
  lastError := PXERR_TABLEEMPTY;
  if debug then
    writeln('DCursor.getRestrictedRecCount: Found no records');

    end;

  end;

{ Set the function to return the number of matching records.          }

  getRestrictedRecCount := numRecs;

{ If a clone cursor was obtained, then delete it.  Make sure that the  }
{ destructor Done is called.                                          }

  if newCursor <> Nil then
    Dispose (newCursor, Done);

  if debug then
    writeln('DCursor.getRestrictedRecCount: Exit, numRecs:',
      numRecs);


end;

(************************************************************************
*
* TYPE: DCursor
*
* MEMBER : getRecCount
*
* DESCRIPTION: Returns the total number of records in the present scope.
*
************************************************************************)
function DCursor.getRecCount : RecordNumber;

begin

  lastError := PXSUCCESS;

  if theLinkType = NONE then
    getRecCount := TCursor.getRecCount

  else
    getRecCount := getRestrictedRecCount
```

```
end;

(******************************************************************
*
* TYPE: DCursor
*
* METHOD: linkTypeIs
*
* DESCRIPTION: Returns the current link type.
*
******************************************************************)
function DCursor.linkTypeIs : LinkType;

begin

  linkTypeIs := userLinkType

end;

(******************************************************************
*
* TYPE: DCursor
*
* METHOD: isValidLink
*
* DESCRIPTION: Determines if the array of fields the user wants
*              to link is valid.
******************************************************************)
function DCursor.isValidLink
  (linkHandles : FieldNumberArray; numberOfHandles : FieldNumber)
: Retcode;

var

  detailFieldHdl : FieldNumber;
  detailKeyedFields : FieldNumber;
  numFields : FieldNumber;

begin

{ Valid only to clear the link.                                  }

  if numberOfHandles = 0 then
  begin
    isValidLink := PXSUCCESS;
    exit
```

```
  end;

{ Get number of detailed keyed fields.                              }

{ If the cursor is opened on the primary table, then get the number of  }
{ primary keys. If the cursor is opened on a secondary index, we assume }
{ that there is only 1 field since we do not allow composite secondary  }
{ indexes.                                                              }

  if indexUsed <> 0 then
    detailKeyedFields := 1
  else
    detailKeyedFields := theDataBase^.getNumPFields(detailTableName);

{ Are there too many handles? Each linked field handle must map to a     }
{ subset of a primary key or a single secondary key.  If there is a      }
{ secondary index and the number of handles is > 1, the link is invalid. }

  if numberOfHandles > detailKeyedFields then
  begin
    lastError := PXERR_NOTENOUGHKEYS;
    isValidLink := lastError;
    exit
  end;

{ Get the number of fields in the master table so we can check that the  }
{ field numbers passed in are valid.                                     }

  numFields := theDatabase^.getFieldCount(masterTableName);


{ Check field numbers for validity and test field type compatibility    }
{ for each pair of linked fields. Remember that N fields in the master   }
{ table link to the first N fields in the detail table if the link is    }
{ not to a secondary index. If the link is to a secondary index, then    }
{ there can only be one linked field in the master table to the field    }
{ that has the secondary index.                                          }

  for detailFieldHdl := 1 to numberOfHandles do
  begin

  { Check field value ranges. It must be a valid field number in the     }
  { master table.                                                        }

    if (linkHandles[detailFieldHdl] < 1) or
        (linkHandles[detailFieldHdl] > numFields) then
    begin
```

7-6 Continued.

```
      lastError := PXERR_FIELDHANDLEOUTOFRANGE;
      isValidLink := lastError;
      exit
   end;

{ Get the field description for each field. Remember that the link is  }
{ to the first N fields of the detail table if a secondary index is    }
{ is not used where N is the number of links.                          }

   masterRecord^.getFieldDesc(linkHandles[detailFieldHdl], masterDesc);

   if indexUsed <> 0 then
     detailRecord^.getFieldDesc(indexUsed, detailDesc)
   else
     detailRecord^.getFieldDesc(detailFieldHdl, detailDesc);

{ Check the field's type to make sure they match.                      }

   if masterDesc^.fldType <> detailDesc^.fldType then
   begin
     lastError := PXERR_INCOMPATABLEFIELDTYPES;
     isValidLink := lastError;
     exit
   end;

{ Check for links to BLOB fields.                                      }

   if (masterDesc^.fldType = fldBlob) or (detailDesc^.fldType = fldBlob)
then
   begin
     lastError := PXERR_CANNOTLINKBLOBFIELDS;
     isValidLink := lastError;
     exit
   end;

{ If they are strings, determine if field size is correct.             }

   if masterDesc^.fldType = fldChar then
     if masterDesc^.fldLen <> detailDesc^.fldLen then
     begin
       lastError := PXERR_DIFFERENTALPAHFIELDLENGTH;
            isValidLink := lastError
     end

   end;  { For }
```

```
  { Set up return values.

    lastError := PXSUCCESS;
    isValidLink := lastError

  end;

(**********************************************************************
*
* TYPE: DCursor
*
* FUNCTION: determineLinkType
*
* DESCRIPTION: Determine if the current link is of 1-1, 1-M, M-M, M-1,
*              or if no link exists ( NONE ).
*
**********************************************************************)
function DCursor.determineLinkType(linkedHandles : FieldNumberArray)
: LinkType;

var

  masterKeyedFields : Integer;
  detailKeyedFields : Integer;

  numMasterKeysLinked : Integer;
  duplicateMap : Boolean;

  count1, count2 : Integer;

begin

{ If no fields are mappped, then there is no link.                   }

  if numberOfLinks = 0 then
  begin
    determineLinkType := NONE;
    exit;
  end;

{ Make sure that the cursor is open.                                 }

  if not isOpen then
  begin
    determineLinkType := NONE;
    exit
  end;
```

```
{ Number of master keyed fields linked to detail, to be determined.      }

   numMasterKeysLinked := 0;

{ Get the number of primary keyed fields in the Master table.            }
   masterKeyedFields := theDataBase^.getNumPFields(masterTableName);

{ Get the number of Detailed keyed fields.                               }

   detailKeyedFields := theDataBase^.getNumPFields(detailTableName);

{ Check which detailed fields are mapped to master KEYED fields.         }

   for count1 := 1 to numberOfLinks do
   begin

      duplicateMap := FALSE;

{ If there is a link to a key field in the master table, then check.     }

      if linkedHandles[count1] <= masterKeyedFields then
      begin

      { Check so that if two embedded keys are mapped to the same master }
      { key field, count will only be incremented once.                  }

         count2 := 1;
         while (count2 <= numberOfLinks) and (not duplicateMap) do
         begin

         if (linkedHandles[count1] = linkedHandles[count2]) and
            (count1 <> count2) then
           duplicateMap := TRUE;

           count2 := count2 + 1
              end;


   end;

   { Number of links mapped to master key field's without duplication.   }

      if not duplicateMap then
        numMasterKeysLinked := numMasterKeysLinked + 1
```

```
{ Determine the link type.                                                   }

{ One-to-One (1-1) Group. This means that the master primary key maps to }
{ the detail primary key.                                                     }


{ If all of the fields in the master table primary key are linked, then  }
{ the link is 1-1 or 1-Many.                                                  }

   if (masterKeyedFields > 0) and (masterKeyedFields = numMasterKeysLinked)
then
   begin

   { If the number of links is greater than the number of fields in the   }
   { detail key and a secondary index is not used, then the link is 1-1.   }
   { Otherwise the link is a 1-Many.                                        }

      if (numberOfLinks >= detailKeyedFields) and (indexUsed = 0) then
         determineLinkType := ONE_TO_ONE
      else
         determineLinkType := ONE_TO_MANY

   end

{ Otherwise it is a Many-1 or Many-Many group.                               }

   else
   begin

   { See comment above for 1-1 group.                                        }

      if (numberOfLinks >= detailKeyedFields) and (indexUsed = 0) then
         determineLinkType := MANY_TO_ONE
      else
         determineLinkType := MANY_TO_MANY
   end;

end;

(*******************************************************************************
*
* TYPE: DCursor
*
* METHOD: link
```

7-6 Continued.

```
*
* DESCRIPTION: Determines if the user's request to link fields between
*              two tables is valid.  If it is, determines the link type
*              and sets internal variables to establish the link.
*
*******************************************************************)
function DCursor.link(linkHandles : FieldNumberArray;
  numberOfHandles : FieldNumber)
: Retcode;

var
  retVal : Retcode;
  i : Counter;

begin

  if debug then
    writeln('DCursor.link: Enter: Number of handles: ', numberOfHandles);

{ If a secondary index is being used, only 1 handle can be passed.        }

  if (indexUsed <> 0) and (numberOfHandles <> 1) then
  begin
    lastError := PXERR_INVALIDLINK;
    link := lastError;
    exit
  end;

{ Make sure cursors have been opened.                                     }

  if (not isOpen) or (not masterHandle^.isOpen) then
  begin
    lastError := PXERR_CURSORNOTOPEN;
    link := lastError;
    exit;
  end;

{ Determine if link is valid.                                             }

  retVal := isValidLink(linkHandles, numberOfHandles);
  if retVal = PXSUCCESS then
  begin

    if debug then
      writeln('DCursor.link: Link is valid');
```

```
{ Set the class up with user's input.                                }

   numberOfLinks := numberOfHandles;

   if numberOfHandles <> 0 then
   begin

   { Save the input field handles.                                   }

      for i := 1 to numberOfHandles do
        linkedFields[i] := linkHandles[i];
      end;

 { Determine the link type.                                          }

   userLinkType := determineLinkType(linkHandles);

 { Set class member.                                                 }

   case userLinkType of
     MANY_TO_ONE, MANY_TO_MANY: theLinkType := GROUP;

     else
             theLinkType := userLinkType;
   end;

   link := PXSUCCESS

 end
 else
   link := retVal;

 if debug then
   writeln('DCursor.link: Exit');

end;

(**********************************************************************
*
* TYPE: DCursor
*
* METHOD: gotoBegin
*
* DESCRIPTION: Moves the cursor to the beginning of the table.
*
**********************************************************************)
function DCursor.gotoBegin : Retcode;
```

7-6 Continued.

```
function DCursor.gotoBegin : Retcode;

begin

{ Use the inherited function.  If it is successful then update the      }
{ status.                                                               }

  TCursor.gotoBegin;

  if lastError = PXSUCCESS then
    curStatus := atBegin;

  gotoBegin := lastError

end;

(*********************************************************************
*
* TYPE: DCursor
*
* METHOD: gotoEnd
*
* DESCRIPTION: Moves the cursor to the end of the table.
*
*********************************************************************)
function DCursor.gotoEnd : Retcode;

begin

{ Use the inherited function.  If it is successful then update the      }
{ status.                                                               }

  TCursor.gotoEnd;

  if lastError = PXSUCCESS then
    curStatus := atEnd;

  gotoEnd := lastError

end;

(*********************************************************************
*
* TYPE: DCursor
*
```

```
* METHOD: gotoRec
*
* DESCRIPTION: Moves the cursor to the record number requested. The record
*              number should be based on the present scope.
*              For example:
*                      gotoRec(10);
*              This moves the cursor to the tenth record within the current
*              scope.  If 10 records do not exist in the current scope,
*              PXERR_OUTOFRANGE will be returned.
*
************************************************************************)
function DCursor.gotoRec(recNum : RecordNumber) : Retcode;


begin

{ If link not set up, then act like the normal cursor.                }

  if theLinkType = NONE then
  begin
    gotoRec := TCursor.gotoRec(recNum);
  end

  else
  begin

  { Determine if records are in the scope.                            }

    if firstRecordInScope = 0 then
    begin
      lastError := PXERR_TABLEEMPTY;
      gotoRec := lastError;
      exit
    end;

  { Is recNum within the current scope's range?                       }

    if (recNum > getRestrictedRecCount) or (recNum < 1) then
    begin
      lastError := PXERR_OUTOFRANGE;
      gotoRec := lastError;
      exit
    end;
```

```
{ Determine the record number with respect to the entire table.        }

  recNum := recNum + firstRecordInScope -1;

{ Move to the record.                                                   }

  gotoRec := TCursor.gotoRec(recNum)

end;

{ If the gotoRec was successful, then we are at a record.               }

  if lastError = PXSUCCESS then
    curStatus := atRecord;

  gotoRec := PXSUCCESS

end;

(********************************************************************
*
* TYPE: DCursor
*
* METHOD: gotoNext
*
* DESCRIPTION: Will move the cursor to the next record within the scope
*              while respecting the limits of the scope.
*
********************************************************************)
function DCursor.gotoNext : Retcode;

var
  curRecNum, restrictNum : RecordNumber;
  theClone : PCursor;

begin

  if debug then
    writeln('DCursor.gotoNext: Enter. firstRecordInScope: ',
      firstRecordInScope);

{ If no link type, then act as normal TCursor.                          }

  if theLinkType = NONE then
  begin
```

```
     ·if debug then
       writeln('DCursor.gotoNext: No Link');
     gotoNext := TCursor.gotoNext;
     if lastError = PXSUCCESS then
       curStatus := atRecord;
     exit;
   end;

{ If no records in scope, then return table empty.                    }

   if firstRecordInScope = 0 then
   begin
     if debug then
       writeln('DCursor.gotoNext: No Scope Yet');

     lastError := PXERR_TABLEEMPTY;
     gotoNext := lastError;
     exit;
   end;

{ If cursor status is atBegin, then goto the first record in the scope.  }

   if curStatus = atBegin then
   begin
     if debug then
       writeln('DCursor.gotoNext: cursor atBegin');

     gotoNext := TCursor.gotoRec(firstRecordInScope);
     if lastError = PXSUCCESS then
     begin
       curStatus := atRecord;
       exit;
     end
   end;

{ If at end of the table, then just return.                           }

   if curStatus = atEnd then
   begin
     if debug then
       writeln('DCursor.gotoNext: Cursor atEnd');

     lastError := PXERR_ENDOFTABLE;
     gotoNext := lastError;
     exit;
   end;
```

7-6 Continued.

```
{ Cursor is either atRecord or atCrack. If we are past the end of the    }
{ scope, we DO NOT want to move this cursor from its current position.    }
{ Thus, we first clone this cursor and move the clone. Move to the next   }
{ record using the inherited function on the cloned cursor.  The reason   }
{ we need to clone the cursor and move it is that if the cursor is        }
{ currently at a crack (after a delete), there is no way to get the       }
{ the current record number.  We must position the cursor ON a record     }
{ before we can get its position.  However, if we position the cursor     }
{ on the next valid record, but we are past the end of the scope we can't }
{ move the cursor back to the crack where it should be.                   }

   if debug then
     writeln('DCursor.gotoNext: Cloning cursor');

{ Clone cursor. Argument specifies that it point to the same record as    }
{ the inherited cursor.                                                   }
   theClone := inherited clone(True);
   theClone^.gotoNext;
   if theClone^.lastError <> PXSUCCESS then
   begin
     if debug then
       writeln('DCursor.gotoNext: Unable to clone or move cloned Cursor: ',
          theClone^.lastError);
     gotoNext := theClone^.lastError;
     dispose(theClone, Done);
     exit;
   end;

{ Decide if we are past the end of the scope. Get the real current        }
{ record number and the number of records in the scope.  If either fails, }
{ then return.                                                            }

   curRecNum := theClone^.getCurRecNum;
   if theClone^.lastError <> PXSUCCESS then
   begin
     if debug then
       writeln('DCursor.gotoNext: GetCurRecNum for clone, error: ',
          lastError);
     gotoNext := theClone^.lastError;
     dispose(theClone, Done);
     exit;
   end;

   if debug then
     writeln('DCursor.gotoNext: Real Record number: ', curRecNum);
```

```
    restrictNum := getRestrictedRecCount;
    if lastError <> PXSUCCESS then
    begin
      gotoNext := lastError;
      dispose(theClone, Done);
      exit;
    end;

{ If current record number is >  first record + number in scope -1,   }
{ then we are past the end of the scope. In this case, simply discard  }
{ the cloned cursor. We never moved the real cursor.                   }

    if curRecNum > (firstRecordInScope + restrictNum - 1) then
    begin
      if debug then
        writeln('DCursor.gotoNext: Past end of scope.');
      lastError := PXERR_ENDOFTABLE;

    end

{ Otherwise, the cloned cursor points to the next valid record. Set this }
{ cursor to the same record as the cloned cursor using the setToCursor   }
{ function. This should work.                                            }

    else
    begin
      if debug then
        writeln('DCursor.gotoNext: Successfully moved');

      lastError := inherited setToCursor(theClone);
      if lastError = PXSUCCESS then
      begin
        curStatus := atRecord;
      end
      else
      begin
        lastError := PXERR_INTERNALERROR;
      end;
    end;

{ Get rid of the cloned cursor. MUST call the Done destructor.          }

    dispose (theClone, Done);

{ Set return value for the function.                                    }

    gotoNext := lastError;
```

```
  if debug then
    writeln('DCursor.gotoNext: Return: ', lastError);

end;

(******************************************************************
*
* TYPE: DCursor
*
* METHOD: gotoPrev
*
* DESCRIPTION: Will move the cursor to the previous record within the scope
*              while respecting the limits of the scope.
*
******************************************************************)
function DCursor.gotoPrev : Retcode;

var
  curRecNum : RecordNumber;
  theClone : PCursor;

begin

  if debug then
    writeln('DCursor.gotoPrev: Enter');

{ If no link type, then act as normal TCursor.                    }

  if theLinkType = NONE then
  begin
    if debug then
      writeln('DCursor.gotoPrev: No Link');

    gotoPrev := TCursor.gotoPrev;
    if lastError = PXSUCCESS then
      curStatus := atRecord;
    exit
  end;

{ If no records in scope, then return table empty.                }

  if firstRecordInScope = 0 then
  begin
    if debug then
      writeln('DCursor.gotoPrev: No Scope');
```

```
    lastError := PXERR_TABLEEMPTY;
    gotoPrev := lastError;
    exit
  end;

{ If cursor status is already at the beginning, then return.            }

  if curStatus = atBegin then
  begin
    if debug then
      writeln('DCursor.gotoPrev: atBegin');
    lastError := PXERR_STARTOFTABLE;
    gotoPrev := lastError;
    exit
  end;

{ If cursor is at end of table then move to last record in the scope.   }
  if curStatus = atEnd then
  begin
    if debug then
      writeln('DCursor.gotoPrev: atEnd');

    lastError := gotoRec(getRestrictedRecCount);
    gotoPrev := lastError;
    if lastError = PXSUCCESS then
      curStatus := atRecord;
    exit
  end;

{ Cursor status is atRecord or atCrack.  Clone the cursor so we can move }
{ to the previous record without changing the current cursor.  See the  }
{ comments in the DCursor.gotoNext function (above) for a complete       }
{ explanation of why we do this.                                         }

  theClone := inherited clone(True);
  theClone^.gotoPrev;
  if theClone^.lastError <> PXSUCCESS then
  begin
    if debug then
      writeln('DCursor.gotoPrev: Unable to clone or move cloned Cursor: ',
        theClone^.lastError);
    gotoPrev := theClone^.lastError;
    dispose(theClone, Done);
    exit;
  end;

{ If the current record number is < the first record in the scope, then  }
```

```
{ we are past the beginning of the scope.                              }

  curRecNum := theClone^.getCurRecNum;
  if curRecNum <  firstRecordInScope then
  begin
    lastError := PXERR_STARTOFTABLE;
  end
```

```
{ Otherwise, the cloned cursor points to the previous valid record. Set }
{ this cursor to the same record as the cloned cursor using the          }
{ setToCursor function. This should work.                                }

  else
  begin
    if debug then
      writeln('DCursor.gotoPrev: Successfully moved');
    lastError := inherited setToCursor(theClone);
    if lastError = PXSUCCESS then
    begin
      curStatus := atRecord;
    end
    else
    begin
      lastError := PXERR_INTERNALERROR;
    end;
  end;
```

```
{ Get rid of the cloned cursor. MUST call the Done destructor.          }

  dispose (theClone, Done);
```

```
{ Set return value for the function.                                    }

  gotoPrev := lastError;

  if debug then
    writeln('DCursor.gotoPrev: Return error: ', lastError);

end;
```

```
(******************************************************************************
 *
 * TYPE: DCursor
 *
 * METHOD: updateLinkedRecs
 *
```

```
* DESCRIPTION: This will update all records within the scope of the
*              detailed table.  The linked fields' values are associated
*              with the current master record.
***********************************************************************)
function DCursor.updateLinkedRecs : Retcode;

var
  retVal : Retcode;
  keyBuffer : PRecord;

begin

{ If no scope, then act as normal TCursor.                              }

  if firstRecordInScope <> 0 then
  begin
    gotoBegin;
    lastError := PXERR_TABLEEMPTY;
    updateLinkedRecs := PXERR_TABLEEMPTY;
    exit;
  end;


{ Does the link require updating the detail records?                    }

  if (theLinkType <> NONE) and (theLinkType <> GROUP) then
  begin

  { Check if the linked fields of the master record have changed.       }

    if didMasterChange(masterHandle^.genericRec) = False then
    begin
      updateLinkedRecs := gotoBegin;
    end;


  { Get the first record in the scope.                                  }

    keyBuffer := New(PRecord, Init(@Self));
    TCursor.gotoRec(firstRecordInScope);
    if lastError <> PXSUCCESS then
    begin
      updateLinkedRecs := lastError;
      if keyBuffer <> nil then dispose(keyBuffer, Done);
      exit;
    end;
```

7-6 Continued.

```
{ Moved the cursor to a record.                                              }

  curStatus := atRecord;

{ Put a copy of the record into the key buffer.                              }

  getRecord(keyBuffer);
  if lastError <> PXSUCCESS then
  begin
    updateLinkedRecs := PXERR_INTERNALERROR;
    dispose(keyBuffer, Done);
    exit
  end;

{ Update all detailed records within the scope with the master              }
{ linked field values.                                                       }

  while TCursor.searchIndex(keyBuffer, pxSearchFirst, numberOfLinks)
          = PXSUCCESS do
  begin

  { Load the detail record with the key fields.                             }

    getRecord(detailRecord);

   updateBufferWithMasterKeys(masterHandle^.genericRec, detailRecord);

  { Call the engine routine to update the current record using the new }
  { record stored in detailRecord.                                       }

    retVal := TCursor.updateRec(detailRecord);
    if retVal <> PXSUCCESS then
    begin
      gotoBegin;
            Dispose(keyBuffer);
            updateLinkedRecs := retVal;
      exit
    end
  end;

  firstRecordInScope := 0;
  Dispose(keyBuffer)

end
else
begin
```

```
      if theLinkType = NONE then
        firstRecordInScope := 1
      else
        firstRecordInScope := 0
    end;

    updateLinkedRecs := gotoBegin;

end;

(************************************************************************
 *
 * TYPE: DCursor
 *
 * METHOD: append
 *
 * DESCRIPTION: Appends a record to the end of the scope's records.
 *
 ************************************************************************)
function DCursor.appendRec(rec : PRecord)   : Retcode;
var
   retVal : Retcode;

begin

{ If either cursor, master or detail, is not open, then return.        }

   if (not isOpen) or (not masterHandle^.isOpen) then
   begin
     lastError := PXERR_CURSORNOTOPEN;
     appendRec := lastError;
     exit
   end;

{ If no link or a group link, then just add the record normally.       }

   if (theLinkType = NONE) or (theLinkType = GROUP) then
     retVal := TCursor.appendRec(rec)

   else
   begin

   { Using the current master record, copy its linked fields into the   }
   { record that was passed in.  This ensures that the links are correct. }

     updateBufferWithMasterKeys(masterRecord, rec);
     retval := TCursor.appendRec(rec);
```

```
  { Check if this is the first record the detailed scope. If so,        }
  { synchronize the detail table with the master table.                 }

    if (firstRecordInScope = 0) and (retVal = PXSUCCESS) then
      sync;

  end;

{ If a record was successfully appended, then the cursor is pointing to }
{ the record.                                                           }

  if retVal = PXSUCCESS then
    curStatus := atRecord;

{ Set function return value.                                            }

  appendRec := retVal

end;

(***********************************************************************
 * TYPE: DCursor
 *
 * METHOD: insert
 *
 * DESCRIPTION: Inserts record within the scope of the detail table.
 *
 ***********************************************************************)
function DCursor.insertRec(rec : PRecord) : Retcode;

var

  retVal : Retcode;

begin

{ If either cursor, master or detail, is not open, then return.         }

  if ( not isOpen) or (not masterHandle^.isOpen) then
  begin
    lastError := PXERR_CURSORNOTOPEN;
    insertRec := lastError;
    exit
  end;

  if (theLinkType = NONE) or (theLinkType = GROUP) then
```

```
      retVal := TCursor.insertRec(rec)

   else
   begin

      updateBufferWithMasterKeys(masterRecord, rec);
      retVal := TCursor.insertRec(rec);

   { Check if this is the first record the detailed scope. If so,   }
   { synchronize the detail with the master.                        }

      if (firstRecordInScope = 0) and (retval = PXSUCCESS) then
        sync;

   end;

{ If a record was successfully inserted, then the cursor is pointing to }
{ the record.                                                           }

   if retVal = PXSUCCESS then
     curStatus := atRecord;

{ Set function return value.                                            }

   insertRec := retVal

end;

(************************************************************************
 *
 * TYPE: DCursor
 *
 * METHOD: deleteRec
 *
 * DESCRIPTION: Deletes the current record in scope and checks if scope
 *              still has any records in it.
 *
 ************************************************************************)
function DCursor.deleteRec : Retcode;
var

   retVal : Retcode;
   deleteLast : Boolean;

begin

   deleteLast := False;
```

```
{ If either cursor, master or detail, is not open, then return.           }

  if ( not isOpen) or (not masterHandle^.isOpen) then
  begin
    lastError := PXERR_CURSORNOTOPEN;
    deleteRec := lastError;
    exit
  end;

  if (theLinkType = NONE) or (theLinkType = GROUP) then
    retVal := TCursor.deleteRec

  else
  begin

  { If no records in the scope, then there is no record to delete.        }

    if firstRecordInScope = 0 then
      retVal := PXERR_TABLEEMPTY

    else
    begin

  { If only one record left in the scope then this is the last one.       }

      if getRecCount = 1 then
            deleteLast := True;

  { Call the engine to delete the current record.                         }

      retVal := TCursor.deleteRec;
      if (retVal = PXSUCCESS) then
      begin

  { If the last record in the scope was deleted, reset it.                }

        if  (deleteLast) then
        begin

              firstRecordInScope := 0;
            retVal := gotoBegin

        end

        else
        begin
```

```
        { The last Record was not deleted. The cursor is now on a crack. }

          curStatus := atCrack
        end

      end { Successful Deletion }

    end

  end; { Possible record to delete. }

{ Set function return value.                                              }

  deleteRec := retVal

end;

(*********************************************************************
*
* TYPE: DCursor
*
* METHOD: update
*
* DESCRIPTION: Updates a record in the current scope.
*
*********************************************************************)
function DCursor.updateRec(rec : PRecord) : Retcode;

var

  retVal : Retcode;

begin

{ If either cursor, master or detail, is not open, then return.        }

  if ( not isOpen) or (not masterHandle^.isOpen) then
  begin
    lastError := PXERR_CURSORNOTOPEN;
    updateRec := lastError;
    exit
  end;

  if (theLinkType = NONE) or (theLinkType = GROUP) then
    retVal := TCursor.updateRec(rec)

  else
```

```
  begin

    updateBufferWithMasterKeys(masterRecord, rec);
    retVal := TCursor.updateRec(rec)

  end;

  updateRec := retval

end;

(*********************************************************************
*
* TYPE: DCursor
*
* METHOD: searchIndex
*
* DESCRIPTION: This function restricts searching to within restricted
*              view.
*
*********************************************************************)
function DCursor.searchIndex
  (keyRec : PRecord; mode : PXSearchMode ; fldCnt : Integer) : Retcode;

begin

{ If no link type or a group link, then we can search the whole table.   }

  if (theLinkType = NONE) or (theLinkType = GROUP) then
    searchIndex := TCursor.searchIndex(keyRec, mode, fldCnt)


  else
  begin

  { There is a 1-1 or 1-Many link.  Update the keyRec passed in        }
  { to include the linked fields from the masterRecord.  This  will    }
  { restrict the search to only those records in the restricted view.  }

    updateBufferWithMasterKeys(masterRecord, keyRec);


  { Since we want to restrict the search we must use all of the fields }
  { in the record that are linked, i.e. if fldCnt is less than the     }
  { number of links reset it to be equal to the number of links.       }
```

```
      if fldCnt < numberOfLinks then
        fldCnt := numberOfLinks;

      searchIndex := TCursor.searchIndex(keyRec, mode, fldCnt)

    end;

  { Update the cursor status.  If the search was successful, or we were   }
  { looking for the closest record, then the cursor is pointing to        }
  { a record.                                                             }

    if (lastError = PXSUCCESS) or
       ((mode = pxClosestRecord) and (lastError = PXERR_RECNOTFOUND)) then
      curStatus := atRecord;

(**********************************************************************
 *
 * TYPE: DCursor
 *
 * METHOD: updateBufferWithMasterKeys
 *
 * DESCRIPTION: This function will take the field values of the master
 *              table that are linked to a detail table and place them
 *              in the appropriate fields of a detail record buffer.
 *
 **********************************************************************)
procedure DCursor.updateBufferWithMasterKeys
    (currentMasterRec : PRecord; recordBuffer : PRecord);

var

  detailFieldHdl, masterFieldHdl : FieldNumber;

  Alpha     : array [0..MaxFieldLen] of char;
  Date      : DateRec;
  Doub      : Double;
  Short     : Integer;
  isNull    : Boolean;
  i         : Counter;

begin

{ Set the detail buffer with the linked fields of the master.            }
```

7-6 Continued.

```
Set the detail buffer with the linked fields of the master.               }

for i := 1 to numberOfLinks do
begin
  masterFieldHdl := linkedFields[i];

{ Set the field handle in the detail table.                               }
{ IF a secondary index is being used, the field number is the index       }
{ number.                                                                  }

  if (indexUsed <> 0) then
    detailFieldHdl := indexUsed

  else
  begin


    detailFieldHdl := i
  end;

{ If the master field is Null, then set the detailed field to be           }
{ null.                                                                    }

  if currentMasterRec^.isNull(masterFieldHdl) then
  begin
    recordBuffer^.setNull(detailFieldHdl)
  end
  else
  begin

  { Otherwise, based on the field type, copy the master field to the      }
  { detail field.                                                         }

  { Get a description of the field in the master record.                  }

    currentMasterRec^.getFieldDesc(masterFieldHdl, masterDesc);

  { Based on the type of field, get the field value out of the master     }
  { record and put it into the passed in record buffer.                   }

    case masterDesc^.fldType of

      fldChar:
      begin
        currentMasterRec^.getField(masterFieldHdl, @Alpha,
```

```
                masterDesc^.fldLen+1, isNull);
              recordBuffer^.putField(detailFieldHdl, @Alpha, masterDesc^.fldLen)
            end;

          fldShort:
          begin
            currentMasterRec^.getInteger(masterFieldHdl, Short, isNull);
            recordBuffer^.putInteger(detailFieldHdl, Short)
          end;

          fldDouble:
          begin
            currentMasterRec^.getDouble(masterFieldHdl, Doub, isNull );
            recordBuffer^.putDouble(detailFieldHdl, Doub )
          end;

          fldDate:
          begin
            currentMasterRec^.getDate(masterFieldHdl, Date, isNull);
            recordBuffer^.putDate(detailFieldHdl, Date);
                end;
        end { Case }
      end { else }

  end; { For }

end;


(***********************************************************************
 *
 * TYPE: DCursor
 *
 * METHOD: didMasterChange
 *
 * DESCRIPTION: This will check if the linked field values of the master
 *              record have changed by examining the master table's
 *              generic record.
 *
 ***********************************************************************)
function DCursor.didMasterChange(recordBuffer : PRecord) : Boolean;

var
  masterField, detailField : FieldNumber;

  masterBlank,  detailBlank : Boolean;
  Changed, isNull : Boolean;
```

```
{ Temporary holders for field data.                                    }

  masterAlpha    : array [0..MaxFieldLen] of char;
  detailAlpha    : array [0..MaxFieldLen] of char;
  masterDate     : DateRec;
  detailDate     : DateRec;
  masterDoub     : Double;
  detailDoub     : Double;
  masterShort    : Integer;
  detailShort    : Integer;

  i : Counter;

begin

  Changed := FALSE;


{ Check each linked field in the master with the record buffer.        }

  for i := 1 to numberOfLinks do
  begin

    masterField := linkedFields[i];

  { See comment in previous procedure.                                 }

    if indexUsed <> 0 then
      detailField := indexUsed
    else
      detailField := i;

  { First check blank values.                                          }

    masterBlank := masterRecord^.isNull(masterField);
    detailBlank := recordBuffer^.isNull(detailField);

  { If both blank then no changes were made.                           }

    if (masterBlank) and (detailBlank) then
      Changed := FALSE

  { Else if one is blank and the other is not, then it has changed.    }

    else if (((not masterBlank) and (detailBlank)) or
            ((masterBlank) and (not detailBlank))) then
      Changed := True
```

```
{ Else need to compare contents since both fields are non blank.        }

   else
   begin

     masterRecord^.getFieldDesc(masterField, masterDesc);

   { Make the comparison based on the field type.                       }

     case masterDesc^.fldType of
       fldChar:
       begin

         masterRecord^.getField(masterField, @masterAlpha,
           masterDesc^.fldLen, isNull);
         recordBuffer^.getField(detailField, @detailAlpha,
           masterDesc^.fldLen, isNull);

       if StrIComp(masterAlpha,detailAlpha) <> 0 then
             Changed := True
       end;

       fldShort:
       begin
         masterRecord^.getInteger(masterField, masterShort, isNull);
         recordBuffer^.getInteger(detailField, detailShort, isNull);
             if masterShort <> detailShort then
           Changed := True
       end;

       fldDouble:
       begin
         masterRecord^.getDouble(masterField, masterDoub, isNull);
         recordBuffer^.getDouble(detailField, detailDoub, isNull);
         if masterDoub <> detailDoub then
           Changed := True
       end;

       fldDate:
       begin
         masterRecord^.getDate(masterField, masterDate, isNull);
         recordBuffer^.getDate(detailField, detailDate, isNull);

     { Cast the dates into longs for comparison. Can do this since       }
     { dates are stored year, month, day.                               }

       if (LongInt(masterDate) <> LongInt(detailDate)) then
```

```
              Changed := TRUE
          end
        end { Case }
      end;

    { Don't continue the For loop if Changed has been set.                    }

      if Changed then
        break;

    end; { For }

    didMasterChange := Changed

end;

(*************************************************************************

*
* TYPE: DCursor
*
* METHOD: findFirstLinkedRecord
*
* DESCRIPTION: This will find the first record in the detailed table whose
*              linked fields match those in the master table's genericRec
*              buffer.
*
*************************************************************************)
function DCursor.findFirstLinkedRecord : Boolean;

var
  retVal : Retcode;

begin

{ Non-linked table. Just goto first record since whole table is scope.   }

  if theLinkType = NONE then
  begin
    TCursor.gotoRec(1);
    if lastError <> PXSUCCESS then
    begin
      findFirstLinkedRecord := False;
      firstRecordInScope := 0
    end
```

```
    begin
      findFirstLinkedRecord := True;
      firstRecordInScope := 1;
      curStatus := atRecord
    end;

    exit
  end;
```

```
{ Set the record buffer with the master keys.                          }

  updateBufferWithMasterKeys(masterRecord, detailRecord);
```

```
{ Find the first record in the detail table. numberOfLinks specifies    }
{ how many fields from the detail table are being linked which is the   }
{ number of fields to use in the search.                                }

  retVal := TCursor.searchIndex(detailRecord, pxSearchFirst, numberOfLinks);

  if retVal = PXSUCCESS then
    findFirstLinkedRecord := True
  else
    findFirstLinkedRecord := False;

end;
```

```
(************************************************************************
*
* TYPE: DCursor
*
* METHOD: sync
*
* DESCRIPTION: This will make a copy of the record in the master table's
*              genericRec buffer and try to find records in the detail
*              table with the same linked field values. If found,
*              firstRecordInScope is set to this record number; otherwise,
*              it is set to zero. If successful, the DCursor will be
*              positioned on the first record in the scope.
*
*************************************************************************)
function DCursor.sync : Retcode;

begin

  if debug then
    writeln('DCursor.sync: Enter');
```

7-6 Continued.

```
{ Cursor must be open.                                                        }

  if not isOpen  then
  begin
    lastError := PXERR_CURSORNOTOPEN;
    sync := lastError;
    exit;
  end;

{ Make a copy of the current master record.                                   }

  masterHandle^.genericRec^.copyTo(masterRecord);
  if (masterHandle^.lastError <> PXSUCCESS) then
  begin
    lastError := masterHandle^.lastError;
    sync := lastError;
    exit;
  end;

if theLinkType <> NONE then
begin

{ Check to see if linked fields in the master have changed.                   }

  if firstRecordInScope <> 0 then
  begin
    TCursor.gotoRec(firstRecordInScope);
    if lastError <> PXSUCCESS then
    begin
      sync := lastError;
      exit
    end;

  { Update the record buffer with the record.                                 }

    TCursor.getRecord(detailRecord);
    if lastError <> PXSUCCESS then
    begin
      sync := lastError;
      exit;
    end;

    if (not didMasterChange(detailRecord)) then
    begin
      sync := PXSUCCESS;
      curStatus := atRecord;
```

```
      exit
    end
  end;

{ There is no scope yet or the master record has changed.         }
{ Find a record that matches the master table's current record.   }

  if debug then
    writeln('DCursor.sync: Finding first record');

  if findFirstLinkedRecord then
  begin

  { Found the record. Save its current record number and point the  }
  { cursor to the record.                                           }

    firstRecordInScope := TCursor.getCurRecNum;
    if lastError <> PXSUCCESS then
    begin
      sync := lastError;
        exit
      end;

      TCursor.gotoRec(firstRecordInScope);
      curStatus := atRecord;

    end
    else
    begin
    { No matching linked record was found. }                        }

      firstRecordInScope := 0;
      gotoBegin;
      sync := PXERR_EMPTYRESTRICTEDVIEW;
      exit;
    end
  end

  else
  begin

{ No link, so whole table is the scope. }                          }

    firstRecordInScope := 1;
    gotoBegin;

  end;
```

```
    sync := PXSUCCESS;

  if debug then
    writeln('DCursor.sync: Exit PXSUCCESS, firstRecordInScope: ',
      firstRecordInScope);

end;




{ Initialization.                                                    }
begin

end.
```

8
Query processing and the Engine

As with maintaining referential integrity, neither the Engine nor the Database framework provide any objects for querying a table. To overcome this, we are providing a query object that allows you to execute simple, single table queries on Paradox tables using the Paradox Engine. If you already are programming with Borland's Database Framework, then you can include this object with other applications that you already might have developed. After we explore the object itself, we will demonstrate how to incorporate its querying capabilities into our application.

We compose each simple query for this application using one or more restrictions that filter records in a table to arrive at a satisfactory answer. For example, we might have a table of employees and each employee record contains the name, age, and salary of the employee. A valid restriction would be all employees who earn more than $60,000. A query can contain more than one restriction. For example, two restrictions might specify employees who make more than $50,000 and who are over 35 years of age. To test the validity of a record within a query, the record must satisfy all restrictions.

Application programs will be able to:

- Create a query object for a table.
- Add a restriction to the query.
- Delete all restrictions from the query.
- Execute the entire query, placing the query result into a specified table.
- Execute the query by retrieving one record at a time. (Note: Our application will not use this feature.)
- Restart the query using the new or same restrictions. (Note: Our application will not use this feature.)

More formally, a query can be specified as follows:

```
<query> ::= <restriction>[,<restriction>].
<restriction> ::= <field id> <operator> <constant>
<field id> ::= int
<operator> ::= {Eq ¦ NotEq ¦ Lt ¦ Le ¦ Gt ¦ Ge}
<constant> ::= {short ¦ double ¦ string}
```

Paradox's *ASK* system, a feature of the interactive Paradox environment, allows a user to query a table using wildcard operators to accomplish search for patterns of alphanumeric strings. It also includes an operator called *LIKE* that will find inexact matches and retrieve information from records that are similar to, but not necessarily the same as, a particular value. Our query system does not handle patterns within restrictions nor does it handle the *LIKE* operator. For these two additions, we would need two procedures, one to check a string against a pattern and another to check to see if two values are *like* each other. As in Paradox, this query object does not query BLOB or Memo fields because the Engine also does not support such searches.

Optimizing a query

In high-level query languages, such as QBE or the Paradox *ASK* Query-by-Example (QBE) system, queries are stated nonprocedurally. There, queries represent *which* records are to be retrieved, not *how* the records are to be retrieved. The query processor within the QBE or Paradox *ASK* database system itself creates a query plan specifying *how* the records are to be accessed to satisfy the intended query. The plan specifies how each referenced table is to be accessed (i.e., by primary index, secondary index, or sequentially) and in which order to access tables in a multi-table query. The processor's Query Optimization module tries to choose the most efficient plan because there might be several query plans that satisfy any query.

Most database tables are not kept in main memory, so any query plan can initiate numerous disk accesses to transfer the pages of a table between the disk and the CPU. Because each of these pages is 4096 bytes, disk access time, already extremely slow compared to memory access time (about 100,000 times slower), usually takes the most time in a query. Therefore, most query optimization systems try to choose a query plan that uses the fewest disk I/O's.

For example, using a table of employees with a social security field as the keyed field of the table, a query wants to find the name of the employee with social security number 123-45-6789. If we let the table consist of, say, 100 pages, the query plan scanning the entire table to search for 123-45-6789 might have to perform 100 disk accesses.

In the Paradox system, because the social security number can be a keyed field in a table, there must exist a primary index for that table. The database also is sorted by social security number. The primary index is a sorted list of keys where each key is the first key on each page in the main database table. Rather than scan an entire table, the query plan can search for the key in the primary index closest to the key the query is asking for. Because the primary index is much smaller than the main table and because the index is also sorted, the search might initiate only one or two disk accesses. Once the primary index is accessed, the page number with 123-45-6789 is found and accessed. Thus, the total number of disk accesses is 2 or 3, rather than 100. Because 100 is much greater than 3, the time difference would be high. It is the job of the query optimizer to perform the query by choosing to access the primary index rather than scan the main table.

Because the query processing module within our application only works with single tables, the query optimizer's job is not too difficult. It does not have to worry about the order of table accesses, only how the table is to be accessed.

Paradox has three major methods for accessing a record within a table: sequential scanning of the table, access via a primary index, and access via a secondary index. Based upon the restrictions given to the query system, the optimizer decides which of these three methods to use. The algorithm for determining the method follows:

1. If there exists a restriction within the keyed field or within the field of the first field of a composite primary key and the restriction includes the = operator, then the primary index is used.

2. If there exists a restriction within a field with a secondary index or first field of a composite secondary key and the restriction includes the = operator, then the secondary index is used.

3. If there exists a restriction within the keyed field or within the field of the first field of a composite primary key and the restriction includes the > or >= operator, then the primary index is used to find the first key in the range and a sequential scan is used because the table is sorted.

4. If there exists a restriction within the keyed field or within the field of the first field of a composite primary key and the restriction includes the = operator, the specifier within the restriction is a pattern, and the pattern begins with a nonpattern character (@ or ..), then the primary index is used to find the first possible key in the range and a sequential scan is used.

5. If there are no restrictions satisfying the previous criteria, a sequential scan is performed.

For sake of brevity, our query system will only implement methods 1, 2, 3, and 5 because these four methods encompass all of the possible ways of accessing Paradox tables. Also, note that, if a restriction with a > or >= operator uses a field upon which a secondary index has been entered, the algorithm does not choose the secondary index. When accessing a secondary index by key, the secondary index points to the record in the main table with that key that then must be accessed. Because the records in the main table can be sorted quite differently from the keys in the secondary index, every keyed access from the secondary index might cause a disk access to retrieve the record in the main table. If many keys in the secondary index satisfy the restriction, many disk accesses may have to be performed. In most cases it is cheaper in disk access terms to scan the main table sequentially.

The query object types described

The **TQuery** object type will allow queries to be specified for Paradox tables. The **Restriction** object type allows us to define the restrictions for a query. Applications will have access to the PXQUERY.PAS file for compiling. A **TQuery** will create an instance for each query performed. Unless otherwise stated, members have public access.

The interface segment of the **PXQuery** unit includes several sets of constants beyond error codes to allow us to define the operators we need for building the restrictions for a query, or define four ways of optimizing the access to a table. Additionally, we define two records: one, **PField-Value**, handles the various types of values we might encounter in a Paradox table; the other, **FieldInfo**, stores the information about each field in the table being queried and is used especially to assist with managing the type and structure of a table's index.

The fields and object types for a query

The following sections describe the various field and object types that can be used in a query.

Fields

FieldInfo This **record** is used to store information about each field in the table being queried.

```
PFieldInfo = ^fieldInfo;
fieldInfo = record
{Pointer to the Engine's TFieldDesc object. }
      fieldDescription : PFieldDesc
{ The restrictions kept as a list in a  }
{ TCollection object. }
      restrictions : RestrictionList;
```

```
{ This number defines the type and number }
{ of an index for the field being queried. }
    indexId : Integer;
```

PFieldValue This **record** is used to store the value within a Paradox field. Paradox stores values as either a string of characters, a double, short, or date type. This **record** defines a record type for these possibilities, which we can use as a restriction for a query. This record defines a new type and can be used like any object type, meaning that the "new" operator can be used, etc.

```
PFieldValue = ^fieldValue;
fieldValue = record
    shortValue : ShortInt;
    dateValue : DateRec;
    doubleValue : Double;
    stringValue : string;
```

The object types

Restriction **Restriction** is an object type that describes the restrictions that the query uses to find records that satisfy the given restrictions. When we declare this object, we also declare that the restrictions are to be stored in our **TCollection** object type, *RestrictionList*. Additionally, **Restriction**'s fields define the value that a field must satisfy and the kind of relational operator used to restrict a query.

Fields

rvalue   rvalue : PFieldValue   **public**

Keeps track of the value that a field must have to satisfy a restriction. This field points to the **fieldValue** record that redefines the various types of values within a Paradox table for our use.

roperator   roperator : opType   **public**

Specifies the relational operator that is being used here. The constants defined by *opType* include the operators shown in TABLE 8-1.

Table 8-1   The constants defined by
***opType* include the following operators.**

Constant	Meaning
OP_EQ	Equal to
OP_NOT_EQ	Not equal to
OP_LT	Less than
OP_LE	Less than or equal to
OP_GT	Greater than
OP_GE	Greater than or equal to

Constructor

Init   constructor Init(theOp : opType; theValue : PFieldValue);

This constructor creates a **Restriction** object according to the values set in *theOp* and *theValue*. The argument *theOp* uses the constants defined in *opType* (see above) and the record *fieldValue*.

TQuery The **TQuery** object type is the main object for querying a table. For such a query to happen, the object needs to open a particular table in a database, then lock the table so that no one else can write to the table during the query. The query is performed using a list of restrictions. Whenever the query successfully matches a restriction, it places the output as a record in a new table for later use or simply returns each record to the user. While this querying object performs single table queries only, you can add more than one restriction to the query. Our user interface allows a user to build a QBE type query for each table in the database.

Fields

theDatabase   the Database : PDatabase   **private**

Points to an opened database. This is passed as an argument.

table   table : String;   **private**

The name of the table to be queried.

numFields   numFields : Integer;   **private**

The number of fields in a table.

numKeyFields   numKeyFields : Integer;   **private**

The number of keyed fields in a table.

tableDescription   tableDescription : PTableDesc;   **private**

Pointer to a description of the fields in a table. This is returned from the Engine function *getDescVector*.

cursor   cursor : PCursor   **private**

Pointer to a **TCursor** object open on a table that allows us to navigate a table.

outputRecord   outputRecord : PRecord;   **private**

Pointer to a record that is passed back via **TQuery.getNextRecord**. This record is appended to the answer table created for each query when *executeAndSave* is called. From this answer table, we can display the results of the query.

optimized   optimized : Boolean;   **private**

Set TRUE if this query has been optimized; otherwise set to FALSE.

fieldList   fieldList : FieldInfoList;   **private**

Specifies a collection of field information structures for the table being queried. There is one structure for each field. This list is a collection of pointers using the **TCollection** object.

locked   locked : Boolean;   **private**

TRUE if the table being queried is locked; otherwise, FALSE.

theAccessMethod   theAccessMethod : accessMethod;   **private**

The private procedure *optimize* chooses the method for accessing a table. *theAccessMethod* is that method.

The constants defining an *accessMethod*, PRIMARY_SCAN, PRIMARY_MATCH, SECONDARY_MATCH, and SCAN, define the following types of accesses to a table during a query:

- PRIMARY_MATCH represents access by keyed lookup using the primary index of the table.
- PRIMARY_SCAN is used when a low and/or high primary key is known.
- SECONDARY_MATCH represents access by keyed lookup using a secondary index of the table.
- SCAN represents access by the main database table in sequential order.

accessField   accessField : FIELDNUMBER;   **private**

The *optimize* procedure defines the FIELDNUMBER of the field used to search the table. The field must be the first field in the primary index, a secondary index, or a composite index.

exactKey   exactKey : PFieldValue;   **private**
highKey   highKey : PFieldValue;   **private**
lowKey   lowKey : PFieldValue;   **private**

If *exactKey* is non-NULL, then we use that key to access a primary or secondary index. Keys can be either ASCII strings, short, double, or dates. *highKey* specifies the highest value a record can have within the field defined by *accessField*; and *lowKey* specifies the lowest value a record can have in the field defined by *accessField*. *lowKey* can be set if the > or >= operators are used in a query; similarly, *highKey* can be set if the < or <= operators are used. These fields are used to optimize a query's search of a table.

Constructor and destructor

Init   constructor Init(db: PDatabase; TableName : String; lockMode : TQLockMode);

This constructor creates a **TQuery** object and opens the specified Paradox table using one of the lock modes defined for this object with **TQLockMode**. **TQLockMode** allows you to set write lock (*TQ_WRITE_LOCK*) or no lock (*TQ_NO_LOCK*) types of locks on the table. We have defined a no lock type of lock because the Engine's **PXLockMode** does not have a constant defined for a no lock situation. If you lock the table during a query, no data will change during your query. If you do not lock the table, then the query might not reflect the latest data; however, the query also will not tie up the table, blocking access to it during a query process. This allows you to set the critical level of a query.

Done   destructor Done;

Closes the query by removing the query's restrictions, field descriptors returned from the table, and any field values if they were non-NULL. Disposes of the table's cursor and releases any lock on the table.

Public methods

addRestrictionChar procedure addRestrictionChar(fieldName : PChar; operator : opType; strp : PChar);

This procedure adds a restriction to a query. The first argument, *field-Name*, specifies the field name to be queried; the second, *opType*, the relational operator; and the third, *strp*, is the null-terminated string that specifies the value to be compared. Patterns to be searched are entered by passing a pointer to the appropriate type whether it be *short*, *double*, or *string*.

This procedure is for fields whose Paradox data type is either date or string. **Nil** values for the input pointers are considered to be a restriction that the field be blank.

This function is overloaded so that it will accept the date string and data types. Dates are entered as strings and converted into **DateRec** records using the **TQuery** private member *ParseDate*. As in a Paradox query, BLOBs and memo fields are not supported within these field restrictions.

addRestrictionShort procedure addRestrictionShort(fieldName : PChar; operator : opType; shortp : PShortInt);

This procedure adds a restriction to a query. The first argument, *fieldName*, specifies the field name to be queried; the second, *opType*, the relational operator; and the third, *shortp*, is the pointer to a short integer that specifies the value to be compared.

This procedure is for fields whose Paradox data type is of a **short** type. **Nil** values for the input pointers are considered to be a restriction that the field be blank.

addRestrictionDouble procedure addRestrictionDouble(fieldName : PChar; operator : opType; doublep : PDouble);

This procedure adds a restriction to a query. The first argument, *field-Name*, specifies the field name to be queried; the second, *opType*, the relational operator; and the third, *doublep*, is the pointer to a double that specifies the value to be compared.

This procedure is for fields whose Paradox data type is of a **double** type. **Nil** values for the input pointers are considered to be a restriction that the field be blank.

removeRestrictions procedure removeRestrictions;

This method removes the restrictions from a query but keeps the query open. Because it does not close the cursor open on the table, this method implicitly resets the query. Without any restrictions, the query is no longer optimized.

executeAndSave function executeAndSave(newTable : String); Retcode;

This function executes the query and places any output from the query in a table specified by the input string *NewTable*.

getNextRecord function getNextRecord : PRecord;

This function returns the next record that satisfies the restrictions for a query. If no record is found, **Nil** is returned.

Private methods

findSecondaryIndexes procedure findSecondaryIndexes;

This method finds the secondary indexes that might exist for a table so that we can use them, if they exist, as a part of our optimization design. This method uses the DOS **findfirst** and **findnext** commands to look for these Paradox index files, then checks to see if the index is up-to-date. Nonmaintained indexes are not updated, so they might be out of date.

checkRestriction function checkRestriction(fieldName : PChar; operator : opType; rtype : restrictionType) : PFieldInfo;

This function checks a given restriction to determine its validity. It checks to see if the database is open, if the field exists within the table to be queried, if the operator is a valid one, and if the data type of the field matches the restriction's data type and returns a pointer to this a *fieldInfo* object. This function is used as part of the *addRestriction...* routines to validate the restriction.

optimize procedure optimize;

This procedure is used to set the type of access method for a query. It is guided by the type of index available for a table as well as the restrictions entered by the user, then selects the optimum method for accessing that table.

canUsePrimary procedure canUsePrimary;

Aiming to optimize a query, this procedure decides if a primary index can be used for searching records.

canUseSecondary procedure canUseSecondary;

Aiming to optimize a query, this procedure decides if a secondary index can be used to search records.

updateHiKey procedure updateHiKey(restrictionp : PRestriction; ftype : PXFieldType);

The field *highKey* delimits the last or highest key in the table that we need to check. The function *updateHiKey* updates the value based on a restriction. It derives this restriction using a pointer to the **Restriction** object that defines the value that a field must have to satisfy a restriction as well as relational operators such as less than, less than or equal to, and so on. This method also uses the Engine's **PXFieldType** enumerated type to specify a valid field type.

updateLowKey procedure updateLowKey(restrictionp : PRestriction; ftype : PXField Type);

The field *lowKey* delimits the first key in the table that can be valid. The function *updateLowKey* updates the value based on a restriction in the same manner as *updateHiKey*.

ParseDate   procedure ParseDate (date : PChar; var drecord : DateRec);

Parses a date as a string into a *Daterec* record. *Daterec* is the default Date record used in converting dates between internal Paradox and *mm/dd/yyyy* or similar formats. Because the actual storage order is reversed to year/month/day sequence, *Daterec* can be cast as a **Longint**, allowing dates to be compared using > and <.

compareDates   function compareDates(var date1 : DateRec;var date2 : DateRec) : opType;

This function compares two dates.

lookupField   function lookupField(fieldName : PChar) : PFieldInfo;

Given a field name, *lookupField* returns a pointer to its information structure *PFieldInfo*.

getFirstRecord   procedure getFirstRecord;

This function, *getFirstRecord*, finds the first possible record in the table being queried that could possibly pass the restrictions for a particular query.

stuffValue   procedure stuffValue(value : PFieldValue);

Stuffs a *fieldValue* into the cursor's generic record so that the record can be used to search for matching records in the table being queried.

validate   function validate : Boolean;

The *validate* routine checks to see if the restrictions involved in the query are all satisfied for the particular record. Returns TRUE if all the restrictions are satisfied; otherwise, it returns FALSE.

compareFieldValue   function compareFieldValue (fieldNum : FIELDNUMBER; value : PFieldValue) : opType;

This function compares the value in a field within the cursor's record against a given value from the query's restrictions.

compareOp   function compareOp(op1 : opType; op2 : opType) : Boolean;

This function compares two operator types (*opType*) for compatibility so that a list of restrictions composes a possible query. The function *compareField-Value* returns whether or not the value in the restriction is greater than, less than, or equal to the value in the field, then calls this function, *compareOp*, which compares the operator returned by *compareFieldValue* with the operators in the restriction to decide if the restriction is a valid match that meets the criteria of a query restriction.

The code for these query objects is found in the file PXQUERY.PAS, which is shown later in FIG. 8-10.

Integrating the query objects and the user interface

With the query objects fully defined and implemented, we now can incorporate it into the application in the normal fashion. We begin be adding a

Windows resource to our POS.RES file that will allow us to build the restrictions for a query. To compose a restriction, we need the following elements: the name of the table to be queried, the fields from that table, a relational operator, and a value to compare with those in the field. We also will need a way of storing a list of these restrictions should a user want to put together a query that quizzes more than one field to satisfy the query's request. Finally, we'll need a way to display the answers to a query.

The first element, the table's name, we simply specify as a choice from the Tools main menu bar option. Once we have done this, we can create two dialog boxes for the remaining elements: one to build a query, the other to display the results. The query building dialog box shown in FIG. 8-1 introduces an interesting use of the combo box control that stuffs the names of the fields for a table into the selection list. The Windows resource for the answers to a query also is a dialog box as shown in FIG. 8-2. Creating them mirrors techniques that already were discussed in the chapter on using the Resource Workshop, so we won't repeat the how-to here, except to note that you will need to remember the control ID constants that each of these dialog boxes assign to the various controls.

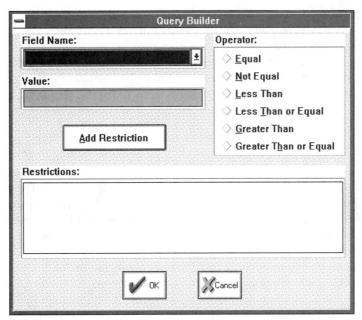

8-1 The query builder dialog box for this application.

Once we have created the menu, we bind the commands to it as expected in our code for the menu's commands as shown in FIG. 8-3. This method's routines are similar for all of our menu bar selections and each includes a call to the *doQuery* method (see FIG. 8-4) to perform a routine that opens the table that we need and itself enables us to build the query.

8-2 The dialog box for viewing the answers that satisfy a query.

The remaining code for example 2 in FIG. 8-3 calls the dialog box that displays the query's answer table so that a user can see the results of the query.

Because our query object performs only simple, single table queries, we need open only one table at a time. Not only does *doQuery* perform this, it also calls the query builder's dialog box so that we can assemble the list of restrictions for a query, execute the query and save any result in an answer table.

Assembling a query for the TQuery object

While the query builder window is not as baroque as those for a Sale operation, we're pretty sure that there's some interesting moments ahead for you as you explore its combo box, input line, and radio buttons. This window allows you to build a list of restrictions for a query using point and click techniques. Sure, you've seen these all before, especially if you're an admirer of the Sale windows. Here's where we use all of those hard won coding techniques in yet another way, one that returns us to the efficiency of coding for a Windows resource.

The query builder

To assemble a query properly, we need three elements for each restriction:

- Field name
- Operator
- Value to match

8-3 These two code excerpts from TMDIPOS.PAS demonstrate how to bind objects to a menu command (Example 1) and implement a method for responding to the menu selection (Example 2).

EXAMPLE 1.

```
{ Procedures to query tables. }

    procedure QueryCustomers(var Msg: TMessage);
      virtual cm_First + id_Query_customers;

    procedure QueryInventory(var Msg: TMessage);
      virtual cm_First + id_Query_Inventory;

    procedure QuerySales(var Msg: TMessage);
      virtual cm_First + id_Query_sales;

    procedure QueryItems(var Msg: TMessage);
      virtual cm_First + id_Query_Items;
```

EXAMPLE 2.

```
**********************************************************************
* CLASS:         TMDIPosWindow
*
* MEMBER:        QueryCustomers
*
* DESCRIPTION:   This function queries the customer table.
**********************************************************************)
procedure TMDIPosWindow.QueryCustomers(var Msg: TMessage);
var
  answerDlg: PCustQueryDialog;
  answerCursor: TCursor;
begin

  if doQuery(CUSTOMER_DB_NAME) then
  begin

{ Open up the ANSWER table. }

    answerCursor.InitAndOpen(getDatabase, ANSWER_DB_NAME, 0, FALSE);
      if(ERROR(answerCursor.lastError, 'opening the answer table') <>
PXSUCCESS) then
      exit;

    answerDlg := new(PCustQueryDialog, Init(@Self, @answerCursor));
```

```
    Application^.ExecDialog(answerDlg);

    answerCursor.Close;
    answerCursor.done;
  end;
end;
```

8-4 This excerpt from TMDIPOS.PAS shows how to write the generic **doQuery** method, which queries a defined table using the restrictions a user has placed on the query.

```
(**********************************************************************
* TYPE:          TMDIPosWindow
*
* METHOD:        doQuery
*
* DESCRIPTION:   This function performs the query.
**********************************************************************)
function TMDIPosWindow.doQuery(tableName: String): Boolean;
var
  queryDlg: PDialog;
  tablesCursor: PCursor;
  theQuery:     TQuery;
begin

{ Construct the query object. }

  theQuery.Init(getDatabase, tableName, TQ_WRITE_LOCK);

{ Did it construct correctly? }
  if(ERROR(theQuery.lastError, 'Creating the query') <> PXSUCCESS) then
  begin

{ No? Then abort the function. }

    theQuery.Done;
    doQuery := FALSE;
    exit;
  end;

{ Open the table. }

  tablesCursor := new(PCursor, InitAndOpen(getDatabase, tableName, 0, True));

{ If open failed, then exit the function. }

  if(ERROR(tablesCursor^.lastError, 'opening table') <> PXSUCCESS) then
  begin
```

```
    doQuery := FALSE;
    exit;
  end;

  queryDlg := new(PQueryBuilder, Init(@Self, tablesCursor, @theQuery));

  if(Application^.ExecDialog(queryDlg) = IDOK) then
  begin

{ Execute the query }

    ERROR(theQuery.executeAndSave(ANSWER_DB_NAME), 'Executing the query');

  end;

{ Call the query's destructor. }

  theQuery.Done;

{ Close the table. }

  tablesCursor^.close;
  dispose(tablesCursor, Done);

  doQuery := TRUE;
end;
```

The combo box contains the field names from whatever table that we open and makes the focused view in that box the first element of a query restriction. The radio buttons offer the options for the various operators to be added to the field name. Finally, a user can enter the value to be matched in this query restriction using an input line. All three sources of information are gathered together and added to a list box of restrictions that we then will pass to the query object for processing. Figure 8-5 lists the illustrative code from the TQBUILD.PAS to show how we build the window for assembling query restrictions.

The constructor for the query builder overrides **TDialog**, adding arguments that point to a cursor open on a table and a query for that table. The code for the constructor shown in FIG. 8-5 demonstrates how to relate the windows resources with the necessary control objects for a combo box, radio buttons, and an edit control. You should note that the routine also points to the open cursor and the query restrictions we are assembling.

There are several methods that this object employs to put together the restrictions for the query object to process when the user clicks the Ok in this dialog box that calls the *doQuery* method itself. The following sections outline their use and the code for them.

8-5 This excerpt from TQBUILD.PAS presents the constructor for the query builder object **TQuery-Builder** that establishes the relationship between the controls in the windows resources and the control objects.

```
(*******************************************************************
* TYPE:         TQueryBuilder
*
* METHOD:       Init     (Constructor)
*
* DESCRIPTION:  Creates an object of this type.
*
*******************************************************************)
constructor TQueryBuilder.Init(AParent: PWindowsObject; ACursor: PCursor;
       AQuery: PQuery);
begin

{ Call constructor of the base class. }

   inherited Init(AParent, 'QUERY_BUILDER');

{ Remember the cursor. }

   tablesCursor := ACursor;

{ Remember the query. }

  theQuery := AQuery;

{ Construct the field name's combo box. }

   fieldNames := new(PComboBox, InitResource(@Self, id_field_names, 26));

{ Construct the restrictions' list box. }

   restrictions := new(PListBox, InitResource(@Self, id_restrictions));

{ Construct the value's edit box. }

   value := new(PEdit, InitResource(@Self, id_values, 255));

{ Construct the objects for the operators. }

   isEqual := new(PRadioButton, InitResource(@Self, id_equal));
   isNotEqual := new(PRadioButton, InitResource(@Self, id_notequal));
   isLess := new(PRadioButton, InitResource(@Self, id_less));
   isLessOrEqual := new(PRadioButton, InitResource(@Self, id_lessorequal));
   isGreater := new(PRadioButton, InitResource(@Self, id_greater));
   isGreaterOrEqual := new(PRadioButton, InitResource(@Self,
   id_greaterorequal));

end;
```

SetupWindow The *SetupWindow* method, shown in FIG. 8-6, loads the combo box with the names of the fields from the table open for this query. To do so, we construct a **TFieldDesc** object and loop through it to read in the field names as a list of strings for the combo box using **TListBox**'s *AddString* method. When we complete this, we dispose of the **TFieldDesc** object appropriately.

8-6 This *SetupWindow* method, excerpted from TQBUILD.PAS, shows how to load a combo box with the names of a table's fields.

```
(*********************************************************************
* TYPE:          TQueryBuilder
*
* METHOD:        SetupWindow
*
* DESCRIPTION:   This procedure is called so the dialog can initialize
*                        its state before it is shown to the user.
*
*********************************************************************)
procedure TQueryBuilder.SetupWindow;
var
  fieldCount: Integer;
  curRec: PRecord;
  desc: TFieldDesc;
  asChar: array[0..26] of char;
begin

{ Construct a TFIeldDesc object. }

  desc.Init;

{ Call the base class. }

  inherited SetupWindow;

{ Get the generic record. }

  curRec := tablesCursor^.genericRec;

{ Load the combo box with the field names from the table }

  for fieldCount := 1 to curRec^.getFieldCount do
  begin
    curRec^.getFieldDesc(fieldCount, @desc);
    strPCopy(asChar, desc.fldName);
    fieldNames^.addString(asChar);
  end;

  desc.Done;
end;
```

IDAdd The procedure shown in FIG. 8-7 gathers and adds the necessary elements of a query—field name, operator, and value—to the restriction list box and adds each restriction to the collection of restrictions that we will pass to the **TQuery** object for processing.

8-7 This *IDAdd* method, excerpted from TQBUILD.PAS, shows how to assemble the restrictions for a query.

```
(*********************************************************************
* TYPE:          TQueryBuilder
*
* METHOD:        IDAdd
*
* DESCRIPTION:   This procedure adds a restriction to the query.
*
*********************************************************************)
procedure TQueryBuilder.IDAdd(var Msg: TMessage);
var
  restString: array [0..300] of char;
  aField: array [0..25] of char;
  anOp: pchar;
  aValue: array [0..255] of char;
  queryOp: opType;
begin

{ Get the field name. }

  if( fieldNames^.getSelString(aField, 26) <= 0) then
  begin
    messageBox(Hwindow, 'You must select a field name', 'Error',
        MB_ICONHAND or MB_OK);
    exit;
  end;

{ Get the operator. }

  if(isEqual^.getCheck = bf_checked) then
  begin
    queryOp := OP_EQ;
    anOP := '=';
    isEqual^.Toggle;
  end
  else if(isNotEqual^.getCheck = bf_checked) then
  begin
    queryOp := OP_NOT_EQ;
    anOP := '<>';
    isNotEqual^.Toggle;
  end
```

```
  else if(isLess^.getCheck = bf_checked) then
  begin
    queryOp := OP_LT;
    anOP := '<';
    isLess^.Toggle;
  end
  else if(isLessOrEqual^.getCheck = bf_checked) then
  begin
    queryOp := OP_LE;
    anOP := '<=';
    isLessOREqual^.Toggle;
  end
  else if(isGreater^.getCheck = bf_checked) then
  begin
    queryOp := OP_GT;
    anOP := '>';
    isGreater^.Toggle;
  end
  else if(isGreaterOrEqual^.getCheck = bf_checked) then
  begin
    queryOp := OP_GE;
    anOP := '>=';
    isGreaterOrEqual^.Toggle;
  end
  else
  begin
    messageBox(Hwindow, 'You must select an operator', 'Error',
        MB_ICONHAND or MB_OK);
    exit;
  end;

  fieldNames^.SetSelIndex(-1);

{ Get the value. }

  if(value^.getText(aValue, 255) = 0) then
    strCopy(aValue, '<BLANK>');

    value^.setText('');

{ Now create the restriction and place it in the list box. }

  strCopy(restString,aField);
  strCat(restString,'    ');
  strCat(restString, anOp);
  strCat(restString, '    ');
  strCat(restString, aValue);
```

```
{ Add the restriction to the TQueryClass restriction list. }

  if(addRestrictionToQuery(aField, queryOp, aValue) = TRUE) then
    restrictions^.addString(restString)
  else
  messageBox(HWindow, 'The value does not match the field''s type.',
    'Can not add restriction', mb_ok or mb_icon information);

end;
```

addRestrictionToQuery As part of the process of assembling the restrictions and placing them in the restriction list box, we also pass the restrictions to the query object itself using this procedure, which is listed in FIG. 8-8. In order that we do this correctly, we ensure that the restriction is passed using the correct *addRestriction* method for the various data types in the table.

8-8 This *addRestrictionToQuery* method, excerpted from TQBUILD.PAS, adds a restriction to the list of restrictions for a query.

```
(*********************************************************************
* CLASS:        TQueryBuilder
*
* MEMBER:       addRestrictionToQuery
*
* DESCRIPTION:  This function adds the restriction to the query's
*       restriction list.  If the restriction could not be added, then the
*       function will return FALSE.
*
*********************************************************************)
function TQueryBuilder.addRestrictionToQuery(fieldName: PChar;
                       queryOp: opType; aValue: PChar): Boolean;
var
  fieldType: PXFieldType;
  fieldSubtype: PXFieldSubtype;
  fieldLen: Integer;
  pToShort: PShortInt;
  pToDouble: PDouble;
  pToChar: PChar;
  aShort: ShortInt;
  aDouble: Double;
  code: integer;
  fldNumber: FIELDNUMBER;
  nameAsString: string;
begin

{ Get the field's data type. }
```

```
  nameAsString := strPas(fieldName);
  fldNumber := tablesCursor^.genericRec^.getFieldNumber(nameAsString);

  if(ERROR(tablesCursor^.genericRec^.getFieldType(fldNumber, fieldType,
      fieldSubtype, fieldLen), 'Getting field type') = PXSUCCESS) then
  begin

{ Depending on the field type, we must call different    }
{ addRestriction functions.                              }

{ a short field }
    if(FieldType = fldShort) then
    begin
      if(aValue[0] = '') then pToShort := nil
      else
    begin
      Val(aValue, aShort, code);
        if (code <> 0) then
        begin
          addRestrictionToQuery := FALSE;
          exit;
        end;
      pToShort := @aShort;
    end;
    theQuery^.addRestrictionShort( fieldName, queryOp, pToShort);
  end

{ Is it a double type field? }

      else if(fieldType = fldDouble) then
      begin
        if(aValue[0] = '') then pToDouble := nil
        else
      begin
        Val(aValue, aDouble, code);
          if (code <> 0) then
          begin
            addRestrictionToQuery := FALSE;
            exit;
          end;
          pToDouble := @aDouble;
      end;
        theQuery^.addRestrictionDouble( fieldName, queryOp, pToDouble);
      end
      else
      begin
```

```
{ a char, date, or BLOb type field. }

        if(aValue[0] = '') then pToChar := nil
        else pToChar := aValue;
        theQuery^.addRestrictionChar( fieldName, queryOp, pToChar);
    end;
  end;
  AddRestrictionToQuery := TRUE;
end;
```

Having assembled the collection of restrictions for a query, the *do-Query* procedure's routine continues by calling **TQuery**'s *executeAndSave* method to perform the query and save the results in an answer table which is displayed using the appropriate dialog box.

The dialog boxes for displaying the results of a query use Windows resources to display the fields of a table and add scrolling buttons to allow a user to scroll through the results. The Resource Workshop provides us with the usual way of creating this dialog box, and the code for each creates the proper control objects and associates them with the fields in the answer table. Because each query builds an answer table that mimics the table descriptors of the table being queried, these dialog boxes contain the edit controls for displaying the data using a generic record. The units and other identifying names for these dialogs are listed in TABLE 8-2.

Table 8-2   The units and other identifying names for the dialogs.

Table Queried	Unit	Object Type	Source code file
INVENTORY	TInvQry	TInvQueryDialog	TINVQRY.PAS
CUSTOMER	TCstQry	TCustQueryDialog	TCSTQRY.PAS
SALE	TSaleQry	TSaleQueryDialog	TSALEQRY.PAS
SALES ITEMS	TSItmQry	TSaleItemQueryDialog	TSITMQRY.PAS

The code listed in FIG. 8-9 demonstrates how to accomplish the Customer answer table's dialog box. The others listed in this chapter follow the same principles. This dialog box is pointed to by **TMDIPosWindows**'s *QueryCustomers* method and displays the results of a query in a dialog window.

In this application, you will note that, while we create a query table, ANSWER.DB, for each query, we also delete the table each time before actually writing the results of any new query. The query processor will produce an error if the table exists. Using the techniques that we've demonstrated in this application, it is possible to create a dialog box that will prompt users for a table name for each query, should they want to save the information. Both the interactive Paradox or PAL can work with these answer tables

8-9 An excerpt from TCSTQRY.PAS, the module that constructs a dialog box for a query and associates it with the answer table for a query on a particular table, here the CUSTOMER table.

```
(******************************************************************
* OBJECT:       TCustQueryDialog
*
* INHERITS:     TCursorDialog
*
* DESCRIPTION:  This is an implementation of a cursor dialog defined in
*               TCursorDialog.
******************************************************************)
  PCustQueryDialog = ^TCustQueryDialog;
  TCustQueryDialog = object(TCursorDialog)

{ A constructor for the class. }

    constructor Init(AParent: PWindowsObject; ACursor: PCursor);

{ Set up the dialog when it comes up.  For this dialog, we want to load }
{ the field values from the record buffer.                             }

    procedure SetupWindow; virtual;


end; { TCustQueryDialog }


{ This section contains the code necessary to make the object work. }

implementation

(******************************************************************
* TYPE:         TCustQueryDialog
*
* METHOD:       Init     (Constructor)
*
* DESCRIPTION:  Creates an object of this type.
*
******************************************************************)
constructor TCustQueryDialog.Init(AParent: PWindowsObject; ACursor: PCursor);
var
  dummyPtr: PControl;
begin

{ Call constructor of the base class. }

  inherited Init(AParent, 'QUERY_CUST', ACursor);
```

8-9 Continued.

```
{ Associate a TFieldStatic with the customer Id on the dialog. }

  dummyPtr := new(PFieldStatic, InitResource(@Self, id_CustID,
    CUST_ID_LEN + 1, getCursor, CUSTOMER_CUSTOMER_ID));

{ Associate a TCurRecStatic with the current record number on the dialog. }

  dummyPtr := new(PCurRecStatic, InitResource(@Self, id_CurRec,
    getCursor));

{ Associate a TTotRecStatic with the total records on the dialog. }

  dummyPtr := new(PTotRecStatic, InitResource(@Self, id_TotRecs,
    getCursor));

{ Now create TFieldEdit boxes for the entry fields on the dialog. }

{ Last name }

  dummyPtr := new(PFieldEdit, InitResource(@Self, id_LastName,
    CUST_NAME_LEN + 1, getCursor, CUSTOMER_LAST_NAME));

{ First name }

  dummyPtr := new(PFieldEdit, InitResource(@Self, id_FirstName,
    CUST_NAME_LEN + 1, getCursor, CUSTOMER_FIRST_NAME));

{ Street }

  dummyPtr := new(PFieldEdit, InitResource(@Self, id_Address,
    STREET_LEN + 1, getCursor, CUSTOMER_ADDRESS));

{ City }

  dummyPtr := new(PFieldEdit, InitResource(@Self, id_City,
    CITY_LEN + 1, getCursor, CUSTOMER_CITY));

{ State }

  dummyPtr := new(PFieldEdit, InitResource(@Self, id_State,
    STATE_LEN + 1, getCursor, CUSTOMER_STATE));

{ ZIP }

  dummyPtr := new(PFieldEdit, InitResource(@Self, id_Zip,
    ZIP_LEN + 1, getCursor, CUSTOMER_ZIP));
```

```
{ Telephone }

  dummyPtr := new(PFieldEdit, InitResource(@Self, id_Telephone,
    TELEPHONE_LEN + 1, getCursor, CUSTOMER_TELEPHONE));

{ Up button }

  dummyPtr := new(PCursorButtonUp, InitResource(@Self, id_Prev,
    getCursor));

{ Down button }

  dummyPtr := new(PCursorButtonDown, InitResource(@Self, id_Next,
    getCursor));

{ First button }

  dummyPtr := new(PCursorButtonFirst, InitResource(@Self, id_Begin,
    getCursor));

{ Last button  }

  dummyPtr := new(PCursorButtonLast, InitResource(@Self, id_Last,
    getCursor));

end;

(************************************************************************
* TYPE:         TCustQueryDialog
*
* METHOD:       SetupWindow
*
* DESCRIPTION:  This procedure is called so the dialog can intialize
*               its state before it is shown to the user.
*
*************************************************************************)
procedure TCustQueryDialog.SetupWindow;
begin

{ Call the base class. }

  inherited SetupWindow;

{ Go to the first record if there is one. }

  getCursor^.gotoBegin;
  getCursor^.gotoNext;
```

```
getCursor^.getRecord(getCursor^.genericRec);
```

```
{ Tell the fields to load their values for the record buffer. }
```

```
  DisplayFields;
```

```
end;
```

should you want to do that. Finally, other third-party vendors offer you the chance to reach out to them for ways to handle reports developed from any of the tables that are in this application. Our implementation of the **TQuery** object is simply the first of many possibilities left for you to explore.

There you have it—all you need to complete a simple query on a single table. Figure 8-10 lists the complete code for the **TQuery** type object.

8-10 The complete code for the query object found in PXQUERY.PAS.

```
(************************************************************************
 *
 * UNIT: PXQuery        File: PXQUERY.PAS
 *
 * DESCRIPTION: This file defines an object type that allows you to perform
 *              simple, single table queries using the Paradox Engine.
 *
 *
 ************************************************************************)

unit PXquery;    { Unit name }

{$N+} { turn on 8087 mode }

interface

uses OOPXENG,
     PXOOPMSG,
     PxEngWin,
     STRINGS,
     WINCRT,
     Objects,
     WinDos;

{ Definitions of the Error Codes that can be returned by the TQuery       }
{ object.                                                                  }

const
  debug = False;
```

```
   PXERR_TQWRONGTYPE        = 701;
   PXERR_TQINVOPERATOR      = 702;
   PXERR_TQINVFIELDNAME     = 703;
   PXERR_TQINTERNALERROR    = 704;
   PXERR_TQDATABASENOTOPEN  = 705;
   PXERR_TQTABLENOTFOUND    = 706;
   PXERR_TQTABLEEXISTS      = 707;
   PXERR_TQINVDATE          = 708;

type

{ Pointer types not defined by Pascal.                          }

   PInteger = ^Integer;
   PDouble = ^Double;

{ Constants to define the operators allowed within restrictions: }
{ The like and not like operators are not supported.  To support }
{ those operators a phonetic function must be included which checks }
{ to see if two values are 'like' each other. OP_INVALID is used when }
{ errors occur.                                                 }

  opType = (OP_EQ, OP_NOT_EQ, OP_LT, OP_LE, OP_GT, OP_GE, OP_INVALID);

{ Constant to define the type of lock put on the table being queried. }
{ Allows flexibility by allowing the user to set a Write lock or no }
{ lock.  The reason for defining a new lock type is because the  }
{ internal PXLockMode enumeration does not have a constant defined }
{ for No Lock.                                                  }

  TQLockMode = (TQ_NO_LOCK, TQ_WRITE_LOCK);

{ The FieldInfoList holds a list of pointers to the individual  }
{ FieldInfo records.                                            }

   FieldInfoList = PCollection;

{ Constants defining the method of table access, PRIMARY_MATCH  }
{ represents access by keyed lookup using the primary index of the }
{ table.  PRIMARY_SCAN is used when a low and/or high primary key is }
{ known. SECONDARY_MATCH represents access by keyed lookup using a }
{ secondary index of the table.  SCAN represents access by the main }
{ database table in sequential order.                           }

  accessMethod = (PRIMARY_SCAN, PRIMARY_MATCH, SECONDARY_MATCH, SCAN);

{ A value within the Paradox system can be either a string of    }
```

8-10 Continued.

```
{ characters, a double, short, or date.  Define a record type for the     }
{ possibilities. This is the value that is used by a restriction.          }
{ This record defines a new type and can be used like any class            }
{ object, the 'new' operator can be used, etc.                             }

   PFieldValue = ^fieldValue;
   fieldValue = record
     shortValue  : Integer;
     dateValue   : DateRec;
     doubleValue : Double;
     stringValue : string;
   end;

{ Constants that define the type of value specified in the restriction.   }

   restrictionType = (RES_SHORT, RES_DOUBLE, RES_DATE, RES_STRING);

(*********************************************************************
*
* OBJECT TYPE: Restriction
*
* INHERITS: TObject
*
* DESCRIPTION:   This object describes a restriction that has been
*                placed on a field. The Query system finds the records
*                that satisfy the given restrictions. Since each restriction
*                is placed into a TCollection, the restriction object must
*                inherit the properties of a TObject defined in the Object
*                Windows Library (OWL).
*********************************************************************)

   PRestriction = ^Restriction;
   RestrictionList = PCollection;
   Restriction = object(TObject)
     { Public }
        rvalue : PfieldValue;   { The value that the field must     }
                                { have to satisfy the restriction.  }
        roperator : opType;     { Relational operator               }

        constructor Init(theOp : opType; theValue : PFieldValue);
        destructor Done; Virtual;

   end;

(*********************************************************************
* OBJECT TYPE: TFieldInfo
```

```
*
* INHERITS: TObject
*
* DESCRIPTION:  This object contains the information about each field
*               in table being queried. The object must inherit the TObject
*               properties since the object is used in a TCollection.
****************************************************************************)

  PFieldInfo = ^TFieldInfo;

  TFieldInfo = object (TObject)

{ Pointer to the field description which contains the name, length,     }
{ and type of the field. This is constructed and returned by the       }
{ Engine.                                                               }

    fieldDescription : PFieldDesc;

{ The restrictions are kept as a list.  We are using the TCollection    }
{ object class in Object Windows. See the BORLAND Object Windows        }
{ Programmer's Guide for more information.                              }

    restrictions : RestrictionList;

{ This number specifies the type and number of an index for this       }
{ field.  If indexId is 0, it means this field is the first field in    }
{ the primary index.  If the indexId is >0 and <FIRST_COMPOSITE_ID,     }
{ this field has a secondary index.  If indexId is greater than         }
{ FIRST_COMPOSITE_ID, this field is the first field in a composite      }
{ index with id indexId.  If indexId is NO_INDEX, this field has no     }
{ index.                                                                }

    indexId : Integer;

{ Destructor. It must be Virtual since it inherits the TObject object.   }

    Constructor Init;
    Destructor Done; Virtual;

  end;  { TFieldInfo }



(****************************************************************************
* OBJECT TYPE: TQuery
*
* INHERITS: None
```

8-10 Continued.
```
*
* DESCRIPTION:  This is the main interface object for querying tables.
******************************************************************)
  PQuery = ^TQuery;
  TQuery = object
{ Public                                                             }

{ Last error from TQuery member function.  This member is associated }
{ with all of the Database Framework objects.                        }

     lastError : Retcode;

{ Constructor which creates the TQuery object.  The parameters       }
{ specify an opened database and a table name within the database.   }
{ The lock mode defaults to a write lock which means no other process }
{ can write to the file while the query is opened.  The lock mode    }
{ means nothing when the Engine is opened in local mode (pxLocal).   }

     constructor Init(db: PDatabase; TableName : String;
         lockMode : TQLockMode);

{ Destructor to close up the query and release the memory used.      }

     destructor Done;

{ There are 3 functions which add a restriction to the query.  The   }
{ first argument specifies the field name for the restriction.  The  }
{ second argument specifies relational operator and the third        }
{ argument is the specifier.  The type of constant should match the  }
{ type of the field. First function is for fields of type string     }
{ and date.  Nil values for the input pointers are considered to     }
{ be a restriction that the field be blank.                    }

     procedure addRestrictionChar(fieldName : PChar; operator : opType;
       strp : PChar);
     procedure addRestrictionShort(fieldName : PChar;  operator : opType;
       shortp : PInteger);
     procedure addRestrictionDouble(fieldName : PChar; operator : opType;
       doublep : PDouble);

{ Removes the restrictions from the query, but keeps the query open. }
{ Implicitly resets the query.                                       }

     procedure removeRestrictions;
```

```
{ by the input string.                                                          }

      function executeAndSave(newTable : String): Retcode;

{ This function returns the next record from the table that satisfies            }
{ the restrictions.  If no record is found, Nil is returned.                     }

      function getNextRecord : PRecord;

   private

{ Pointer to opened database.  This is passed as an argument.                    }

      theDatabase : PDatabase;

{ Name of the table to be queried.                                              }

      table : String;


{ Number of fields and keyed fields in the table.                               }

      numFields : Integer;
      numKeyFields : Integer;

{ Pointer to a description of the fields in the table.  This is                 }
{ returned from the Engine function getDescVector.                              }

      tableDescription : PTableDesc;

{ Cursor used to move through the table being queried.                          }

      cursor : PCursor;

{ A record that is passed back via TQuery.getNextRecord.                        }

      outputRecord : PRecord;

{ True, if the query has been optimized; False, otherwise.                      }

      optimized : Boolean;

{ Collection of the field information structures for the table.  One            }
{ structure for each field. The list is actually a collection of               }
{ pointers using the TCollection object.                                       }
```

8-10 Continued.

```
    fieldList : FieldInfoList;

{ TRUE, if the query file is locked.                                      }

    locked : Boolean;

{ The optimizer chooses the method of accessing the table. If            }
{ exactKey is non-NULL, then we use that key to access an index.         }
{ Keys can be either ascii, shorts, doubles, or dates. theAccessField    }
{ specifies the field to use to access the table.  The field must be     }
{ the first field in the primary index, a secondary index, or a          }
{ composite index.  highKey specifies the highest value a record can     }
{ have within field accessField. highKey can be set if the < or <=       }
{ operators are used.  lowKey is set accordingly.                        }

    theAccessMethod : accessMethod;
    accessField : FIELDNUMBER;
    exactKey : PFieldValue;
    highKey  : PFieldValue;
    lowKey   : PFieldValue;


                        { PRIVATE Methods }

{ Finds the secondary indexes that exist for the given table.            }

    procedure findSecondaryIndexes;

{ Checks a given restriction to determine its validity.                  }

    function checkRestriction(fieldName : PChar; operator : opType;
                    rtype : restrictionType) : PFieldInfo;

{ Optimizes the query and sets the access_method and access_key          }
{ variables which specify how the table is to be accessed.               }

    procedure optimize;

{ Decides if the primary index can be used for searching records.        }
{ If index can be used, accessKey points to the key to use.              }

    procedure canUsePrimary;

{ Decides if a secondary index can be used for searching records.        }

    procedure canUseSecondary;
```

```
{ highKey determines the last key in the table that we need to        }
{ check.  The function updateHiKey updates the value based on a        }
{ restriction.                                                         }

    procedure updateHiKey(restrictionp : PRestriction; ftype : PXFieldType);

{ lowKey determines the first key in the table that may be valid.      }
{ The function updateLowKey updates the value based on a restriction.  }

    procedure updateLowKey(restrictionp : PRestriction; ftype : PXFieldType);

{ Parses a date as a string into a date record.                        }

    procedure ParseDate (date : PChar; var drecord : DateRec);

{ Compares 2 dates.                                                    }

    function compareDates(var date1 : DateRec;var date2 : DateRec) : opType;

{ Given a field name, returns a pointer to its information structure.  }
{ (PfieldInfo).                                                        }

    function lookupField(fieldName : PChar) : PFieldInfo;

{ This function finds the first possible record in the database to check }
{ that could possibly pass the restrictions.                           }

    procedure getFirstRecord;

{ Stuffs a fieldValue into the cursor's generic record so the record can }
{ be used to search for matching database records.                     }

    procedure stuffValue(value : PFieldValue);

{ The validate routine checks to see if the restrictions involved in   }
{ the query are all satisfied.                                         }

    function validate : Boolean;

{ Compares a field within the cursor's record against a given value.   }

    function compareFieldValue (fieldNum : FIELDNUMBER; value : PFieldValue)
        : opType;

{ Compares 2 operator types (opType) for compatibility.                }

    function compareOp(op1 : opType; op2 : opType) : Boolean;
```

```
  end;    { TQuery Object }

implementation

{ Definitions of symbolic constants.                                      }

const
  FIRST_COMPOSITE_ID = 255;
  NO_INDEX = -1;
  PRIMARY_INDEX = 0;

{ Simple Counter type                                                     }

type
  Counter = Integer;

(*********************************************************************
 *
 * CLASS: Restriction
 *
 * MEMBER: Init
 *
 * DESCRIPTION: Initializes the Restriction object with the given
 *              parameters.
 *
 *********************************************************************)
constructor Restriction.Init(theOp : opType; theValue : PFieldValue);
begin
  rvalue := theValue;
  roperator := theOp;
end;

(*********************************************************************
 *
 * CLASS: Restriction
 *
 * MEMBER: Done
 *
 * DESCRIPTION: Destroys the restriction object.
 *
 *********************************************************************)
destructor Restriction.Done;
begin
if debug then writeln('Restriction: Done');
if rvalue <> Nil then
  dispose (rvalue)
```

```
end;

(*********************************************************************
*
* CLASS: TFieldInfo
*
* MEMBER: Init
*
* DESCRIPTION: Initializes the field information object.
*
**********************************************************************)
constructor TFieldInfo.Init;
begin

{ The restrictions for each field are kept as a collection of         }
{ pointers to restriction objects. Initialize the collection here.    }
{ Init takes 2 parameters, the number of pointers to start with and   }
{ the number of pointers to add when the collection is full.          }

  restrictions := New(PCollection, Init(1,1));

{ The fieldDescription object is returned by the Engine when getDescVector}
{ is called.                                                          }

  fieldDescription := Nil;

end;


(*********************************************************************
*
* CLASS: TFieldInfo
*
* MEMBER: Done
*
* DESCRIPTION: Destroys the field information object.
*
**********************************************************************)
destructor TFieldInfo.Done;
begin
if debug then writeln('TFieldInfo.Done: Enter');

  if FieldDescription <> Nil then
    dispose (fieldDescription);

  if restrictions <> Nil then
    dispose (restrictions, Done);
```

8-10 Continued.

```
if debug then writeln('TFieldInfo.Done: Exit');

end;

(*********************************************************************
*
* CLASS: TQuery
*
* MEMBER: Init
*
* DESCRIPTION: Initializes the query for a table.
*
*********************************************************************)
constructor TQuery.Init
  (db : PDatabase; { Pointer to an opened database }
   tableName : String; { Table to be queried}
   lockMode : TQLockMode); { Lock Mode }

var
  rc : Retcode;
  i : Counter;
  info : PFieldInfo;

begin

{ Get a description of the fields in the table.  If the table does   }
{ not exist, an error will be returned.                              }

  tableDescription := db^.getDescVector(tableName);

{ If pointer is not nil, call was successful.                        }

  if tableDescription <> Nil then
  begin

  { Set data members.                                                }

    theDatabase    := db;
    exactKey       := nil;
    highKey        := nil;
    lowKey         := nil;
    optimized      := FALSE;
    table          := tableName;
    locked         := FALSE;
    lastError      := PXSUCCESS;
    cursor         := nil;
    fieldList      := nil;
```

```
{ Use TDatabase member function to get the number of fields in the      }
{ table and the number of fields in the primary key (if any).           }

  numFields := theDatabase^.getFieldCount(tableName);
  if (theDatabase^.lastError <> PXSUCCESS) then
  begin
    lastError := theDatabase^.lastError;
    exit;
  end;
  numKeyFields := theDatabase^.getNumPFields(tableName);
  if (theDatabase^.lastError <> PXSUCCESS) then
  begin
    lastError :=theDatabase^.lastError;
    exit;
  end;

{ Get the cursor that will be used to retrieve records. It will be      }
{ opened in the first call to getNextRecord.                            }

  cursor := New(PCursor, Init);

{ Allocate a FieldInfo array for each field in the table.  The          }
{ fieldList structure will contain pointers to the information          }
{ about the fields in the table and the restrictions entered for        }
{ each field.                                                           }

  fieldList := New(PCollection, Init(numFields, 1));

  for i := 0 to numFields - 1 do
  begin

  { Allocate the field information object.  Note that the Init          }
  { constructor MUST be called since a PFieldInfo object inherits the   }
  { TObject object.                                                     }

    info := New(PFieldInfo, Init);

  { Save the field descriptor returned from the getDescVector call      }
  { above. The tableDescription object is a TCollection of              }
  { field descriptor pointers.                                          }

    info^.fieldDescription := tableDescription^.At(i);

  { If this is the first field within the table and there is a          }
  { primary index for the table, then set the indexId member to         }
  { PRIMARY.  Otherwise, set it to NO_INDEX and then check for          }
  { secondary indexes.                                                  }
```

8-10 Continued.

```
      if (i = 0) and (numKeyFields > 0) then
            info^.indexId := PRIMARY_INDEX
      else
            info^.indexId := NO_INDEX;

   { Add the information structure to the field information list    }
   { using the TCollection functions.                              }

      fieldList^.AtInsert(i, info);

   end; { For each Field }

   { Find out which secondary indexes exist for the table.         }

   findSecondaryIndexes;


   { Lock the file if the user specified it.  We can't tell if the }
   { database has been opened in the local or networked environment. }
   { If the lock mode specified is TQ_WRITE_LOCK, try locking the   }
   { file. If the return code is PXERR_NETNOTINIT, assume that the  }
   { database was opened locally and do not return an error.        }

                      -              -

   if lockMode = TQ_WRITE_LOCK then
   begin
     rc := theDatabase^.lockNetFile(table, pxWL);
     if (rc <> PXERR_NONETINIT) and (rc <> PXSUCCESS) then
            lastError := rc
     else
            locked := TRUE
   end

 end

{ Table does not exist, tableDescription was Nil.                  }

 else
 begin
   theDatabase := nil;
   lastError := PXERR_TQTABLENOTFOUND;
 end;

end;
```

```
(**********************************************************************
*
*
* OBJECT TYPE: TQuery
*
* MEMBER: Done (Destructor)
*
* DESCRIPTION: Finishes a simple query for a table and deletes
*              the appropriate data structures.
***********************************************************************)

destructor TQuery.Done;
var
  i : Counter;
  info : PFieldInfo;

begin
if debug then writeln('TQuery.Done: Enter');

{ If database is Non-NULL, the query has been successfully initialized.  }

  if theDatabase <> Nil then
  begin

  { Delete the descriptors returned from the engine.                     }
    if debug then writeln('deleting table description');
      dispose (tableDescription);

  { Delete the field information structure.  This will also delete each  }
  { information structure in the fieldList collection.                   }

    if fieldList <> Nil then
    begin
      if debug then writeln('freeing fieldList');
      fieldList^.FreeAll;
    end;

  { Delete the cursor if it was opened.                                  }

    if cursor <> Nil then
    begin
      if debug then writeln('deleting cursor');
      dispose (cursor, Done);
    end;

  { Delete the fieldValues if they were non-null.                        }
```

```
     if exactKey <> Nil then
       dispose (exactKey);

     if lowKey <> Nil then
       dispose (lowKey);

     if highKey <> Nil then
       dispose (highKey);

   { If the file was locked, then unlock it.  It can only be locked        }
   { in write mode.                                                         }

     if locked then
       theDatabase^.unlockNetFile(table, pxWL);

   end;
   if debug then writeln('TQuery.Done: Exit');

end;


{***********************************************************************
*
*
* OBJECT TYPE: TQuery
*
* MEMBER: ParseDate
*
* DESCRIPTION: Translates a string as a date to a DateRec record.
*
***********************************************************************}

procedure TQuery.ParseDate (date : PChar; var drecord : DateRec);

var
  bad : Integer;
  slash : PChar;
  P : PChar;

begin
{ Initialization                                                         }

  slash := '/';
  lastError := PXERR_TQINVDATE;
```

```
{ Look for first / in the date. This terminates the month.                   }

    P := StrPos(date, slash);
    if P <> Nil then
    begin

    { Change the / to a Null and then translate the string to an integer    }
    { value.                                                                 }

        date[P-date] := #0;
        val(date, drecord.month, bad);

    { Bad is set to 0 if string was successfully translated.                 }

        if bad <> 0 then
            exit;

    { Update the pointer so it is 1 char past the /.                         }

        date := date + (P - date + 1);

    { Now Look for next / which should delimit the day. And then process     }
    { as above.                                                              }
        P := StrPos(date, slash);
        if P <> Nil then
        begin
            date[P-date] := #0;
            val (date, drecord.day, bad);
            if bad <> 0 then
                exit;

            date := date + (P - date + 1);
            val (date, drecord.year, bad);
            if bad <> 0 then
                exit;

        end
    end;

{ So far, so good. Check to make sure its a valid day, month and year.       }
{ We don't check for real valid dates, i.e. 2/31/93 is valid here but        }
{ not a real valid date.                                                     }

    if (drecord.day < 1) or (drecord.day > 31) or
        (drecord.month < 1) or (drecord.month > 12) or
        (drecord.year < 0) or (drecord.year > 9999) then
```

```
    exit;

{ If the year value is >0 and <100 add 1900 to the year.  This code must  }
{ change at the year 2000.                                                 }

  if (drecord.year > 0) and (drecord.year < 100) then
    drecord.year := drecord.year + 1900;

{ If we got here, it's a valid date.                                       }

  lastError := PXSUCCESS;

end;


(**************************************************************************
*
* OBJECT TYPE: TQuery
*
* MEMBER: addRestrictionShort
*
* DESCRIPTION: Adds a restriction to the query involving a short integer
*              value.
*
**************************************************************************)
procedure TQuery.addRestrictionShort
  (fieldName : PChar; operator : opType; shortp : Pinteger);

var
{ A pointer to the restriction object created                             }

  restriction : PRestriction;

{ A pointer to the field information structure                            }

  fptr : PFieldInfo;

{ A restriction value is saved as a fieldValue structure                  }

  value : PFieldValue;

begin

{ Check the validity of the restriction.  If the restriction is valid,    }
{ a pointer to a fieldInfo structure is returned.  The structure contains }
{ the information for the particular field.  The third parameter           }
```

```
{ specifies the data type or the input restriction.  A NULL pointer is    }
{ returned if the restriction is not valid                                }

    fptr := checkRestriction(fieldName, operator, RES_SHORT);

    if fptr <> Nil then
    begin
    { Save the short value in the fieldValue structure. If it is NULL, then }
    { the restriction is searching for BLANKS                               }

      if (shortp = Nil) then
        value := Nil
      else
      begin
        value := New(PFieldValue);
        value^.shortValue := shortp^
      end;

    { Create the new restriction object.                                    }

      restriction := New(PRestriction, Init(operator, value));

    { Save the restriction in the restriction list using the Insert        }
    { function.  It is a built-in function within the TCollection object    }
    { library                                                               }

      (fptr^.restrictions)^.Insert(restriction);

      lastError := PXSUCCESS;
    end;

    { If check restriction failed, it set lastError to the error.           }

end;


(************************************************************************
*
* OBJECT TYPE: TQuery
*
* MEMBER: addRestrictionDouble
*
* DESCRIPTION: Adds a restriction to the query involving a double value.
*
************************************************************************)
procedure TQuery.addRestrictionDouble
    (fieldName : PChar; operator : opType; doublep : PDouble);
```

8-10 Continued.

```
var
  restriction : PRestriction;
  fptr : PFieldInfo;
  value : PFieldValue;

begin

{ See addRestrictionShort for a description of the code.  This works the  }
{ same way.                                                               }

  fptr := checkRestriction(fieldName, operator, RES_DOUBLE);
  if fptr <> Nil then
  begin
    if doublep = Nil then
      value := Nil
    else
    begin
      value := New(PfieldValue);
      value^.doubleValue := doublep^;
    end;

    restriction := New(PRestriction, Init(operator, value));
    (fptr^.restrictions)^.Insert(restriction);
    lastError := PXSUCCESS;
  end

end;

(****************************************************************************
 *
 * OBJECT TYPE: TQuery
 *
 * MEMBER: addRestrictionChar
 *
 * DESCRIPTION: Adds a restriction to the query involving a alphanumeric
 *              or date value.
 *
 ****************************************************************************)

procedure TQuery.addRestrictionChar
  (fieldName : PChar; operator : opType; strp : PChar);

var
  restriction : PRestriction;
  fptr : PfieldInfo;
  value : PFieldValue;
```

```
      day, month, year : Integer;

begin

{ See addRestrictionShort for a description of the code.  This works the  }
{ same way.                                                               }

   fptr := checkRestriction(fieldName, operator, RES_STRING);
   if fptr <> Nil then
   begin
      if strp = Nil then
         value := Nil
      else
      begin
         value := New(PFieldValue);

      { If the field data type is alphanumeric, save the value as a string. }

         if fptr^.fieldDescription^.fldType = fldChar then
         begin

         { Save the string in a fieldValue structure                       }

            value^.stringValue := strPas(strp);
            restriction := New(PRestriction, Init(operator, value));
            (fptr^.restrictions)^.Insert(restriction)


         end
         { If the field is a date field, then attempt to translate the date  }
         { into a DateRec record.                                            }

         else if fptr^.fieldDescription^.fldType = fldDate then
         begin

         { Parse the input string for 'month/day/year'.  Place the parsed    }
         { values into the appropriate values.                               }

            ParseDate(strp, value^.dateValue);
            if lastError <> PXSUCCESS then
               exit;

         { Create a restriction and save it.                               }

            restriction := New(PRestriction, Init(operator, value));
                  (fptr^.restrictions)^.Insert(restriction);
         end
```

```
        { If the else is taken, then the field type is wrong.                }
        else
        begin
                lastError := PXERR_TQINTERNALERROR;
                if debug then writeln('addRestrictionChar: Internal error');
        end
      end
    end
end;

(***********************************************************************
 *
 * OBJECT TYPE: TQuery
 *
 * FUNCTION: checkRestriction
 *
 * DESCRIPTION: Checks the validity of an input restriction.
 *
 ***********************************************************************)
function TQuery.checkRestriction
   (fieldName : PChar; operator : opType; rtype : restrictionType)
 : PFieldInfo;

var

  info : PFieldInfo;    { Pointer to the field information structure      }

begin

{ Make sure the database is opened.                                       }

  if theDatabase = Nil then
  begin
    lastError := PXERR_TQDATABASENOTOPEN;
    checkRestriction := Nil;
    exit;
  end;

{ Make sure that the field exists and retrieve its field number within    }
{ the table.  Use the lookupField function which returns Nil if the field }
{ name was not found.                                                     }

  info := lookupField(fieldName);
  if info = Nil then
  begin
    lastError := PXERR_TQINVFIELDNAME;
```

```
        checkRestriction := Nil;
        exit
    end;

{ Make sure that the operator is valid.                                      }

    if (operator <> OP_EQ) and (operator <> OP_NOT_EQ) and
       (operator <> OP_LT) and (operator <> OP_LE) and
       (operator <> OP_GT) and (operator <> OP_GE) then
    begin
        lastError := PXERR_TQINVOPERATOR;
        checkRestriction := Nil;
        exit;
    end;

{ Make sure that the type of the field matches the type of specifier.  If }
{ the field is a date field, it must match a string input.                }

    case rtype of
        RES_DOUBLE:
            if (info^.fieldDescription^.fldType <> fldDouble) then
            begin
                lastError := PXERR_TQWRONGTYPE;
                info := Nil;
            end;

        RES_SHORT:
            if (info^.fieldDescription^.fldType <> fldShort) then
            begin
                lastError := PXERR_TQWRONGTYPE;
                info := Nil;
            end;

        RES_STRING:
            if (info^.fieldDescription^.fldType <> fldDate) and
               (info^.fieldDescription^.fldType <> fldChar) then
            begin
                lastError := PXERR_TQWRONGTYPE;
                info := Nil;
            end;

        else
        begin
            lastError := PXERR_TQINTERNALERROR;
            info := Nil
        end
    end;
```

```
{ Return Value is pointer to the information structure                    }

  checkRestriction := info

end;

(***********************************************************************
*
* OBJECT TYPE: TQuery
*
* MEMBER: removeRestrictions
*
* DESCRIPTION: Removes the restrictions from the query.
*
***********************************************************************)

procedure TQuery.removeRestrictions;

var
  i : Counter;
  info : PFieldInfo;
begin

if debug then writeln('removeRestrictions: Enter: nfields: ', numFields);

{ For each field, if it has a restriction, then delete them using the    }
{ TCollection function FreeAll.  This will dispose of each restriction in }
{ the collection of restrictions.                                         }

  for i := 0 to numFields - 1 do
  begin

    info := FieldList^.At(i);
    if info^.restrictions <> Nil then
    begin
      if debug then writeln('removeRestrictions: FreeAll field: ', i);
      info^.restrictions^.FreeAll;
    end
  end;

{ The query is no longer optimized since there are no restrictions.       }

  optimized := FALSE;

  lastError := PXSUCCESS;
if debug then writeln('removeRestrictions: Exit');
```

```
end;

(*********************************************************************
* OBJECT TYPE: TQuery
*
* MEMBER: getNextRecord
*
* DESCRIPTION: Gets the next valid record, if any.
*
*********************************************************************)
function TQuery.getNextRecord : PRecord;

var
   eof, validRec : Boolean;
   compare : opType;

begin
   eof := False;
   validRec := False;

{ If the query has not been optimized, then optimize it by getting the   }
{ first record that satisfies the query.                                  }

   if not optimized then
     getFirstRecord;

{ On entrance to this function, the cursor is pointing to the next        }
{ record that has not yet been checked.  On first entry the cursor        }
{ points to the first record found by the member function                 }
{ getFirstRecord.  Loop until a valid record is found, i.e., a record     }
{ that passes all restrictions, or the end of the file is reached. The    }
{ end of file can also be reached if a PRIMARY_SCAN is being done and     }
{ a record is reached that has a higher key than the variable highKey.    }

   while (not eof) and (not validRec) and (cursor^.lastError = PXSUCCESS) do
   begin

     { Copy the record the cursor is pointing to into the generic TRecord }
     { of the cursor.  This gives access to the record. If an error is     }
     { returned then go to the next iteration of the loop which will fail. }

       cursor^.getRecord(cursor^.genericRec);
       if cursor^.lastError <> PXSUCCESS then
         continue;

     { Check to see if the record is valid, i.e., passes all restrictions. }
     { TRUE is returned if the record is valid.                            }
```

Integrating the query objects and the user interface **289**

```
    validRec := validate;

{ If the record is not valid, then check to see if the end of file has  }
{ been reached or if no more records can possibly satisfy the           }
{ restrictions.                                                         }

  if not validRec then
  begin
    case theAccessMethod of

    { Search is for an exact match using a primary or secondary }
    { index.                                                    }

          PRIMARY_MATCH, SECONDARY_MATCH:
      begin

      { If the key in the record of the cursor is higher than }
      { the key in exactKey, there are no more records to search.       }

        compare := compareFieldValue(accessField, exactKey);
        if compare = OP_GT then
              eof := True;
      end;

    { Scanning the table in record order.  If the table has         }
    { a primary key, then the table is sorted by the key.           }

    PRIMARY_SCAN:
    begin

    { If the key in the record of the cursor is higher than the key }
    { in highKey, there are no more records to search. }

      if highKey <> Nil then
      begin
        compare := compareFieldValue(accessField, highKey);
        if compare = OP_GT then
          eof := TRUE
      end
    end;

    { Scanning the table in record order with no restrictions.  No code  }
    { to execute, but good programming to take care of all cases.        }

      SCAN:
```

```
      begin
      end;


             { Always add a default case.  Good for debugging. }

      else
      begin
        cursor^.lastError := PXERR_TQINTERNALERROR;
        if debug then writeln('getNextRecord: internal error: bad access
method');
        eof := TRUE;
      end
    end
  end;

  { Move the cursor to the next record for the next iteration.          }

  if not eof then
    cursor^.gotoNext;
end;

{ If a valid record was found, return a pointer to the record. The      }
{ record is in the cursor. Otherwise, the end of file switch has been   }
{ set or the cursor could not be moved to the next record, so return a  }
{ Nil pointer.                                                          }

  if validRec then
    getNextRecord := cursor^.genericRec
  else
    getNextRecord := Nil;

end;

(*********************************************************************
*
* OBJECT TYPE: TQuery
*
* MEMBER: getFirstRecord
*
* DESCRIPTION:  This function moves the cursor to the first record that
*               could possibly satisfy all restrictions.
*
*********************************************************************)
procedure TQuery.getFirstRecord;
var
  info : PFieldInfo;
```

```
begin

{ If the query has not been optimized, then optimize it and open the    }
{ cursor to be used to retrieve records.                                 }

  if not optimized then
  begin
    optimize;
    optimized := True;

    { If the cursor has been opened, then close it.  It may have been    }
    { opened for a previous query.                                       }

    if cursor^.isOpen then
      cursor^.close;

    { Open the cursor based on the access method that was determined by  }
    { the optimization routine. accessField specifies the field to be    }
    { used, and its indexId is used to open the cursor.                  }

    info := fieldList^.At(accessField);
    cursor^.open(theDatabase, table, info^.indexId, False);

  end;
{ Find the record to start the scan.                                     }

if cursor^.lastError = PXSUCCESS then
begin

{ Based on the access method of the table, search for the first         }
{ record.  To search by key, we first stuff the key value into the       }
{ internal cursor's record buffer.  Then we pass the record buffer to    }
{ the search function.                                                   }

  case theAccessMethod of
    PRIMARY_MATCH:
    begin
    { Search for exact key match specified in exactKey. Only search      }
    { within the first field of the primary key since the restriction    }
    { specified is on the first field only.  There is no optimization     }
    { for multiple field primary keys. }

     stuffValue(exactKey);
     cursor^.searchIndex(cursor^.genericRec, pxSearchFirst, 1);
    end;
```

```
PRIMARY_SCAN:
begin
{ Position the cursor at the record closest to lowKey if it exists; }
{ otherwise, start at the first record in the file.                 }

        if lowKey <> Nil then
        begin
        stuffValue(lowKey);
        cursor^.searchIndex(cursor^.genericRec, pxClosestRecord, 1);
  { Return from searchIndex may be PXERR_RECNOTFOUND              }
  { which means an exact match wasn't found, but there           }
  { is a closest record greater than the given key               }

        if cursor^.lastError = PXERR_RECNOTFOUND then
           cursor^.lastError := PXSUCCESS;
        end
        else
        begin
  { Go to first record in file by using gotoBegin which          }
  { positions cursor BEFORE first record and gotoNext which      }
  { positions cursor ON first record.                            }

           cursor^.gotoBegin;
           cursor^.gotoNext;
        end
end;


SECONDARY_MATCH:
begin
{ If the index being searched is a non-composite index,          }
{ then look for an exact match.  If the index is a composite     }
{ index then the key being used to search is only a partial      }
{ key. Partial key means the key used to search is not the entire }
{ key.  In this case search for the closest record with the      }
{ partial key. The last param to searchIndex specifies that only 1 }
{ field is used.                                                 }

        stuffValue(exactKey);
  info := fieldList^.At(accessField);
        if (info^.indexId > FIRST_COMPOSITE_ID) then
        begin
        cursor^.searchIndex(cursor^.genericRec, pxClosestRecord, 1);

  { See above comment about PXERR_RECNOTFOUND.                   }

  if cursor^.lastError = PXERR_RECNOTFOUND then
```

```
            cursor^.lastError := PXSUCCESS;
        end
        else
        begin
          cursor^.searchIndex(cursor^.genericRec, pxSearchFirst, 1);
        end
      end;

      SCAN:
      begin
      { Go to first record.  See above comment.                    }

        cursor^.gotoBegin;
        cursor^.gotoNext;
      end
    end
  end

{ Cursor was not opened; and so, return an error.                  }

  else
  begin
    cursor^.genericRec := Nil;
  end;

  lastError := cursor^.lastError;
end;


{*******************************************************************
*
* OBJECT TYPE: TQuery
*
* MEMBER: stuffValue
*
* DESCRIPTION: Puts a value into the generic record so a keyed search can
*              be done.
*
*******************************************************************}
procedure TQuery.stuffValue  (value : PFieldValue);

var
  info : PFieldInfo;
  pdox_fld : FIELDNUMBER;

begin
```

```
{ Use the generic record in the cursor and use putXX to put the key      }
{ into the record.  It is done based on the field type of the field used }
{ in the access.  accessField specifies the index into the fieldList     }
{ Since fieldList is an array which starts at 0, the actual field number  }
{ is accessField+1. If the input value is Nil, then set the field        }
{ within the record to be blank by using the setNull function.           }

  pdox_fld := accessField + 1;

  if value = Nil then
    cursor^.genericRec^.setNull(pdox_fld)

  else
  begin
    info := fieldList^.At(accessField);
    case info^.fieldDescription^.fldType of
      fldShort : cursor^.genericRec^.putInteger(pdox_fld, value^.shortValue);
      fldDouble: cursor^.genericRec^.putDouble(pdox_fld, value^.doubleValue);
      fldChar:   cursor^.genericRec^.putString(pdox_fld, value^.stringValue);
      fldDate:   cursor^.genericRec^.putDate(pdox_fld, value^.dateValue);
       else
          cursor^.lastError := PXERR_TQINTERNALERROR;
    end
  end;
  lastError := cursor^.lastError;
end;


(***********************************************************************
 *
 * OBJECT TYPE: TQuery
 *
 * FUNCTION: optimize
 *
 * DESCRIPTION: Determines the method for retrieving records.
 *
 ***********************************************************************)
procedure TQuery.optimize;

begin
{ Initialize the variables used in optimization.                         }

  TheAccessMethod := SCAN;
  highKey := Nil;
  lowKey := Nil;

{ Determine if the primary index can be used.                            }
```

```
  canUsePrimary;

{ The variable accessMethod is set to PRIMARY_MATCH if a keyed lookup   }
{ can be used.  This is the best and cheapest way for performing the    }
{ query. It can also be set to PRIMARY_SCAN if there exists a low or     }
{ high key that can be scanned for.                                      }

  if theAccessMethod = PRIMARY_MATCH then
    exit;

{ Determine if a secondary index can be used.                           }

  canUseSecondary;

{ theAccessMethod is set to SECONDARY_MATCH if a keyed lookup can be     }
{ used, or it was set to PRIMARY_SCAN in canUsePrimary. Both of these    }
{ methods are cheaper than a sequential scan in terms of disk accesses.  }

  if (theAccessMethod = SECONDARY_MATCH) or (theAccessMethod = PRIMARY_SCAN)
then
    exit;

{ If neither method can be used, then a scan of the database is          }
{ performed.  The first field is used to open the table.                 }

  theAccessMethod := SCAN;
  accessField := 0;

end;

(*********************************************************************
 *
 * OBJECT TYPE: TQuery
 *
 * MEMBER: canUsePrimary
 *
 * DESCRIPTION: Determines if a primary index can be used
 *                to find the restricted records.
 *
 *********************************************************************)
procedure TQuery.canUsePrimary;

var
  restriction : PRestriction;
  exactMatch : Boolean;
  i : Counter;
```

```pascal
  info : PFieldInfo;

begin
{ Initialize.  Information needed is for the first field, i.e. = 0.        }

  info := FieldList^.At(0);
  exactMatch := False;

{ Number of keyed fields must be greater than 0 and there must be a        }
{ restriction on the first field.                                          }

  if (numKeyFields > 0) and (info^.restrictions^.Count > 0) then
  begin
{ The index id to open the table is 0 for the primary index.  See          }
{ TCursor::open.                                                            }

    accessField := 0;

{ The first field in the table must be keyed.  We see if there is an        }
{ Equals operator on the key. Even if the primary key is composed of        }
{ more than 1 field, we still can use the restriction within the            }
{ first field.                                                              }

{ Scan list of restrictions. If we find an OP_EQ operator, we are           }
{ finished.                                                                 }

    i := 0;
    while (i < info^.restrictions^.Count) and (not exactMatch) do
    begin

{ Get a pointer to the i'th restriction using the At member of             }
{ TCollection.                                                             }

      restriction := info^.restrictions^.At(i);

      case restriction^.roperator of

        OP_EQ:
        begin

{ Can use a keyed lookup for this restriction.                             }

          exactKey := restriction^.rvalue;
          theAccessMethod := PRIMARY_MATCH;
          exactMatch := TRUE;
        end;

        OP_LT, OP_LE:
```

```
      begin

      { Otherwise the operator is a range operator which can be used     }
      { to start or end a scan.                                          }

        theAccessMethod := PRIMARY_SCAN;
        updateHiKey(restriction, info^.fieldDescription^.fldType);
      end;

      OP_GT, OP_GE:
      begin
        theAccessMethod := PRIMARY_SCAN;
        updateLowKey(restriction, info^.fieldDescription^.fldType);
      end

    end; { Case }

    i := i + 1;    { Next restriction }

  end   { While }
 end
end;

(*************************************************************************
*
* OBJECT TYPE: TQuery
*
* MEMBER: canUseSecondary
*
* DESCRIPTION: Determines if a secondary index can be used
*              to find the restricted records.
*************************************************************************)
procedure TQuery.canUseSecondary;

var
  i, j : Counter;
  exactMatch : Boolean;
  restriction : PRestriction;
  info : PFieldInfo;

begin
  exactMatch := False;

{ Loop until we find an indexed field (non-primary) with an OP_EQ     }
{ restriction or until we run out of fields.                          }
```

```
   i := 0;
   while (not exactMatch) and (i < numFields) do
   begin

      info := FieldList^.At(i);


{ If this field has restrictions and has an index (indexId > 0), we      }
{ look to see if there is an OP_EQ operator.                             }


      if (info^.restrictions^.Count > 0) and (info^.indexId > 0) then
      begin

      { Loop for each restriction or until we get a match.               }

         j := 0;
         while (j < info^.restrictions^.Count) and (not exactMatch) do
         begin

            restriction := info^.restrictions^.At(j);

         { If the operator is OP_EQ, then we can do an exact match.       }

            if restriction^.roperator = OP_EQ then
            begin
               exactMatch := TRUE;

            { Save the information needed for the execution of the query.  }

               theAccessMethod := SECONDARY_MATCH;
               accessField := i;
               exactKey := restriction^.rvalue;



            end;

            j := j + 1;
         end
      end;

   { Increment the field iterator.                                       }
      i := i + 1;

   end
end;
```

8-10 Continued.

```
(*********************************************************************
*
* OBJECT TYPE: TQuery
*
* MEMBER: executeAndSave
*
* DESCRIPTION: Executes the entire query and saves the output in the
*              file specified.
*
*********************************************************************)
function TQuery.executeAndSave  (newTable : String) : Retcode;

var
  i : Counter;
  rc : Retcode;
  outputCursor : PCursor;    { Cursor used to fill output table }
  orecord : PRecord;         { Record used to find valid records }

begin

{ If the table already exists, delete it.                             }

  if theDatabase^.tableExists(newTable) then
  begin
    rc := theDatabase^.deleteTable(newTable);
    if rc <> PXSUCCESS then
    begin

    { Couldn't delete the table, so return an error.                  }

      lastError := rc;
      executeAndSave := rc;
      exit

    end
  end;

{ Lock the table before creating it.  This ensures that other queries or }
{ processes cannot create or update the file.  If the Engine started was }
{ not in Network mode=PxNet, this call will return PXERR_NONETINIT which }
{ is OK.  Any other error is returned to the user.  There is no direct   }
{ way to tell if the Engine was started in the network mode or local    }
{ mode.                                                                 }

  rc := theDatabase^.lockNetFile(newTable, pxFL);
  if (rc <> PXSUCCESS) and (rc <> PXERR NONETINIT) then
```

```
    begin
      lastError := rc;
      executeAndSave := rc;
      exit;
    end;

{ Create the table. The TDatabase member function createTable takes a    }
{ Table Descriptor as input. Simply use the Table Descriptor for the     }
{ table being queried since the output table contains all of its fields. }

    theDatabase^.createTable(newTable, tableDescription);
    if theDatabase^.lastError <> PXSUCCESS then
    begin
      lastError := theDatabase^.lastError;
      executeAndSave := lastError;
      exit;
    end;

{ Table was created.  Open it by opening a cursor for it in the default  }
{ mode.  Check any errors. InitAndOpen takes 4 parameters, the database, }
{ the name of the table, an index id (we use 0 since we are opening the  }
{ table through no index), and the last parameter specifies if every     }
{ change should be written to disk.  In this case, that would slow down   }
{ the query.                                                              }

   outputCursor := New(PCursor, InitAndOpen(theDatabase, newTable, 0, False));
    if outputCursor^.lastError <> PXSUCCESS then
    begin
      lastError := outputCursor^.lastError;
      executeAndSave := lastError;
      exit
    end;

{ Get the records from the original table.  Make sure the cursor used to }
{ retrieve the records is at the first record. As each record is         }
{ returned from getNextRecord, add it to the output table.               }

    orecord := getNextRecord;
    while orecord  <> Nil do
    begin

    { Copy the record retrieved into the cursor of the output table and  }
    { then add the record to the table.                                   }

      outputCursor^.genericRec^.copyFrom(orecord);

    { Always check for errors.                                            }
```

```
   if theDatabase^.lastError <> PXSUCCESS then
   begin
     lastError := theDatabase^.lastError;
     executeAndSave := lastError;
     exit;
   end;

 { Add the retrieved record to the output file.                          }

   outputCursor^.appendRec(outputCursor^.genericRec);
   if theDatabase^.lastError <> PXSUCCESS then
   begin
     lastError := theDatabase^.lastError;
     executeAndSave := lastError;
     exit
   end;
   orecord := getNextRecord;
       end;

{ Close the file by disposing of the cursor and using the TCursor        }
{ destructor.                                                            }

   Dispose (outputCursor, Done);

{ Unlock the file just loaded.  If the file is not on a network, this    }
{ function will have no effect.                                          }

   theDatabase^.unlockNetFile(newTable, pxFL);

   lastError := PXSUCCESS;
   executeAndSave := lastError;


end;


(************************************************************************
*
* OBJECT TYPE: TQuery
*
* MEMBER: updateHiKey
*
* DESCRIPTION: If input restriction value is less than
*              the high key, update the high key.
*
************************************************************************)
```

```
**********************************************************************)
procedure TQuery.updateHiKey
   (restrictionp : PRestriction; ftype : PXFieldType);

begin
{ If highKey has not been initialized, then just set input value to be  }
{ the highKey.                                                          }

   if highKey = Nil then
     highKey := restrictionp^.rvalue

{ Otherwise, do the comparison.                                         }

   else
   begin

   { Compare values in highKey and restriction based on the field type.  }

     case ftype of
       fldChar:
         begin

       { StrComp returns -1 if the first string is less than the second.  }

           if restrictionp^.rvalue^.stringValue < highKey^.stringValue then
             highKey := restrictionp^.rvalue;

         end;

       fldShort:
         if restrictionp^.rvalue^.shortValue < highKey^.shortValue then
           highKey := restrictionp^.rvalue;

       fldDouble:
         if restrictionp^.rvalue^.doubleValue < highKey^.doubleValue then
           highKey := restrictionp^.rvalue;

       fldDate:
       begin

       { compareDates returns -1 if the first date is less than the second.}

         if compareDates(restrictionp^.rvalue^.dateValue, highKey^.dateValue)
= OP_LT then
           highKey := restrictionp^.rvalue

       end
```

8-10 Continued.

```
      else
        lastError := PXERR_TQINTERNALERROR;

    end  { case of }
  end  { Comparison }
end;

(*************************************************************************
 *
 * OBJECT TYPE: TQuery
 *
 * MEMBER: updateLowKey
 *
 * DESCRIPTION: If input restriction value is greater than
 *              the low key, update the low key.
 *
 *************************************************************************)
procedure TQuery.updateLowKey
   (restrictionp : PRestriction; ftype : PXFieldType);

begin
  if lowKey = Nil then
    lowKey := restrictionp^.rvalue

  else
  begin

  { Compare values in lowKey and restriction based on the field type.    }

    case ftype of

      fldChar:
        if restrictionp^.rvalue^.stringValue > lowKey^.stringValue then
          lowKey := restrictionp^.rvalue;

      fldShort:
        if restrictionp^.rvalue^.shortValue > lowKey^.shortValue then
          lowKey := restrictionp^.rvalue;

      fldDouble:
        if restrictionp^.rvalue^.doubleValue > lowKey^.doubleValue then
          lowKey := restrictionp^.rvalue;

      fldDate:
      begin
        if compareDates(restrictionp^.rvalue^.dateValue,
```

```
                 highKey^.dateValue) = OP_GT then
             lowKey := restrictionp^.rvalue
        end

        else
          lastError := PXERR_TQINTERNALERROR;
      end { case of }
    end
  end
end;
```

```
(***********************************************************************
*
* OBJECT TYPE: TQuery
*
* MEMBER: findSecondaryIndexes
*
* DESCRIPTION: Finds the secondary indexes associated with the table. Uses
*              the DOS findfirst, and findnext commands to look for the
*              indexes.  There is no function within the Engine that does
*              this.
*
***********************************************************************)
procedure TQuery.findSecondaryIndexes;

var

  indexPath : array [0..fsPathName] of char;

{ Directories.  The table specified may point to another directory.        }

        tableAsPChar:  array [0..fsPathName] of char;
  tableDir      : array [0..fsDirectory] of char;
  tableName     : array [0..fsFileName] of char;
  tableExt      : array [0..fsExtension] of char;
  thisDir       : array [0..fsDirectory] of char;

  findResult    : TSearchRec;
  IndexId       : FieldNumber;        { Handle for index }
  fieldName     : String;
  fieldArray    : FieldNumberArray;   { List of field numbers in index }
  numIndexFields
                : Integer;
  sensitivity   : Boolean;
  rc            : Retcode;
  tempCursor    : PCursor;
```

8-10 Continued.
```
   info             : PFieldInfo;

begin

{ copy the String table name to a pchar type }

        strPCopy(tableAsPChar, table);

{ Split the Table name into its components in case the table is in    }
{ another directory.                                                  }

   FileSplit(tableAsPChar, tableDir, tableName, tableExt);

{ If table is another directory, then change to it for fast searching. }
{ First character of tableDir will not be the string terminator.       }

   if tableDir[0] = #0 then
   begin
     GetCurDir(thisDir, 0);    { 0 = Current Drive }
     SetCurDir(tableDir);

   { If it failed, then set error and get out.                        }

     if DosError <> 0 then
     begin
       lastError := PXERR_TQINTERNALERROR;
       exit
     end;
   end;

{ Secondary indexes have the file extension .Xzz where zz is the number }
{ of the index.  findfirst procedure finds the first file with name     }
{ name. First, copy the name of the table and then the extension.       }

   StrCopy(indexPath, tableName);
   StrCopy(indexPath, 'X*');

{ Loop until there are no more files with the .Xzz extension.         }

   findfirst(indexPath, $0, findResult);
   while DosError = 0 do
   begin

   { We need to get the information about the index.  There are two    }
   { routines to obtain this information, getCompKeyInfo and getSKeyInfo, }
   { but it turns out that getCompKeyInfo works for both types.        }
```

```
{ getSKeyInfo is really not needed.  findResult.Name contains the file }
{ name of the index.  numIndexFields, Sensitivity, FieldArray and       }
{ IndexId are all set by the call to getCompKeyInfo.                     }

   rc := theDatabase^.getCompKeyInfo(findResult.Name, fieldName,
               numIndexFields, sensitivity, fieldArray, indexId);

   if rc = 0 then
   begin
   { Get pointer to the information structure for the field. We          }
   { subtract 1 for the index into fieldList since collections start at  }
   { 0, but fields start at 1.                                           }

      info := fieldList^.At(fieldArray[1]-1);

   { An index exists.  We need to determine if the index is up-to-date.  }
   { Non-maintained indexes are not updated so they may be out-of-date.  }
   { To check the validity of the index try and open a cursor on the     }
   { index.                                                              }

      tempCursor := New (PCursor,
                      InitAndOpen(theDatabase, table, indexId, FALSE));
      if tempCursor^.lastError = PXSUCCESS then
      begin

      { Index is up-to-date, save its handle in the field information    }
      { list.                                                            }
             info^.indexId := indexId;
      end

      { Otherwise index is out-of-date.                                  }

      else
        info^.indexId := NO_INDEX;
   end;

{ Find the next DOS file that has the same extension as was set in       }
{ findfirst.                                                             }

   findNext(findResult)

end; { while }

{ Move back to original directory if need be.                           }

   if thisDir[0] <> #0 then
   begin
```

8-10 Continued.

```
    SetCurDir(thisDir);
    if DosError <> 0 then
    begin
      lastError := PXERR_TQINTERNALERROR;
      exit;
    end
  end;

  lastError := PXSUCCESS;

end;
(************************************************************************
*
* OBJECT TYPE: TQuery
*
* MEMBER: lookupField
*
* DESCRIPTION: Looks up the name of a field in the
*              field information list.
*
************************************************************************)
function TQuery.lookupField  (fieldName : PChar): PFieldInfo;

var
  i : Counter;
  info : PFieldInfo;
  fieldAsString : String;

begin

  info := Nil;

  fieldAsString := strPas(fieldName);

{ Loop for all the table's fields or until the field is found.            }

  i := 0;
  lookupField := Nil;
  while i < numFields do
  begin

  { The name of the field is pointed to by the 'fieldDescription' member. }

    info := FieldList^.At(i);
    if fieldAsString = info^.fieldDescription^.fldName then
    begin
```

```
    { Save return value and set the loop terminator.                    }

      lookupField := info;
      i := numFields;

    end;
    i := i + 1
  end
end;

(*********************************************************************
 *
 * OBJECT TYPE: TQuery
 *
 * MEMBER: compareDates
 *
 * DESCRIPTION: Compares 2 DateRec objects.
 *
 *********************************************************************)
function TQuery.compareDates
   (var date1 : DateRec; var date2 : DateRec) : opType;

begin

{ Since DateRecs are stored year/month/day, they can be compared as    }
{ LongInt's.                                                           }

  if LongInt(date1) < LongInt(date2) then
    compareDates := OP_LT
  else if LongInt(date1) = LongInt(date2) then
    compareDates := OP_EQ
  else
    compareDates := OP_GT;

end;

(*********************************************************************
 *
 * OBJECT TYPE: TQuery
 *
 * MEMBER: compareFieldValue
 *
 * DESCRIPTION: Compares a field within the cursor's record against a given
 *              value.
 *
 *********************************************************************)
function TQuery.compareFieldValue
```

```
  (fieldNum : FieldNumber; value : PFieldValue) : opType;

var
  answer  : opType;
  fnull   : Boolean;      { Dummy variable which is passed to getField}
  compare : Integer;
  info    : PFieldInfo;
  intval  : Integer;
  dval    : Double;
  strval  : String[MaxNameLen+1];
  dateval : DateRec;
  rc      : Retcode;

begin
{ Perform the comparison based on the type of the field. The type is    }
{ found within the field information structure.                         }
if debug then writeln('compareFieldValue: Enter: field: ', fieldNum);

  info := fieldList^.At(fieldNum);
  case info^.fieldDescription^.fldType of

  { Field is a SHORT, getField uses the INT16 data type.                }

    fldShort:
    begin

    { Use the record within the cursor and place the fields value into  }
    { sval.  fnull is set to TRUE if the field is blank.                }

      rc := cursor^.genericRec^.getInteger(fieldNum+1, intval, fnull);
      if rc = PXSUCCESS then
      begin

      { Check the value in the field against the value in the           }
      { restriction. If value is Nil, then check for BLANK.             }

        if value = Nil then
        begin
          if fnull then
            answer := OP_EQ
          else
            answer := OP_GT;
        end
        else if (intval < value^.shortValue) then
          answer := OP_LT
        else if (intval > value^.shortValue) then
```

```
        answer := OP_GT
      else
        answer := OP_EQ
    end

{ getInteger failed.                                                          }

    else
    begin
      lastError := cursor^.lastError;
      answer := OP_INVALID
    end
  end;

{ Field is a DOUBLE.                                                          }

  fldDouble:
    begin

{ Use the record within the cursor and place the field's  value into  }
{ dval.                                                                }

      rc := cursor^.genericRec^.getDouble(fieldNum+1, dval, fnull);
      if debug then writeln('compareFieldValue: double, field is: ', dval);
      if rc = PXSUCCESS then
      begin
        if value = Nil then
        begin
          if fnull then
            answer := OP_EQ
          else
            answer := OP_GT
        end
        else if dval < value^.doubleValue then
          answer := OP_LT
        else if dval > value^.doubleValue then
          answer := OP_GT
        else
          answer := OP_EQ
      end

{ getDouble failed. }
      else
      begin
        lastError := cursor^.lastError;
        answer := OP_INVALID
      end
```

8-10 Continued.
```
  end;

{ Field is a STRING. }

  fldChar:
  begin

    { Use the record within the cursor and place the field's value }
    { into strval. fnull is set to TRUE if the field is BLANK. }

    rc := cursor^.genericRec^.getField(fieldNum+1, @strval,
                         info^.fieldDescription^.fldLen+1, fnull);

     if rc = PXSUCCESS then
     begin

     { If value is Nil, check for BLANK field. }

      if value = Nil then
      begin
        if fnull then
           answer := OP_EQ
        else
           answer := OP_GT;
      end
      else
      begin

    { Compare field value to restriction value by StrComp          }

        if strval < value^.stringValue then
           answer := OP_LT
        else if strval > value^.stringValue then
           answer := OP_GT
        else
           answer := OP_EQ
      end
    end

    { get failed.                                                   }

    else
    begin
      lastError := cursor^.lastError;
    end
  end;
```

```
{ Field is a DATE.                                                         }

  fldDate:
  begin
    rc := cursor^.genericRec^.getDate(fieldNum+1, dateval, fnull);
    if rc = PXSUCCESS then
    begin

    { If value is Nil, check for BLANK field.                             }

      if value = Nil then
      begin
        if fnull then
          answer := OP_EQ
        else
          answer := OP_GT
      end
      else
      begin
        answer := compareDates(dateval, value^.dateValue);
      end
    end
    else
    begin

    { get failed.                                                         }
      lastError := cursor^.lastError;

    end
  end;

  else
    lastError := PXERR_TQINTERNALERROR

end; { case of }

  compareFieldValue := answer;
  if debug then writeln('compareFieldValue: Exit: ');

end;

(*******************************************************************************
*
* OBJECT TYPE: TQuery
*
* MEMBER: compareOp
```

8-10 Continued.

```
* DESCRIPTION: Determine whether 2 operators are compatible.
*
*********************************************************************)
function TQuery.compareOp  (op1, op2 : opType) : Boolean;

var
  valid : Boolean;

begin
if debug then writeln('compareOp: Enter');
  valid := False;

{ The first input opType was determined by comparing 2 values. Valid   }
{ opTypes are OP_EQ, OP_LT, OP_GT depending on whether the first value  }
{ is equal to, less than, or greater than the second.  The second input }
{ opType is the operator from the restriction. This function determines }
{ whether the 2 opTypes are compatible.                                 }

  case op1 of

  { OP_EQ is compatible with OP_EQ, OP_LE, and OP_GE.                    }

    OP_EQ:
      case op2 of
        OP_EQ, OP_LE, OP_GE: valid := True;
      end;

  { OP_LT is compatible with OP_LT, OP_LE, and OP_NOT_EQ.                }

    OP_LT:
      case op2 of
        OP_LT, OP_LE, OP_NOT_EQ: valid := TRUE;
      end;



  { OP_GT is compatible with OP_GT, OP_GE, and OP_NOT_EQ.                }

    OP_GT:
      case op2 of
        OP_GT, OP_GE, OP_NOT_EQ: valid := TRUE;
      end;

    else
      lastError := PXERR_TQINTERNALERROR;

  end;
```

```
    compareOp := valid;
    if debug then writeln('compareOp: Exit: ', valid)


end;

(*********************************************************************
*
* OBJECT TYPE: TQuery
*
* MEMBER: validate
*
* DESCRIPTION: Determine whether the restrictions in effect satisfy
*              a particular record in the objects cursor.
*
*********************************************************************)
function TQuery.validate : boolean;

var
  i, j : Counter;
  restriction : PRestriction;
  valid : boolean;
  compare : opType;
  info : PFieldInfo;

begin
if debug then writeln('validate: enter');
  valid := True;

{ On entry, the TQuery 'cursor' data member is pointing to the record   }
{ that needs to be checked.

{ Check the restrictions for each field.  Continue until all of the     }
{ restrictions are checked and valid or a restriction is not valid.     }

  i := 0;
  while (i < numFields) and (valid) do
  begin

  { Get a pointer to the information structure for this field.          }

    info := fieldList^.At(i);

  { If the field has a restriction list, iterate through the list and   }
  { check each restriction.                                             }
```

8-10 Continued.

```
   j := 0;
   while (j < info^.restrictions^.Count) and (valid) do
   begin

   { Get a pointer to the restriction using the TCollection At function. }

     restriction := info^.restrictions^.At(j);

   { Compare the field in the cursor's record against the value in the   }
   { restriction.  The cursor's record is set in the functions           }
   { getFirstRecord and getNextRecord.                                   }

     compare := compareFieldValue(i, restriction^.rvalue);

   { compareField returns OP_GT, OP_LT or OP_EQ based on whether the      }
   { restriction value is greater than, less than or equal to the value  }
   { in the field of the cursors record.                                 }

   { Based on the comparison and the relational operator, decide if the   }
   { restriction is valid.                                               }

     valid := compareOp(compare, restriction^.roperator);
       j := j + 1;
   end;

     i := i + 1;
   end;

   validate := valid;
if debug then writeln('validate: exit: ', valid)
end;

begin
end.
```

Appendix
Source code listings

The code listings discussed in this appendix gather together all source code not completely listed elsewhere. In chapter 4, we presented all of the code for the objects that we created for this application that can be reused. Chapters 7 and 8 presented the complete listings for each file related to the objects that we wrote for referential integrity and queries because they each contained material separate from the user interface and its incorporation of the Engine. The disk contains the full listings of the code used to write the user interface and join it with our new types and the Engine itself.

Starting out

TABLEDIC.PAS contains all of the code for all of the tables used in this application.

TABLEDIC.CPP contains utility routines used by the program, including the definitions for the various pictures used as part of the validation routines for this application.

The heart of the matter

TMDIPOS.PAS features the code that responds to all of the menu's commands.

The windows and dialogs

TSALWIN.PAS, TCSTDLG.PAS, THISTWIN.PAS, and TINVDLG.PAS contain the complete code for each of the dialog boxes and windows of the applications functions except those for queries.

Querying the database

TSALEQRY.PAS, TCSTQRY.PAS, TSITMDRY.PAS, and TINVQRY.PAS show how to write the query answer dialog boxes.

Index

A

addRestrictionChar function, 248
addRestrictionDouble function, 248
addRestrictionShort function, 248
addRestrictionToQuery function, 133
alphanumeric field, 7
appendRec function, 186
application design
  database, 19-22
  defining fields and table relations, 23-28
  establishing requirements, 18-19
  planning process, 17-36
  table code, 28-36
  tables, 22-23
applications (*see also* source code)
  hardware/software requirements, xvii
  planning, 3-4

B

binary field, 8
binary large object (BLOB), 3, 8
BNClicked procedure, 88
Borland Windows Custom Controls (BWCC), 37

C

canUsePrimary procedure, 249
canUseSecondary procedure, 249
checkRestriction function, 249
child windows, 45
close function, 186
columns, 5
compareDates function, 250

compareOp function, 250
createIdNumber function, 158-160
currency field, 7

D

data types, 6-8
  alphanumeric, 7
  binary, 8
  currency, 7
  date, 7
  memo, 7-8
  numeric, 7
  short, 7
database
  columns, 5
  designing, 19-22
  fields (*see* fields)
  maintaining integrity with Engine, 181-240
  records, 5
  relational, 1-15
  rows, 5
  tables (*see* tables)
database management system, xiii
date field, 7
DCursor object, 184-188
  constructors, 185-186
  destructors, 185-186
  fields, 184-185
  integrating into user interface, 189
  linking, 185
  methods, 186-188
  using with Engine, 188
DCURSOR.PAS, 192-240
default values, 10

deleteRec function, 187
detail table, 6
determineLinkType function, 188
dialog boxes, 45
  creating, 47-50
didMasterChange function, 188
DisplayFields procedure, 98, 107, 126, 153, 158
doMove procedure, 88, 89

E

Engine (*see* Paradox Engine)
entity integrity, 181-182
executeAndSave function, 248

F

fields, 5
  datatypes, 6-8
  DCursor, 184-185
  defining, 23-28
  naming, 9
  query processing, 244-247
  validity checking, 9-10, 163, 167-168
findFirstLinkedRecord function, 188
findSecondaryIndexes function, 249
foundation screens, 46-59
  new customer, 46-50
  new sale, 53-56
  select customer, 51-53
  TSALWIN.PAS, 56-59
functions (*see* specific function names)

G

getClassName function, 89
getCurRecNum function, 187
getCursor function, 80, 88, 97, 107, 126, 172
getDatabase function, 75
getDouble function, 153
getEngine function, 75
getFieldNumber function, 97, 107
getFirstRecord function, 250
getFldType function, 153
getNextRecord function, 249
getRealCurRecNum function, 186
getRecCount function, 187
getRestrictedRecordCount function, 188
getString function, 153
gotoBegin function, 187
gotoEnd function, 187
gotoNext function, 187
gotoPrev function, 187
gotoRec function, 187

H

hardware, requirements, xvii
HaveValuesChanged function, 80, 126 (*see also* wm_HaveValuesChanged)

I

IDAdd procedure, 133
IDDel procedure, 155, 160-161
IDNew procedure, 155, 158
indexes and indexing
  primary objects, 11-12
  secondary objects, 12
Initialize procedure, 187
insertRec function, 186
integrity constraints, 181-184
  entity, 181-182
  referential, 182-184
isEmpty function, 186
isValidLink function, 188

L

link function, 186
linking, 185
linkTypeIs function, 186
lookupField function, 250

M

main menu bar, 38-39, 41-45
  History choice, 38
  Inventory choice, 39
  Sales choice, 38
  TMDIPOS.PAS, 44-45
  Tools choice, 39
  Window choice, 39
memo field, 7-8
menus (*see also* screens)
  child windows, 45
  dialog boxes, 45
  main bar, 38-39, 41-45
  POS.PAS, 43
  screen design, 39-45
  TMDIPOS.PAS, 44-45
  user interface, 37-38

N

numeric field, 7

O

object-oriented programming (OOP), 2
objects, 10-12, 61-142 (*see also* specific object names)
  listing, 11
  new objects and their ancestors, 67-69
  new objects and messages, 69-74
  new objects and their code, 74-142
  primary index, 11-12
  secondary index, 12
  table, 11
  TCURBTN.PAS, 90-97
  TCURDLG.PAS, 127-133
  TCURWIN.PAS, 71, 81-83
  TFEDIT.PAS, 99-106

TFLIST.PAS, 108-114
TFSTAT.PAS, 116-125
TINVDLG.PAS, 72-73
TMDIDBF.PAS, 76-79
TQBUILD.PAS, 134-142
WMDBF.PAS, 74
ObjectWindows, xiv
OOP (*see* object-oriented programming)
open function, 186
optimize procedure, 249

P

PAL (*see* Paradox Application Language)
Paradox Application Language (PAL), xiii
Paradox Engine, 13
    data validity checking, 163-180
    initializing, 147-149
    integrating user interface, 143-162
    maintaining database integrity, 181-240
    opening tables, 149
    POS.PAS, 144-146
    positioning cursor, 149
    query processing, 241-316
    TFEDIT.PAS, 157
    TFSTAT.PAS, 154-155
    TINVDLG.PAS, 158-159
    TMDIDBF.PAS, 147-148
    TMDIPOS.PAS, 150
ParseDate procedure, 250
POS.PAS, 43, 144-146
primary index object, 11-12
procedures (*see* specific procedure names)
putString function, 156, 158
PXQUERY.PAS, 166-316

Q

query processing, 241-316
    fields, 244-247
    integrating with user interface, 250-316
    object types, 244-250
    optimizing, 242-244
    PXQUERY.PAS, 166-316
    TCSTQRY.PAS, 263-266
    TMDIPOS.PAS, 253-255
Query-by-Example (QBE), 242

R

records, 5
referential integrity, 182-184
relational database, 1-15
    application planning, 3-4
    design planning, 2
    overview, 2-3
removeRestrictions procedure, 248
Resource Workshop, xiv, 37-59
rows, 5

S

SaveFields procedure, 80, 98, 107, 115, 126, 156, 158
screens (*see also* menus)
    designing, 39-45
    foundation, 46-59
    validity checking, 169
    Windows, 40-41
searchIndex function, 187
secondary index object, 12
setNull function, 156
SetupWindow procedure, 133, 153
short field, 7
software, requirements, xvii
source code
    DCURSOR.PAS, 192-240
    POS.PAS, 43, 144-146
    PXQUERY.PAS, 166-316
    TABLEDIC.PAS, 30-35
    TCSTQRY.PAS, 263-266
    TCURBTN.PAS, 90-97
    TCURDLG.PAS, 127-133
    TCURWIN.PAS, 71, 81-83
    TFEDIT.PAS, 99-106, 157
    TFLIST.PAS, 108-114
    TFSTAT.PAS, 116-125, 154-155
    TINVDLG.PAS, 72-73, 158-159, 174-175
    TMDIDBF.PAS, 76-79, 147-148
    TMDIPOS.PAS, 36, 44-45, 150, 253-255
    TPOSUTILS.PAS, 167
    TQBUILD.PAS, 134-142
    TSALWIN.PAS, 56-59, 176, 190-191
    WMDBF.PAS, 74
stuffValue function, 250
sync function, 186

T

TABLEDIC.PAS, 30-35
table objects, 11
tables, 4
    code preparation, 28-36
    designing, 22-23
    detail, 6
    field relations and, 23-28
    linking, 5-6, 183
    opening with TRecord, 149
    setting up, 13-14
    TABLEDIC.PAS, 30-35
    TMDIPOS.PAS, 36
    validity checking, 163
TAddCustDialog object, 174-175
TAddCustomer object, 173
TApplication object, 43, 143
TButton object, 55, 89-97
TCollection object, 29, 245
TComboBox object, 98, 106
TControl object, 67, 152, 153

TCSTQRY.PAS, 263-266
TCURBTN.PAS, 90-97
TCURDLG.PAS, 127-133
TCurRecStatic object, 69, 72, 114-115
TCursor object, 64, 90-97, 99-106, 115, 149, 151-153, 155-158, 160-162, 184, 187
TCursorButton object, 68, 72, 88-97, 155
TCursorButtonDown object, 68, 88
TCursorButtonFirst object, 68, 88
TCursorButtonLast object, 68, 89
TCursorButtonUp object, 68, 88
TCursorDialog object, 68, 70, 72, 115, 125-133, 151, 153, 155, 176, 178
TCursorWindow object, 54, 68, 70, 73, 75, 80-88
TCURWIN.PAS, 71, 81-83
TCustQueryDialog object, 262-266
TDatabase object, 63, 144, 147, 149, 162
TDialog object, 47, 55, 67, 69, 70, 115, 126, 151, 153, 255
TEdit object, 55, 89, 97, 99-106, 172-173
TEngine object, 62-63, 144, 147, 149
TFEDIT.PAS, 99-106, 157
TFieldDesc object, 26, 29, 61, 65, 187, 257
TFieldEdit object, 68, 72, 73, 89, 98-106, 151, 153, 157, 172, 173
TFieldListbox object, 69, 98, 106-107, 108-114
TFieldStatic object, 69, 72, 107, 114-125, 152-153
TFilterValidator object, 164-165, 170
TFLIST.PAS, 108-114
TFSTAT.PAS, 116-125, 154-155
TINVDLG.PAS, 72-73, 158-159, 174-175
TInventoryDialog object, 72, 149, 151, 155, 158-159, 161-162
TInventoryWindow object, 56, 189
TInvQueryDialog object, 262
TItemsWindow object, 56, 176, 179-180, 189, 190-191
TListBox object, 67, 257
TLookupValidator, 170
TMDIDBF.PAS, 76-79, 147-148
TMDIDBFWindow object, 43, 68, 143-144, 147-148
TMDIPOS.PAS, 36, 44-45, 150, 253-255
TMDIPosWindow object, 43, 146-149, 253-255
TMDIWindow object, 43, 67, 74-75, 144
TObject object, 29, 62
TObjectWindows object, 70
TPosApplication object, 43, 143
TPOSUTILS.PAS, 167
TPXPictureValidator object, 67, 165-168, 171
TQBUILD.PAS, 134-142, 256-262
TQuantityDialog, 176-178
TQuery object, 244, 246, 252
TQueryBuilder object, 69, 126, 133-142, 256-262
TRangeValidator object, 67, 170, 173, 176-177
TRButton object, 66, 68, 89
TRecord object, 64-65, 98, 149, 153, 162
TSaleItemQueryDialog object, 262

TSaleItemr object, 175
TSaleQueryDialog object, 262
TSaleWindow object, 54, 56, 177, 189
TSALWIN.PAS, 56-59, 176, 190-191
TScroller object, 126
TSelectItemDialog object, 151-152, 155
TStatic object, 55, 89, 106, 107, 153
TStringLookupValidator object, 170-171
TTableDesc object, 61
TTotRecStatic object, 69, 72, 114-115
TValidator object, 66, 164-169
TWindow object, 54, 55, 67, 69, 70, 90-97
TWindowsObject object, 70, 126

U

updateBufferWithMasterKeys function, 188
updateHiKey function, 249
updateLinkedRecs function, 186
updateLowKey function, 249
updateRec function, 187
user interface
    integrating DCursor into, 189
    integrating query objects into, 250-316
    integrating validity checking into, 171-173
    integrating with Engine, 143-162
user interface menus, 37-38

V

validate function, 250
validity checking, 9-10, 163-180
    initiating, 173-180
    integrating into user interface, 171-173
    TINVDLG.PAS, 174-175
    TPOSUTILS.PAS, 167
    TSALWIN.PAS, 176
    types of for tables/fields, 163
values
    default, 10
    expected, 10
    range, 10
    required, 10
    uniqueness, 10

W

windows screen, 40-41
    control bars, 41
    frame, 40
    menu bar, 40
    message bar, 41
    scroll bar, 40-41
    status bar, 41
    title bar, 40
WMDBF.PAS, 74
wm_DisplayFields, 69, 70, 73, 80, 98, 126
wm_HaveValuesChanged, 70, 73, 98, 107, 155
wm_SaveFields, 70, 73, 80, 98, 107, 115, 126, 155

About the Authors

Michael Vernick
MEE, Cornell University
Centerfield Corporation, Miller Place, NY

Mike's consulting work takes him from Wall Street to Tokyo. When he is not recovering from jet lag, Mike works at finishing his doctorate in computer science at the State University of New York at Stony Brook, getting married, and driving a Mazda Miata.

Robert Signore
BS, Computer Science, SUNY at Stony Brook
Q+E Software, Raleigh, NC

Rob has recently taken a position in Raleigh, NC, known for high-tech companies and fierce thunderstorms. In addition to being a contributing author for Batch File Programming with DOS 5.0, Rob published a series of articles about TurboVision in the Borland Informant. Rob has also begun to make a major contribution to the local economy of North Carolina: he's building a new house.

Michael O. Stegman
Ph.D., English, SUNY at Stony Brook
Shoreham-Wading River High School, Shoreham, NY

Mike is in demand as a speaker at local, state, and national conventions of teachers on topics that range from fairy tales to computers in an English classroom. He has published scholarly articles on the American poet Wallace Stevens and the Trappist monk and writer Thomas Merton. Mike drives a Jeep Cherokee, but not the green one, and recently had his house re-sided.

Other Bestsellers of Related Interest

STACKER®: An Illustrated Tutorial
—2nd Edition—Dan Gookin

Turn your single hard disk into two with this professional guide. Updated through Stacker 3.0, it contains information not found in the manuals. You'll use such features as Express or Custom Setup for Windows and DOS; Windows Stackometer™—a set of real-time gauges showing hard disk capacity, compression ratio, and fragmentation levels. Plus, you'll use Unstack™, a time-saving utility that decompresses files and automatically returns systems to their original state. 208 pages, 50 illustrations. Book No. 4447, $19.95 paperback only

CONVERTING MICROSOFT C TO
MICROSOFT C/C++ 7.0—Len Dorfman

This book/disk package is designed to help real-world Microsoft C programmers make a smooth transition to Microsoft C/C++. It introduces you to the principles of object-oriented programming and shows you how to develop commercial-quality class libraries using Microsoft C/C++. Ready-to-run source code is included on the companion disk. The author also discusses many of C/C++ 7.0's most exciting new features, including High-Performance Object Technology (HOT), the inline assembler, and more. 288 pages, 100 illustrations, 3.5" disk. Book No. 4341, $34.95 paperback only

MICROSOFT ACCESS PROGRAMMING
—Namir C. Shammas

This hands-on introduction to Microsoft Access database programming is designed for anyone who's familiar with the BASIC language. It's a practical tutorial approach—complete with ready-to-use program code and professional tips, tricks, and warnings. You get up-to-date information on the built-in online help that Microsoft Access offers . . . how to craft the visual interface of a form . . . how to fine-tune the control settings to alter their appearance or behavior . . . and much more. 304 pages, 158 illustrations, 3.5" disk. Book No.4333, $32.95 paperback only

LAN PERFORMANCE OPTIMIZATION
—Martin A. W. Nemzow

Resolve your most stubborn network performance problems with this practical resource for LAN managers and consultants. This book/disk package will help you locate and eliminate bottlenecks in local area networks quickly. The diagnostic tools provided are equally effective with Banyan Vines, Novell Netware, UB Access One, Unix, Sun, NFS, IBM LAN Server, Microsoft LAN Manager, Ethernet, Token Ring, and FDDI network operating systems. 230 pages, 90 illustrations, 5.25" disk. Book No. 4310, $29.95 paperback only

WRITING DR DOS® BATCH FILES
—Ronny Richardson

Boost the performance and increase the efficiency of the DR DOS operating system with this first and only book/disk package on batch file programming for DR DOS. After a complete batch file programming tutorial, you'll discover how to create your own batch files using DR DOS commands and the batch file utilities included on the FREE 3.5" companion disk. A screen compiler, a batch file utility kit, and a quick-reference summary of the DR DOS command language round out this thoroughly practical, easy-to-follow guide. 464 pages, 79 illustrations, 3.5" disk. Book No. 4289, $32.95 paperback only

BUILD YOUR OWN 486/486SX AND SAVE A
BUNDLE—2nd Edition—Aubrey Pilgrim

This hands-on guide makes it possible for you to build your own state-of-the-art, 100% IBM-compatible PC for about one-third the retail cost or less with little more than a few parts, a screwdriver, and a pair of pliers. So don't shell out huge sums of money for a PC at your local retail outlet. This book will allow you to enjoy the speed and power of a 486—and still put food on the table. 256 pages, 58 illustrations. Book No. 4270, $19.95 paperback, $29.95 hardcover

WINDOWS® BITMAPPED GRAPHICS
—Steve Rimmer

Stocked with ready-to-run source code in C, and illustrated with many fine examples of bitmapped output, this complete programmer's reference gives you all the practical information you need to work effectively with Windows-compatible graphics formats, including Windows BMP, TIFF, PC Paintbrush, GEM/IMG, GIF, Targa, and MacPaint. You get a toolbox of portable source code designed to help you integrate these standards into your Windows applications plus a whole lot more. 400 pages, 82 illustrations. Book No. 4265, $26.95 paperback, $38.95 hardcover

BUILDER LITE: Developing Dynamic Batch Files—Ronny Richardson

With this software and Richardson's accompanying user's manual, even beginners will be able to build and test sophisticated batch files in as little as 10 minutes. Richardson's step-by-step tutorial demonstrates how to write batch files that manipulate displays, create menus, make calculations, customize system files, and perform looping operations. This isn't a demo package, either. Builder Lite was developed by Doug Amaral of hyperkinetix, inc., especially for this book. 368 pages, 61 illustrations, 3.5" disk. Book No. 4248, $32.95 paperback, $44.95 hardcover

DOS SUBROUTINES FOR C AND ASSEMBLER—Leo J. Scanlon
and Mark R. Parker

Fully tested and guaranteed to make programming faster and easier, this collection of subroutines will work on any IBM-compatible computer running DOS. It's a valuable source code toolbox that experienced C and assembly language programmers can draw on to save the hours or days it can take to create subroutines from scratch. Beginners also will appreciate this book because it's an easy-to-use source of pre-tested, error-free code that demonstrates the correct way to prepare programs. 360 pages, 125 illustrations, 3.5" disk. Book No. 4239, $34.95 paperback, $44.95 hardcover

WINDOWS™ BATCH FILE PROGRAMMING—Namir C. Shammas

Create and run Windows-based batch files quickly and easily with this book/disk package. You'll find detailed coverage of the shareware product WinBatch—included on disk along with WinEdit, a shareware text editor—and the commercial package BridgeBatch. Plus, you'll find a step-by-step tutorial that shows how to input and output with batch files, construct highly interactive dialog boxes, manipulate text in files, and manage files, directories, and disk drives. 384 pages, 147 illustrations, 3.5" disk. Book No. 4238, $32.95 paperback only

DR. BATCH FILE'S ULTIMATE COLLECTION—Ronny Richardson

Boost productivity, enhance DOS performance, and save hundreds of unnecessary keystrokes with this practical library of programs—no programming skills required. Assembled here and on the FREE 3.5" companion disk are over 120 of the most useful batch files available for creating and using keyboard macros, saving and reusing command lines, tracking down viruses in COMMAND.COM, and much more. 440 pages, 146 illustrations, 3.5" disk. Book No. 4220, $29.95 paperback, $39.95 hardcover

TURBO PASCAL® MEMORY MANAGEMENT TECHNIQUES—Len Dorfman and
Marc J. Neuberger

Gain and maintain control over the memory requirements of the programs you write. This book explores many of the memory options used by C programmers. Plus, a memory management library is provided on disk. You'll learn to write Pascal application programs that fully utilize EMS, XMS, and virtual memory techniques—with special emphasis on optimizing the virtual memory system's seamless interface to the world of expanded, extended, and hard disk memory management. 304 pages, 100 illustrations, 3.5" disk. Book No. 4193, 32.95 paperback only

MASTERING HARVARD GRAPHICS FOR WINDOWS—Donald Richard Read

This comprehensive tutorial takes you through using Harvard Graphics for Windows to create dazzling charts, graphics, screen shows, and even animated displays. Divided into three sections, it will help you increase personal productivity, get more done in less time at a lower cost, and produce professional presentations that make your point more effectively. In addition, you'll find helpful sections on installing the program on your computer . . . configuring output devices for use with Harvard Graphics for Windows . . . and using the program with OS/2 version 2.0. 280 pages, 417 illustrations. Book No. 4186, $22.95 paperback only

UPGRADE YOUR COMPUTER PRINTER AND SAVE A BUNDLE—Horace W. LaBadie, Jr.

Explore the affordable upgrade opportunities available for several popular printer makes and models including Apple Laser-Writers, the Hewlett-Packard Series, HP Desk-Jet, Canon Bubble Jets, Okidata, and others. You'll look at added font and graphics capabilities, spoolers and buffers, printer sharing and network boxes, interface converters, and caching drives, as well as software solutions such as PostScript and others. 288 pages, 245 illustrations. Book No. 4144, $19.95 paperback, $29.95 hardcover

BUILD YOUR OWN COMPUTER ACCESSORIES AND SAVE A BUNDLE—Bonnie J. Hargrave and Ted Dunning

Here are step-by-step instructions for 27 useful network management and computer diagnostic devices. Practical guidance for building accessories makes complex network operations easier and faster. Plus, you'll find a special section on the tools necessary for basic soldering and cabling operations, information on how to read circuit diagrams and schema-tics, a list of component suppliers, and estimated costs for each project. 376 pages, 222 illustrations. Book No. 4134, $19.95 paper-back, $29.95 hardcover

GLOSSBRENNER'S GUIDE TO SHAREWARE FOR SMALL BUSINESSES—Alfred Glossbrenner

Now, in as little time as one hour, you can use a personal computer to keep track of your customers, ride herd on your inventory, and run your business with a degree of control you may have only dreamed about. This valuable book/disk package clears away the miscon-ceptions surrounding today's computer jargon and products, offers solid advice on how to select IBM-compatible hardware, and reviews and recommends dozens of today's hottest shareware programs—all at the lowest pos-sible prices! 432 pages, 64 illustrations, 5.25" disk. Book No. 4059, $27.95 paperback, $37.95 hardcover.

Prices Subject to Change Without Notice.

Look for These and Other Windcrest/McGraw-Hill Books at Your Local Bookstore

To Order Call Toll Free 1-800-822-8158
(24-hour telephone service available.)

or write to Windcrest/McGraw-Hill, Blue Ridge Summit, PA 17294-0840.

Title	Product No.	Quantity	Price

☐ Check or money order made payable to Windcrest/McGraw-Hill

Charge my ☐ VISA ☐ MasterCard ☐ American Express

Acct. No. _____ Exp. _____

Signature: _____

Name: _____

Address: _____

City: _____

State: _____ Zip: _____

Subtotal $ _____

Postage and Handling
($3.00 in U.S., $5.00 outside U.S.) $ _____

Add applicable state and local
sales tax $ _____

TOTAL $ _____

Windcrest/McGraw-Hill catalog free with purchase; otherwise send $1.00 in check or money order and receive $1.00 credit on your next purchase.

Orders outside U.S. must pay with international money in U.S. dollars drawn on a U.S. bank.

Windcrest/McGraw-Hill Guarantee: If for any reason you are not satisfied with the book(s) you order, simply return it (them) within 15 days and receive a full refund.

BC

Order Form for Readers
Requiring a Single 5.25" Disk

This Windcrest/McGraw-Hill software product is also available on a 5.25"/360K disk. If you need the software in 5.25" format, simply follow these instructions:

- Complete the order form below. Be sure to include the exact title of the Windcrest/McGraw-Hill book for which you are requesting a replacement disk.

- Make check or money order made payable to *Glossbrenner's Choice*. The cost is **$7.00** (**$10.00** for shipments outside the U.S.) to cover media, postage, and handling. Pennsylvania residents, please add 6% sales tax.

- Foreign orders: please send an international money order or a check drawn on a bank with a U.S. clearing branch. We cannot accept foreign checks.

- Mail order form and payment to:

    Glossbrenner's Choice
    Attn: Windcrest/McGraw-Hill Disk Replacement
    699 River Road
    Yardley, PA 19067-1965

Your disks will be shipped via First Class Mail. Please allow one to two weeks for delivery.

 ....

Windcrest/McGraw-Hill
Disk Replacement

Please send me a replacement disk in 5.25"/360K format for the following Windcrest/McGraw-Hill book:

Book Title _____

Name _____

Address _____

City/State/ZIP _____

DISK WARRANTY

This software is protected by both United States copyright law and international copyright treaty provision. You must treat this software just like a book, except that you may copy it into a computer in order to be used and you may make archival copies of the software for the sole purpose of backing up our software and protecting your investment from loss.

By saying "just like a book," McGraw-Hill means, for example, that this software may be used by any number of people and may be freely moved from one computer location to another, so long as there is no possibility of its being used at one location or on one computer while it also is being used at another. Just as a book cannot be read by two different people in two different places at the same time, neither can the software be used by two different people in two different places at the same time (unless, of course, McGraw-Hill's copyright is being violated).

LIMITED WARRANTY

Windcrest/McGraw-Hill takes great care to provide you with top-quality software, thoroughly checked to prevent virus infections. McGraw-Hill warrants the physical diskette(s) contained herein to be free of defects in materials and workmanship for a period of sixty days from the purchase date. If McGraw-Hill receives written notification within the warranty period of defects in materials or workmanship, and such notification is determined by McGraw-Hill to be correct, McGraw-Hill will replace the defective diskette(s). Send requests to:

Customer Service
Windcrest/McGraw-Hill
13311 Monterey Lane
Blue Ridge Summit, PA 17294-0850

The entire and exclusive liability and remedy for breach of this Limited Warranty shall be limited to replacement of defective diskette(s) and shall not include or extend to any claim for or right to cover any other damages, including but not limited to, loss of profit, data, or use of the software, or special, incidental, or consequential damages or other similar claims, even if McGraw-Hill has been specifically advised of the possibility of such damages. In no event will McGraw-Hill's liability for any damages to you or any other person ever exceed the lower of suggested list price or actual price paid for the license to use the software, regardless of any form of the claim.

McGRAW-HILL, INC. SPECIFICALLY DISCLAIMS ALL OTHER WARRANTIES, EXPRESS OR IMPLIED, INCLUDING, BUT NOT LIMITED TO, ANY IMPLIED WARRANTY OF MERCHANTABILITY OR FITNESS FOR A PARTICULAR PURPOSE.

Specifically, McGraw-Hill makes no representation or warranty that the software is fit for any particular purpose and any implied warranty of merchantability is limited to the sixty-day duration of the Limited Warranty covering the physical diskette(s) only (and not the software) and is otherwise expressly and specifically disclaimed.

This limited warranty gives you specific legal rights; you may have others which may vary from state to state. Some states do not allow the exclusion of incidental or consequential damages, or the limitation on how long an implied warranty lasts, so some of the above may not apply to you.

If you need help
with the enclosed disk . . .

The enclosed 3½-inch diskette contains all of the Pascal code discussed in this book, including the complete listings from the appendix. Make a subdirectory on your hard drive to copy the files to:

    C:\> MD *directory_name*

where *directory_name* is the name of the directory that you want to create. Next, make this new directory the current directory:

    C:\> CD *directory_name*

where *directory_name* is the name of the directory that you just created. Then, copy the files to this directory:

    C:\> XCOPY *d*:*.* /S

where *d* is the letter of the floppy drive containing the companion diskette. This command will copy all of the files from the companion diskette, retaining the subdirectory structure found on the diskette.

IMPORTANT

Read the Disk Warranty terms on the previous page before opening the disk envelope. Opening the envelope constitutes acceptance of these terms and renders this entire book-disk package nonreturnable except for replacement in kind due to material defects.